T0327479

# The Permanent Portfolio

## *Harry Browne's Long-Term Investment Strategy*

**CRAIG ROWLAND**
**J. M. LAWSON**

**WILEY**
John Wiley & Sons, Inc.

Published by John Wiley & Sons, Inc., Hoboken, New Jersey.
Published simultaneously in Canada.

For general information on our other products and services or for technical support, please contact our Customer Care Department within the United States at (800) 762-2974, outside the United States at (317) 572-3993 or fax (317) 572-4002.

Wiley also publishes its books in a variety of electronic formats. Some content that appears in print may not be available in electronic books. For more information about Wiley products, visit our web site at www.wiley.com.

*Library of Congress Cataloging-in-Publication Data:*
Rowland, Craig, 1971-
  The permanent portfolio : Harry Browne's long-term investment strategy / Craig Rowland, J. M. Lawson. – 1st ed.
      p. cm.
  Includes index.
  ISBN 978-1-118-28825-2 (cloth); ISBN 978-1-118-33156-9 (ebk);
  ISBN 978-1-118-33377-8 (ebk); ISBN 978-1-118-33488-1 (ebk)
1.   Portfolio management. 2.   Investments.  I. Lawson, J. M., 1970-  II. Title.
  HG4529.5.R69 2012
  332.6—dc23
                                                             2012015383

Printed in the United States of America

10 9 8 7 6 5 4 3 2 1

# Contents

# Foreword

I nvesting is complicated. It's difficult. You need expert help if you're going to build your wealth so that you can retire on time. Or at least that's what you've been told.

There's a vast financial industry with a vested interest in convincing you that to be a successful investor you have to:

- Follow the daily movements of the markets.
- Learn how to analyze the nitty-gritty details of stocks and bonds.
- Buy and sell constantly to maximize profit.

The truth is that none of this matters. The truth is that smart investing is simple. And easy.

I believe that most investors are better off putting their money into low-cost index funds. (An index fund is a mutual fund that tracks the broad movements of a stock-market index, such as the S&P 500.) Over the long term, this passive investing approach has been shown to produce above-average returns for patient investors. Why? There are many reasons, but primarily because investing in index funds costs much less than nearly any other method.

In fact, Stanford University professor William Sharpe famously demonstrated that passive investing with low-cost index funds *must* produce better results than traditional investing. The average return of both methods is the average return of the market. But because traditional investing costs so much, investors taking that path necessarily see smaller returns on their investments. (To read more, see http://tinyurl.com/sharpe-rocks.)

But there are other ways to explore passive investing besides index funds.

Three years ago, I read a book called *Fail-Safe Investing* by Harry Browne. This tiny volume, first published in 1999, champions a method of passive investing that Browne called the Permanent Portfolio. And while it's a little more complicated than simply investing in index funds, the ideas are still fairly simple.

According to Browne, the Permanent Portfolio should provide three key features: safety, stability, and simplicity. He argues that your permanent portfolio should protect you against all economic futures while also providing steady returns. It should also be easy to implement.

There are many ways to approach safe, steady investing, but Browne has some specific recommendations:

- Hold 25% of your portfolio in U.S. stocks, to provide a strong return during times of prosperity.
- Hold 25% in long-term U.S. Treasury bonds, which do well during prosperity and during deflation (but which do poorly during other economic cycles).
- Hold 25% in cash in order to hedge against periods of "tight money" or recession.
- Hold 25% in precious metals (gold, specifically) in order to provide protection during periods of inflation.

To use the Permanent Portfolio, you simply divide your investment capital into four equal chunks, one for each asset class. Once each year, you rebalance your portfolio. If any part of your portfolio has dropped to less than 15% of the whole, or grown to over 35% of the total, then you reset all four parts to 25%.

That's it. That's all the work involved.

Because this asset allocation is diversified, the entire portfolio performs well under most circumstances. Browne writes:

*"The portfolio's safety is assured by the contrasting qualities of the four investments—which ensure that any event that damages one investment should be good for one or more of the others. And no investment, even at its worst, can devastate the portfolio—no matter what surprises lurk around the corner—because no investment has more than 25% of your capital."*

Browne's arguments sounded crazy at first – far too simplistic! – but with time, I've come to believe he's on to something. In fact, over the past three years I've gradually realized that what I need to is move from investing in index funds to establishing a permanent portfolio for myself. Why haven't I done so?

The high price of gold, for one. Plus, I've never really been sure how to implement Browne's Permanent Portfolio in real life. I mean, what are the actual steps for making it happen? *Fail-Safe Investing* is a good book, but it's long on theory and short on actual details. I'm not a professional investor; sometimes I need to have somebody hold my hand.

That's where *this* book comes in.

*The Permanent Portfolio* is an easy-to-access how-to manual for putting Browne's investment strategy into practice. This book doesn't just cover the theories behind this method; it also gives details for putting the theories to work in the Real World.

Nobody knows where the economy is headed. Nobody knows if economic prosperity looms on the horizon – or if we're in for decades of rampant inflation. And because nobody knows what's ahead, nobody knows the best way to save for retirement (or any other purpose).

But with the Permanent Portfolio, you don't *have* to see the future. You don't need a crystal ball to divine the best place to put your money. Instead, you hedge your bets against all possibilities. Sexy? Nope. Safe? You bet. And now that Craig Rowland and J.M. Lawson have explained exactly how to put the Permanent Portfolio into practice, I intend to do so. Perhaps *you* will, too.

J.D. Roth
July 2012

# Preface: Life Is Uncertain

What if everything you had been told about investing was wrong? What if investment predictions were just for entertainment purposes and had no connection to what actually happens in the markets? What if no one really had any idea what was going to happen tomorrow, much less next year?

This situation is the scourge of investors. When we think the economy is doing great, it suddenly turns sour. The bad market that lingers on forever suddenly turns upward. The sure-thing investment we heard about from our broker goes bust. Instead of building our savings, it feels more like it's being taken at the point of a gun. Life is uncertain, and that includes the investment markets.

But perhaps we're just looking at the problem of investing the wrong way. If the investing world is so uncertain and unpredictable, why not build an investing strategy around this idea? Why not strike out the notion that the future can be predicted and instead invest in a way that assumes surprises are *normal*?

That's what this book is about: investing for surprises. Or perhaps we should say investing for how the real world *actually works*.

Several decades ago, the late financial author Harry Browne created an ingenious investing strategy that is strikingly simple, yet extremely sophisticated. This investment strategy was called the "Permanent Portfolio," and it was designed to be set up one time and maintained with minimal effort *permanently*. The strategy was not designed around predicting the future or outsmarting other investors. Instead, it embraced the idea of the unpredictable, the unknowable, and the surprises that the real world always seems to generate. It assumed that nobody can predict the future and that protecting your life savings with an all-season investment strategy should be the primary goal.

How has this approach worked in practice? Very well. Over the last 40 years the strategy has returned between 9 and 10 percent a year. Even more remarkably, the worst loss it has ever had in a single year was only around −5 percent. This even includes the recent 2008 financial crisis during which the portfolio was basically flat while the stock market sank over 36 percent in value. Even better, the portfolio now has over 30 years of empirical data behind it from those who have used it to weather all types of markets (good, bad, and ugly). But despite these extremely impressive results, the portfolio is incredibly simple to implement. At the basic level, it's just four investment asset classes. That's it. This book will tell you how to implement this simple portfolio and avoid investing mistakes that are extremely expensive and are probably putting your life savings at risk *right now*.

In addition, you will also learn about different implementation options that can fit any situation. You'll also be exposed to some important topics such as storing part of your life savings in a foreign account to protect against natural and/or manmade disasters.

Finally, you will learn about many common pitfalls in the investing world such as the risks associated with active management, investment industry costs, dangerous assumptions in much of what passes for conventional investment wisdom, and how to actually enjoy investing without it being a constant source of worry.

"Talk about irony!"

Uncertainty is what makes life interesting. When you learn how to make market uncertainty your friend, you will find that you are on your way to both better investment returns and a more peaceful state of mind. If it sounds implausible that uncertainty could be the basis for a *relaxed* approach to investing, then please read on. Investing can be relaxing and stress free and we'll show you how to make it that way.

Together, we are melding our own experiences and insights into a strategy that, despite being three decades old at this point, provides a robust investing framework even today. Our goal is to provide you with exposure to ideas about diversification that you may not have come across before, along with a higher degree of skepticism toward the investment industry.

There is a way to save and invest that will allow you to reach your goals safely and it's in this book. We will do our best to make the trip interesting and useful. Thank you for joining us.

# Acknowledgments

I would like to thank the following people, who have helped tremendously in creating this book:

Newt Rumble, CPA for reviewing of tax related information and state/local tax treatment questions; Mike Barber for his input on Canadian implementation ideas; Dan Mohr, CPA for proofreading and tax accountant review of information presented; Loren Dohm for proofreading and input.

I would also like to acknowledge Otto Hueppi, managing director for Swiss American Advisors, for providing information and insight into Swiss banking opportunities today for Americans. Additionally, Bron Suchecki at the Perth Mint for his information on the background and history of the mint, knowledge of the gold industry, and review of the chapter on the overseas gold allocation methods. Mike O'Kane, head bullion trader at the New Zealand mint for providing background information on gold storage options in New Zealand. Claudio Grass at Global Gold, AG for providing background on non-banking gold storage options in Switzerland. Frank Trotter, President of Everbank, for background information on gold storage options for U.S. bank custody accounts.

Andy Knippenberg, of John Wiley & Sons, who put us in contact with the publisher. Also at Wiley, Tiffany Charbonier for keeping things organized on the administrative side; Meg Freeborn, Development Editor, for speedy edits and content advice; Senior Production Editor Donna Martone, and Executive Editor Bill Falloon, Wiley Executive Editor, for accepting our proposal and helping to bring it to publication.

Andy Bryant for our conversations relating to investing, business, and market theory. J. D. Roth, operator of the blog "Get Rich Slowly" (www.getrichslowly.org), who provided book proposal advice and wrote the Foreword.

Thanks also to Matthew Wilson and Jeff Sponaugle, both for proofreading and input from an investor's point of view and C. J. Domerchie for his backstories on subjects that were relevant to the book. Thanks for being great friends as well.

John Chandler is also acknowledged for many interesting conversations on the formulation of the Permanent Portfolio strategy and background into Harry Browne and his ideas. Our exchanges through the years have always been educational.

Thank you Pamela Wolfe Browne, Harry Browne's widow, for allowing me to host his investing podcasts all these years and continue to keep his investing ideas alive.

Kendall Earl for being so patient while I worked on this project.

Brian Rowland, for proofreading and exchanging ideas on content. Also to Brian and Keith for being great brothers. Thanks to Mom and Dad for raising me well despite my own efforts to thwart them, several of which almost succeeded.

To all the blog and internet forum participants that have provided so many interesting and fun conversations on the topic of the Permanent Portfolio all these years.

C. R.

As a co-author of what I hope will be a readable and useful guide to personal investment management, I can only echo all of Craig's acknowledgements above. No book covering as many topics as this one comes together without the collaboration of many minds and the contributions from many people, and I offer my thanks and appreciation to all who helped us along the way.

Writing a book like this one takes a lot of time and energy. When you have three small children at home and a full-time job as I do, it would be impossible to undertake a project like this one without a partner who cares about you and believes in what you are doing. My wife Crystal has been instrumental in encouraging me and supporting me as this book has come together, and I want to especially thank her. Her love has been a consistent inspiration to me.

J. M. L.

## About the Illustrator

Special thanks to illustrator Chad Crowe. When we decided we wanted an illustrator, we were looking for someone that could do drawings to poke fun at the industry in the style of *How to Lie With Statistics*, which is a classic book. Of the many dozens of submissions, Chad stood clearly above them all.

Chad is an immensely talented illustrator that has done drawings for many periodicals including *The Washington Post* and *The Wall Street Journal*. He was able to take our concepts and turn them into hilarious cartoons on time and on budget. Check out his website at www.chadcrowe.com.

# CHAPTER 1

# What Is the Permanent Portfolio?
## *Golden Beginnings*

The Permanent Portfolio is an investment strategy designed to grow and protect your life savings under any set of economic conditions. It will work during good and bad markets, and it will even work in markets experiencing extremely serious and unexpected events.

The idea for the portfolio was first proposed in the 1970s by the late Harry Browne, who had gained fame by betting against the dollar with his first book *How You Can Profit from the Coming Devaluation.* The premise of that book, published in 1970, was that the United States would soon break the last vestiges of the gold standard and the resulting inflation would be so bad that gold and certain other hard asset prices would skyrocket. Harry Browne therefore advised readers to purchase assets like gold and silver, and to invest in strong currencies like the Swiss franc as hedges against inflation.

As it turned out, in 1971 President Nixon in fact *did* break the gold standard and the results were spectacular. Starting from $35 an ounce at the time of Nixon's announcement, gold ended the decade near $850 an ounce (over $2,200 in 2012's dollars). Assets like silver and the Swiss franc experienced very high returns as well.

That market call was quite good and there was now a real need to protect those profits once the bad inflation of the 1970s ended.

## A Simple Idea

In response to the need to diversify their profits, Harry Browne and his team, which included Terry Coxon, John Chandler, and Charles Smith, began working out early versions of a new strategy. This strategy would allocate their money not just into assets like gold, but into stocks, bonds, natural resources, and cash as well. Further, unlike Browne's prior bets on the market moving in a certain direction, the new strategy would avoid market timing entirely and be completely passive—something almost unheard of in the investing world at the time outside of a few lone voices.

Browne's new strategy would be called the Permanent Portfolio. The original strategy held the following:

- Stocks
- Bonds
- Cash
- Gold
- Silver
- Swiss francs
- Natural resources

This mix of assets was reached after extensive research into market history, economics, and the potential for a passive strategy to perform well under any environment. This research even included computer analysis, which at the time in the late 1970s wasn't yet in wide use due to the expense involved. Harry Browne, who was interested in the emerging personal computer technology, even did the programming necessary to conduct the research.[1]

As the Permanent Portfolio idea began to take shape, readers of Harry Browne's newsletter—*Harry Browne's Special Reports*—were puzzled by his recommendation to consider owning stocks and bonds in a portfolio (which had done poorly in the 1970s inflation). Yet, Browne stuck to his advice that strong diversification would be a good long-term strategy.

Harry Browne and Terry Coxon then wrote a book in the early 1980s, *Inflation-Proofing Your Investments*, that (contrary to its title) presented a comprehensive review of this new way of thinking about investing that would do well when inflation came back under control. This is actually a pretty remarkable thing for an investment advisor to do. He built his career in the 1970s advocating hard asset investing (like gold) to fight inflation and all of the sudden he advises readers to sell a portion of their hard assets and buy something completely opposite like stocks or bonds? This was heresy!

Well, Browne turned out to be exactly right. In fact, gold soon did settle down by the early 1980s from the previous highs as inflation came under control and the stock market took off in response.

Over time, Browne simplified the Permanent Portfolio to make it easier to implement and more balanced. This effort culminated in Harry Browne's

---

[1] Personal interview with John Chandler, Harry Browne's former newsletter publisher and colleague.

1987 book *Why the Best Laid Investment Plans Usually Go Wrong.* This book, which is probably one of the best ever written on the flaws in many popular investment strategies, reduced the portfolio down to the core components that are still in use today.

## A Simple Allocation

Now that the background of the strategy has been discussed, we can look more closely at the approach that evolved into the following deceptively simple asset allocation:

25 percent—Stocks
25 percent—Bonds
25 percent—Cash
25 percent—Gold

The allocation above is the strategy in its most basic conceptual form. Now, how you implement these 25 percent allocations is just as important as the allocation itself. This book will help you understand how to do that.

## Simply Great Results

Don't let the apparent simplicity of the allocation fool you. Even though it appears simple, it is far from *simplistic.* The allocation actually reflects a sophisticated understanding of economics and financial history. It is this understanding of economics and financial history that allows it to perform so well under so many market conditions and provide strong diversification.

If you walk away from this book with anything, it should be the idea that you do not need a complicated investment strategy to do well in the markets. In fact, it's just the opposite. A simple strategy will often outperform complicated ones over time. It will do it with less risk, less management, lower costs, and more profits to compound. The Permanent Portfolio still remains not only one of the most simple asset allocations you are likely to encounter, but also one of the best in terms of risk versus return.

# CHAPTER 2

# The 16 Golden Rules of Financial Safety

## *Golden Rules and Uncertainty*

O ver the years, Harry Browne developed a set of rules he used to guide his own investing decisions and offered them as general guidelines for all investors in his book *Fail-Safe Investing*. Browne called these maxims the 16 Golden Rules of Financial Safety. These Golden Rules are integral to the design of the Permanent Portfolio and represent timeless advice borne out of witnessing all manner of events in the markets. This chapter provides a summary of the rules that will be helpful in understanding the philosophy behind the Permanent Portfolio.

First, know that the markets are uncertain. There is no way to escape this basic premise. You must accept the idea that the markets are uncertain just as the *rest* of life is. Yet, investors often find the most trouble through the innocent belief that they have somehow conquered uncertainty. Ironically, it is only when an investor learns to *embrace* uncertainty rather than trying to *conquer* it that a strategy can be adopted to deal with it realistically.

> The Permanent Portfolio is a strategy to embrace uncertainty in the markets.

The Permanent Portfolio is a strategy to embrace uncertainty in the markets. It is not just a way to invest, it is an entire philosophy about how to grow and protect your money from risks that can have devastating results. Part of the Permanent Portfolio philosophy involves following the rules outlined below, and one of the benefits of this approach is that it will make it very hard to lose your life savings no matter what the markets decide to do. These rules are the foundation of virtually all of the advice you will read in this book, and the logic of the Permanent Portfolio is more easily understood after an investor has spent some time familiarizing himself with these rules.

## Rule #1: Your Career Provides Your Wealth

Most of the money you make in your lifetime will come from your profession. It's true that investing can be very powerful in growing your money, but it's normally your career that provides the funds that allow you to invest in the first place and continue adding to your nest egg over time. It is easy to be drawn in by stories of people who experience sudden financial windfalls from speculative investment activity, but investors should understand that these stories are noteworthy *because they are so rare*. It is much more important to focus on making the earnings from one's profession as productive as possible and not hold out hope of making a 10,000 percent gain on your investments in a short period. Investing should be a process of taking part of the earnings from your career and allowing them to grow safely. It should not be a process that takes your hard earned money and allows it to be lost in the markets through risky bets.

## Rule #2: Don't Assume You Can Replace Your Wealth

Never assume you can earn back money that is lost through bad investments. A large investment loss can represent years, or even *decades*, of hard work. When losses of this magnitude occur, investors often find that it is not possible to replace the lost wealth no matter how long they work or how much additional money they save. Taking big risks with money you worked hard to earn is literally gambling with years of your life that you can't get back.

The past cannot be repeated and the circumstances that allowed you to earn and save your money will never be the same again. Be careful with the money you worked hard to earn and never assume you can just go back and earn it all again, because you probably can't.

## Rule #3: Recognize the Difference between Investing and Speculating

Investing is the process of taking a clear strategy and implementing it with discipline and focus with an emphasis on *long-term* results. Speculating is the process of engaging in trading for short-term profits, looking for hot stock tips, day trading, market timing, or other highly risky approaches (and there are many of them).

> If you are engaging in trading that seems just one step away from walking down to the local horse track and putting it all on Scarlet Maverick's Escapade, you are speculating.

If you are engaging in trading that seems just one step away from walking down to the local horse track and putting it all on Scarlet Maverick's Escapade, you are speculating. People often take bad risks with their investments that would be obvious if they were *honest* with themselves about what they were actually doing. Many speculative activities are entered into more for entertainment than anything else—just like going to the horse track is more about having an exciting experience than about actually making money (for the gambler anyway—the horse track makes plenty of money off of gamblers' never-ending desire to try to pick a winner).

Where an investor has a plan, the speculator only has hope. Don't bet your life savings on hope.

## Rule #4: No One Can Predict the Future

It is strange that people who would never think of visiting a psychic each morning for advice will happily listen to a commentator or investing guru tell them what the future holds for the markets. No area of life can be predicted with certainty. It doesn't matter what degrees the experts have, where they work, what they did in the past, or who invests with them. No qualification or credentials give any person on the planet the ability to predict the future.

Investors will make more money by ignoring investing gurus than by listening to them. If you believe that any person can reliably predict what the market is going to do next, ask yourself why such a person would bother making media appearances talking about the latest hot stock? Why waste time telling *you* about it instead of just going out and profiting themselves?

## Rule #5: No One Can Time the Market

If you watch an investment guru long enough, you will probably find that he makes some good calls and some bad calls. However, very few of these gurus can reliably beat the broader market *consistently* over time. If an investment guru can't consistently beat the broader market over time, then of what value is his advice for the typical investor? Who wants to see large gains one year turn into large losses the next year because a guru lost his touch?

Unfortunately, it is the clients of the guru who usually experience the actual losses when the advice blows up. As mentioned earlier under Rule #4, if someone is really that good at profiting from market timing then why is he selling *you* this information? Why not just keep quiet and rake in all of the easy wealth himself?

Market timing doesn't work and it doesn't matter who is doing it or how scientific it sounds. If market timing did work then everyone would be doing it and we'd all be rich.

## Rule #6: No Trading System Will Work as Well in the Future as It Did in the Past

The Securities and Exchange Commission (SEC) requires all mutual funds to state the following: *"Past performance does not guarantee future results."* It is short and correct. A system that worked great 10 times in the past gets attention from people, while the one that failed 10 times doesn't. But the finite nature of markets dictates that a winning system can't continue winning forever—in theory the traders using the system would simply own the entire market if they kept winning. The reality, of course, is that trading systems never get that close to world domination—often they don't even get that close to breaking even.

There have been countless, *countless*, trading systems through the years that tried to beat the markets and never once have they worked well enough to survive. Each generation comes up with its own variants of these systems, yet today's hot trading system never seems to work any better than all of the ones that came before it. The sad truth is that once you hear about a system that is supposedly foolproof it is often only a short time later that the system's lucky streak ends, taking a chunk of your savings with it.

## Rule #7: Don't Use Leverage

Leverage is when you borrow money to invest with strategies such as the use of margin loans. *Using leverage in your investments is the single fastest way to lose everything you own.* When you use leverage it may work when the markets are doing well, but if the markets do poorly it can quickly destroy your life savings.

For instance, under the terms of a typical margin loan agreement, if the investor's assets purchased with borrowed funds fall below a certain level the broker has the ability to go into the investor's account and sell any assets necessary to recoup the amount of the margin loan (even those assets not invested on margin). The broker is not obligated to obtain the investor's permission before taking this action and the investor may still owe the broker money if the assets that were sold were not sufficient to cover the losses.

Further, why would a broker loan you money to invest for a small interest payment when the broker could use that same money to invest itself? What do they know that you don't? Stay far away from any kind of leverage or investment products that use leverage. The mirage of easy riches conceals a long history of ruined investors.

## Rule #8: Don't Let Anyone Make Your Decisions

Investing can seem complicated because the financial industry spends millions each year trying to convince you it is. The reality though is that investing can be simple and easy to do once you learn to ignore all of the noise in the markets.

There are cases where certain types of legal and financial planning advice can be of tremendous value (estate and tax planning are two such areas). However, it is important to understand the difference between professional advice that allows you to make better decisions and simply turning over your money to a third party to make your decisions for you.

A third party managing your money often adds very little value, but they may be taking large risks with your money or (in rarer cases) conducting outright fraudulent behavior without you having any way of knowing about it. Whether it is a professional money manager or a trusted relative, there are risks when you turn over your wealth to a third party to manage on your behalf. The risks are especially high when you give them signature authority to directly access and withdraw funds inside the account, which no investor should ever do.

It's important to remember that nobody cares more about your money than you do. Make your own decisions about how your money will be invested.

## Rule #9: Don't Ever Do Anything You Don't Understand

For most investors, the more complicated an investment is, the more likely it is to lead to losses due to unknown or poorly understood risks. Despite this reality, many investors have been convinced that the more complicated an investment is, the more sophisticated it must be. It is important to know your limits and not let overconfidence lead you into something you know little or nothing about.

> It is important to know your limits and not let overconfidence lead you into something you know little or nothing about.

For example, when Craig was raising venture capital money he often saw that the best ideas and successful companies could quickly explain what they do. Their ideas were simple to understand and the business could be easily evaluated for risks. Yet there were many (unsuccessful) entrepreneurs who had horribly complicated ideas that were very difficult to understand. Invariably, experienced venture capitalists would completely avoid these complicated investments. These investors know from hard-earned experience that complicated investments that they don't fully understand rarely turn out well.

If you don't understand how an investment works within about five minutes,[1] walk away. Even if you miss a hot new opportunity because you don't fully understand it, there will be duds that you will also avoid by staying away. The most successful investors on the planet have no shame in admitting they avoided an investment that they didn't understand. So don't let anyone make you feel guilty for staying away from something that doesn't make sense to you.

## Rule #10: Don't Depend on Any One Investment, Institution, or Person for Your Safety

In the 2008 banking crisis, some institutions that existed for over a century went bankrupt almost overnight inflicting large losses on investors. In the same year Bernie Madoff, one of the founders of the NASDAQ stock exchange, was revealed to have been running a multibillion-dollar Ponzi scheme that caused tremendous losses to investors, many of whom had entrusted him with their life savings. The process above repeated itself in 2011 when another large firm, MF Global, went bankrupt and many investors found that their accounts had apparently been plundered by corrupt management.

The sort of financial mismanagement, incompetence, and fraud described above has happened throughout history. No bank, brokerage, or company lasts forever. By spreading your wealth around you ensure that if something unexpected happens your life savings won't be entirely wiped out.

---

[1] Vanguard CEO William McNabb on Restoring Investor's Trust, June 2010, https://retirementplans.vanguard.com/VGApp/pe/PubVgiNews?ArticleName=TrustSpeech.

## Rule #11: Create a Bulletproof Portfolio for Protection

The best long-term investment strategies are often those that can weather the most extreme market conditions without incurring serious damage and at the same time grow your money no matter what is going on in the economy. One of the best portfolios to diversify against the widest array of risks and extreme market conditions is the Permanent Portfolio strategy outlined in this book.

## Rule #12: Speculate Only with Money You Can Afford to Lose

Any money being used for speculation should be money that you can lose entirely and it won't affect your life plans. Part of Harry Browne's overall investment strategy is what he called the "Variable Portfolio." The Variable Portfolio is for money you can afford to lose and is held separately from your core Permanent Portfolio. If you don't have money you can afford to lose, or simply don't feel like speculating in the markets, then there may be no need for a Variable Portfolio in your overall investment strategy.

## Rule #13: Keep Some Assets Outside the Country in which You Live

Geographic diversification protects you from natural and manmade disasters that could impact your life savings. It also protects you against a government that may try to solve its financial problems by confiscating citizens' private property.

By storing some assets outside of the country where you live, you have protection against these events. Further, you will have the ability to evaluate your options during any kind of extraordinary domestic political or economic crisis that many others wouldn't have. Such protection may seem unnecessary, but history is filled with examples of unexpected crises causing investors to incur large losses due to a concentration of investments in their home country. As this book will explain, mitigating such risks is not difficult if geographic diversification steps are taken before a crisis occurs.

## Rule #14: Beware of Tax-Avoidance Schemes

Governments around the world provide many legal ways of reducing taxes (such as tax-deferred retirement savings). There are, however, many tax-avoidance schemes that are flat-out illegal and are likely to lead to financial and even criminal penalties. Unfortunately, many operators of tax-avoidance strategies are either simply ignorant of tax law or crooks looking to steal your money.

There are ways to build a solid portfolio and minimize taxes without hassle. There is no need to bring the stress of risky tax avoidance advice into your life when so many legitimate avenues already exist. Don't let your desire to save some money on taxes put everything you own in jeopardy (including your freedom).

## Rule #15: Enjoy Yourself with a Budget for Pleasure

This rule can be boiled down to the following: You don't know how much time you have on this planet. While you shouldn't be a spendthrift leaving nothing to live on in retirement, you should also realize that being miserly into old age might mean that you never get to enjoy the fruits of your efforts. Find a balance that allows you to enjoy what you worked so hard to earn without leaving you penniless in your old age.

## Rule #16: Whenever You're in Doubt about a Course of Action, It's Always Better to Err on the Side of Safety

If you have trouble understanding an investment, or are nervous about a particular course of action, *take the most conservative approach possible*. If that means doing nothing but putting your money into U.S. Treasuries earning little interest, that is better than taking a risky bet that may wipe out your life savings. It is easier to live on a little less from conservative investing than to take a big loss in your personal savings doing things that you have doubts about.

## Investing and the Rules of Life

Harry Browne summarized these rules in his book *Fail-Safe Investing* in the following way:

> *The rules of safe investing are little different from the rules of life: recognize that you live in an uncertain world, don't expect the impossible, and don't trust strangers. If you apply to your investments the same realistic attitude that produced your present wealth, you needn't fear that you'll ever go broke.*

Many of these rules seem like common sense, and they *are*. But when money is involved human emotions kick in and drive many bad decisions due to greed, fear, envy, and so on. Don't ever let your emotions lead you to do something with your life savings that you will later regret.

In investing there are many good ways to make money and a multitude of ways to lose it all. You need to be exceedingly careful about how you invest your hard-earned money. The rules in this chapter and the advice in this book can help protect you from many dangers to your life savings.

## Recap

The 16 Golden Rules of Financial Safety are the foundation of the Permanent Portfolio philosophy. Once you accept that the markets are uncertain, you can then begin to develop a strategy to deal with that uncertainty. That's what this book is about.

# CHAPTER 3

# Permanent Portfolio Performance
## *Testing Theories*

When discussing any investment strategy, the question of how it has performed in the past always comes up. The process of looking at historical data to determine how a particular investment strategy may perform going forward is called "backtesting." It's a good idea, however, to be cautious about drawing any firm conclusions about an investment strategy based solely on backtesting data. A better approach is to use backtesting as a tool to prove or disprove general ideas about a strategy, rather than to mechanically project past performance into the future.

Backtesting can tell an investor how well an investment strategy's *theories* have worked in practice during historical periods. Thus, if something failed to work in the past there may be good reason to believe that it won't work in the future either. Repeating mistakes and leaving to faith something that has failed once before is a bad (and likely expensive) strategy. Backtesting then can be an excellent tool to *disprove* theories or to provide a tentative validation of the way a theory would have worked in practice in the past. This approach is, however, quite different from simply noting that an investment strategy has gone up every year for the past 10 years and using that observation as evidence that the strategy will go up for the *next* 10 years.

The value of the Permanent Portfolio performance data presented here is that it demonstrates how well the economic theories behind the strategy have worked historically. The portfolio was first conceived in the late 1970s and put into its final form in the mid-1980s. In other words, at this point we have more than 30 years of empirical data to review to determine how the portfolio's theories have performed under real-world conditions.

While this chapter provides performance data for the Permanent Portfolio, it also provides a framework for assessing other portfolio strategies as well. Two important questions that backtesting data can help to answer are: How do investing strategies fail and what actually causes them to fail?

So how *has* the Permanent Portfolio done compared to other investment strategies? What sets it apart? Let's take a look.

## Growth, No Large Losses, and Real Returns: The Holy Trinity

According to historical data, the Permanent Portfolio strategy has provided investment returns of 9 to 10 percent a year for the past 40 years.[1] The worst loss in any year was around −5 percent back in 1981.

Although these figures are impressive, average annual returns don't tell the whole story when it comes to long-term returns. We all must actually *live* through the periods that are going to determine our future investing track record. This means we also want to see what the Permanent Portfolio investor can expect both in total returns and how nerve wracking those returns were.

Table 3.1 shows the returns of the Permanent Portfolio going back to the early 1970s.

Table 3.1 is interesting for what it shows, but it's also interesting for what it doesn't show.

First, the portfolio has provided respectable growth. An average of 9.5 percent a year is on par with investment portfolios that are much riskier. In fact, it's nearly identical to a portfolio that is 100 percent stocks (which returned 9.8 percent annualized over the same period), even though an all-stock portfolio is *extremely* risky.

Secondly, the portfolio didn't deliver any large losses. You'll see that the number of negative years is very low. Not only did the portfolio have few down years, but the losses in the down years were also quite small. The portfolio's worst year was in 1981, when it lost about −4.9 percent (−12.6 percent adjusted for inflation). Yet, this was just a scratch compared to the severe losses investors experienced in that year in other approaches. Even with this small loss, however, a Permanent Portfolio investor would have recouped all of his losses the very next year as the markets found a new equilibrium among the portfolio's assets and the steady upward growth resumed.

Third, look at the real returns column that shows the portfolio's returns after adjusting for inflation. For the most part it is positive over the entire period, which means that no matter what was going on in the markets, the Permanent Portfolio was able to deliver returns to investors significantly in excess of the rate of inflation. This includes good, bad, and ugly markets. In

---

[1] Source © 2012 Morningstar. All rights reserved. Used with permission in all tables. Gold prices tracking London PM Fix December average for that year.

TABLE 3.1 Nominal and Real Returns 1972 to 2011

| Year | Nominal Returns | Real Returns (Adjusted for Inflation) |
|------|------|------|
| 1972 | 18.9 | 15.0 |
| 1973 | 14.5 | 5.4 |
| 1974 | 14.5 | 2.0 |
| 1975 | 7.0 | 0.1 |
| 1976 | 10.5 | 5.3 |
| 1977 | 4.3 | −2.3 |
| 1978 | 10.5 | 1.4 |
| 1979 | 36.7 | 20.6 |
| 1980 | 17.6 | 4.5 |
| 1981 | −4.9 | −12.6 |
| 1982 | 20.2 | 15.8 |
| 1983 | 4.9 | 1.0 |
| 1984 | 3.5 | −0.5 |
| 1985 | 17.8 | 13.5 |
| 1986 | 17.7 | 16.4 |
| 1987 | 8.1 | 3.5 |
| 1988 | 4.7 | 0.3 |
| 1989 | 14.0 | 8.9 |
| 1990 | 0.8 | −5.0 |
| 1991 | 12.7 | 9.4 |
| 1992 | 3.0 | 0.1 |
| 1993 | 11.4 | 8.4 |
| 1994 | −0.9 | −3.5 |
| 1995 | 19.2 | 16.3 |
| 1996 | 5.6 | 2.2 |
| 1997 | 8.2 | 6.4 |
| 1998 | 11.9 | 10.1 |
| 1999 | 3.5 | 0.8 |
| 2000 | 3.5 | 0.1 |
| 2001 | −0.7 | −2.2 |
| 2002 | 4.5 | 2.0 |
| 2003 | 13.4 | 11.3 |
| 2004 | 7.2 | 3.9 |
| 2005 | 7.8 | 4.2 |
| 2006 | 11.3 | 8.6 |
| 2007 | 11.9 | 7.5 |
| 2008 | −2.0 | −2.1 |
| 2009 | 12.7 | 9.7 |
| 2010 | 12.0 | 10.3 |
| 2011 | 13.3 | 10.1 |
| **Annualized Returns** | 9.5 | 4.9 |

*Numbers rounded to nearest tenth in this and other charts.

short, the Permanent Portfolio is a "real return" portfolio. Real returns are a very important, but frequently overlooked, way of evaluating and comparing investment strategies.

These three points reflect basic performance characteristics of the Permanent Portfolio that few other investment strategies have been able to pull off with as much safety and stability. Some portfolios do not grow money at a rate appreciably above inflation because they are too cautious, while other portfolios may provide high growth but tend to suffer periodic large losses due to the overall risk in the strategy. Finally, some portfolios may provide protection against large losses and decent non-inflation adjusted returns, but can't beat inflation over all periods (resulting in a different type of loss that will be discussed later).

The most significant difference between the Permanent Portfolio and other approaches is that the Permanent Portfolio gives you real growth *and* protection of your money. Let's take a closer look at these points.

## Respectable Growth

An annual growth rate of 9 to 10 percent is about what the U.S. stock market has averaged in recent decades (though with much more volatility). To have a portfolio that can deliver 9 to 10 percent annual growth offers serious compounding power. Table 3.2 illustrates what that kind of growth looks like over time.

Over an investor's lifetime, a growth rate in the 9 to 10 percent range can provide a very comfortable retirement (or even early retirement). Best of all, with the Permanent Portfolio these returns can be obtained with very little stress.

Most reviews of investment performance stop here with an overview of historical performance. However, a portfolio's rate of growth is just *one*

TABLE 3.2  Growth of $10K at Average Annual Return of 9.5 Percent with No Future Contributions

| Year | Amount |
| --- | --- |
| 1 | $ 10,000 |
| 2 | $ 10,950 |
| 5 | $ 15,742 |
| 10 | $ 24,782 |
| 20 | $ 61,416 |
| 30 | $152,203 |
| 40 | $377,193 |

*aspect* of portfolio performance that needs to be considered. There are at least two other important components of overall performance, which are discussed below.

## No Large Losses

It's easy to get distracted by an investment's promise of high returns. What one often finds, however, is that high historical returns were obtained by taking huge risks. These risks just happened to work out well for investors (you don't hear all of the stories about the investors who didn't do so well over the same period). Investing based on recent high returns often works out disastrously (it's called "performance chasing"). Periods of high gains are often followed by periods of sub-par returns or even large losses.

Even one year of large losses can be very difficult to recover from (especially for someone who is nearing retirement or already retired). Consider Table 3.3, which shows various losses and how much you would need to fully recover if they should occur.

Investors should understand the math involved here because it is not symmetrical. For example, recovering from a 50 percent loss can be very

**TABLE 3.3  A Large Loss in a Portfolio can Take Years to Recover from in a Portfolio**

Investors should Balance Growth with Protection of Their Assets

| Portfolio Loss | Return to Get Back to Even |
| --- | --- |
| −5% | +5.3% |
| −10% | +11.1% |
| −15% | +17.6% |
| −20% | +25% |
| −25% | +33.3% |
| −30% | +42.9% |
| −35% | +53.8% |
| −40% | +66.7% |
| −45% | +81.8% |
| −50% | +100% |
| −55% | +122.2% |
| −60% | +150% |
| −65% | +185.7% |
| −70% | +233.3% |
| −75% | +300% |
| −80% | +400% |
| −85% | +566.7% |
| −90% | +900% |
| −95% | +1900% |
| −100% | Never! |

difficult because an investor in that situation will need a 100 percent return just to get back to where he started! Even a 40 percent loss (as happened recently in 2008 to U.S. stocks) requires a 66.7 percent gain to get back to even. Depending on how an investor reacts to these kinds of losses, the recovery could happen in a few years if the investor is patient enough to wait, or it could never happen if the investor bails out due to the stress generated by excessive portfolio volatility.

This problem of large losses hobbling a portfolio potentially for years is why investors want to avoid it. The only way to protect against these kinds of losses is to either take almost no risk (which also means limiting potential gains) or use strong diversification within a portfolio.

> It is an unusual investor who can calmly sit through a −30 percent or worse decline in the value of his portfolio.

Fortunately, the Permanent Portfolio has some of the simplest and strongest diversification available to protect against large losses and excessive portfolio volatility. Don't underestimate the importance of a portfolio avoiding large losses. It is an unusual investor who can calmly sit through a −30 percent or worse decline in the value of his portfolio. What often happens is that investors will bail out of a volatile investment strategy at the worst possible time (usually near a market low). However, by never placing yourself in a situation where you would need to endure large losses, you will be ahead of most investors and can ride out inevitable market volatility with less fear.

On one occasion when Craig was working as a network engineer he was discussing network architecture with a very experienced designer, Dr. Jose Nabielsky. Dr. Nabielsky responded to a question about the role of high performance in system design with the following comment: "Speed is fine, just be sure you can take the turns." The translation is that high performance is only one part of network design; it also has to be reliable at all times to handle inevitable problems.

What does this have to do with investing? A lot. It's tempting to get enchanted with high performance returns in a portfolio. But, having a portfolio that shows red-hot performance is only one measure you need to consider (and probably not the most important one). Investors also need to know what happens when things don't go according to plan. *Can your investment portfolio take the turns?* Or does it go flying off a cliff into a fiery death at the first twist in the road?

Red-hot historical returns are not impressive on their own. It is easy to go into a spreadsheet with historical data and hindsight to come up with a portfolio that outperformed everything else, *but that doesn't mean the portfolio will do that in the future.* If investing was that easy there would only be one mutual fund—The Hot Historical Return Fund—and everyone would invest all of their money in it.

Designing a portfolio for high returns alone eventually leads to disaster. Portfolios need the ability to generate growth, but must also have the ability to weather the unexpected storms, including investors' inevitable bouts of fear when the whole market seems to be falling apart. *Portfolios need to take the turns.*

### Real Inflation-Adjusted Returns

When discussing an investment's performance, it's important to understand the difference between non-inflation adjusted returns (called "nominal returns") and inflation-adjusted returns (called "real returns"). *Only real returns matter.*

In simple terms, inflation is the loss of purchasing power of a currency over time. In this era, the U.S. Federal Reserve has remained committed to maintaining a low but steady rate of inflation in the 2 to 3 percent range (although over the past 40 years it's been more like 4.4 percent on average).

This policy toward inflation means that an investor typically must earn at least 4.4 percent per year on his investments just to stay even. While there is plenty to complain about with respect to this arrangement, for purposes of determining how we are going to invest our hard-earned money, we need to simply accept that this is how the system works and adjust our strategy to deal with it.

As discussed, in the United States the rate of inflation has averaged around 4.4 percent a year since the early 1970s. The early 1970s is used as the starting point because that is when the United States broke the last chain of the gold standard. This is when President Nixon ended the international convertibility of the U.S. dollar into gold (President Roosevelt had taken away the ability of U.S. citizens to exchange their dollars for gold in 1933). After President Nixon ended the peg of the U.S. dollar to gold, inflation was able to quickly get traction as the U.S. dollar rapidly lost value. While all of the dynamics driving inflation are too involved to fully explore here, for purposes of the Permanent Portfolio it is important to simply understand that U.S. inflation in recent decades has been a deliberate policy decision by the government. Dealing with this steady erosion of purchasing power is one of the most serious challenges facing any investment strategy.[2]

One of the insidious aspects of inflation is that if a person does nothing at all with his savings and decides to simply keep it under his mattress, he could, on average, see 4.4 percent of its value disappear each year *automatically.*

> One of the insidious aspects of inflation is that if a person does nothing at all with his savings and decides to simply keep it under his mattress, he could, on average, see 4.4 percent of its value disappear each year *automatically.*

What happens over time to a dollar that loses 4.4 percent a year in purchasing power? Table 3.4 illustrates (rounded to nearest penny).

Simply put, if you stuffed $100 under your mattress today, after 10 years you'd look under your mattress and find approximately $67 in purchasing power. Where did the $33 go? While we can't necessarily say where the lost purchasing power *went*, we can say with certainty that it is no longer under your mattress, and that's all you are really concerned about.

---

[2] Consumer Price Index (CPI) rose on average 4.4 percent since 1972 once the gold standard was totally abandoned. Under the gold standard, from the founding of the country until 1933, there was very slight *deflation* and no loss of purchasing power.

TABLE 3.4 Inflation Erodes
Purchasing Power Over Time

| Year | Future Value |
| --- | --- |
| 1 | $1.00 |
| 2 | $0.96 |
| 5 | $0.84 |
| 10 | $0.67 |
| 20 | $0.43 |
| 30 | $0.27 |
| 40 | $0.17 |

Think of the process of inflation as a very tall ladder that has been set on fire from the bottom. If you don't climb fast enough, you'll eventually be consumed in flames.

Note, however, that the inflation figures above are just historical *averages*. Let's suppose that we're experiencing above-average inflation such as the U.S. experienced during the 1970s, when inflation rates went into double digits in some years. Such an inflationary period can be a disaster for savers. What would happen to the money under your mattress if inflation were running at 10 percent annually instead of the 4.4 percent average?

Table 3.5 is an eye-opener. With 10 percent annual inflation, inside of 10 years you would lose over 60 percent of the purchasing power of your savings, and after 40 years you would basically be wiped out. One dollar in today's terms would buy just two cents of future goods under that scenario. Inflation is dangerous.

What's the takeaway? *If your portfolio doesn't at least earn the rate of inflation each year you are losing money.* An investment portfolio not only needs to provide good nominal returns (without large losses), it must also provide good *real* returns, and must do so over all time periods, including periods of high inflation. Pulling this off consistently is harder than it looks.

TABLE 3.5 Higher Inflation Rates
Quickly Destroy Purchasing
Power

| Year | Future Value |
| --- | --- |
| 1 | $1.00 |
| 2 | $0.90 |
| 5 | $0.66 |
| 10 | $0.39 |
| 20 | $0.14 |
| 30 | $0.04 |
| 40 | $0.02 |

Investors can't afford to just match inflation; they need to *beat it*. No exceptions.

Investors can't afford to just match inflation; they need to *beat it*. No exceptions. To not do this means that inflation will definitely erode your life savings down to dangerously low levels over the years.

## Only Real Returns Matter

It's important to emphasize again that only real returns matter to an investor. The good news is that the Permanent Portfolio can provide you with both consistent real returns, as well as a smooth ride along the way. This matter of consistent real returns is why Table 3.1 at the beginning of the chapter is so important. The portfolio didn't just earn solid returns; it was able to do it no matter what inflation was doing in the broad economy. Over the last 40 years the Permanent Portfolio has had real annual returns in the 3 to 6 percent range over all rolling 10-year periods. That means that there is no 10-year period over the past 40 years where the portfolio failed to beat inflation by at least 3 percent, and the portfolio was able to beat inflation by as much as 6 percent over some periods.

A popular investment strategy is to allocate 60 percent of a portfolio's assets to stocks and 40 percent to bonds. We will call this approach the "60/40 portfolio." This portfolio is a fine strategy and has performed reasonably well over most periods. However, what you find with this type of portfolio is that it will have some periods when the portfolio lags inflation or barely keeps pace. The periods of high inflation in the 1970s, for example, caused stock-and-bond-only portfolios to see multi-year periods of negative real returns. In other words, investors were losing money over extended periods. In fact, just about any portfolio that only held stocks and bonds during the 1970s performed poorly on an inflation-adjusted basis, no matter what percentage allocations it used

When comparing any strategy to the Permanent Portfolio, it is normally the multi-year returns that are the most telling. Table 3.6 illustrates several multi-year comparisons of how the Permanent Portfolio's performance compared to a 60/40 portfolio. A start year of 2000 would mean how the portfolio did from 2000–2002 for 3 years, 2000–2004 for 5 years, and 2000–2009 for 10 years. The table is showing what returns you would have received if you had invested in that year and waited 3, 5, or 10 years into the future.

TABLE 3.6 Multi-year Real Returns for Permanent Portfolio Compared to 60/40 Stock/Bond Portfolio from 1972 to 2011

| | Permanent Portfolio | | | 60/40 Portfolio | | |
|---|---|---|---|---|---|---|
| Start Year | 3 Year | 5 Year | 10 Year | 3 Year | 5 Year | 10 Year |
| 1972 | 7.3% | 5.4% | 3.6% | −10.3% | −0.8% | −1.6% |
| 1973 | 2.4% | 2.0% | 3.6% | −8.3% | −4.5% | −0.9% |
| 1974 | 2.4% | 1.3% | 3.2% | 1.0% | −2.1% | 1.9% |
| 1975 | 1.0% | 4.7% | 3.0% | 6.5% | 3.1% | 5.1% |
| 1976 | 1.4% | 5.7% | 4.3% | −0.4% | 1.5% | 5.5% |
| 1977 | 6.1% | 1.8% | 5.3% | −4.3% | −2.5% | 5.6% |
| 1978 | 8.5% | 5.3% | 5.9% | 1.5% | 2.9% | 6.6% |
| 1979 | 3.3% | 5.2% | 5.8% | 0.4% | 6.2% | 7.8% |
| 1980 | 1.9% | 1.2% | 4.7% | 6.1% | 7.2% | 9.7% |
| 1981 | 0.7% | 2.9% | 3.7% | 7.4% | 9.6% | 8.3% |
| 1982 | 5.2% | 9.0% | 6.1% | 11.9% | 14.4% | 11.2% |
| 1983 | 4.5% | 6.6% | 4.6% | 12.9% | 10.4% | 9.8% |
| 1984 | 9.6% | 6.4% | 5.3% | 13.8% | 9.5% | 9.2% |
| 1985 | 11.0% | 8.4% | 5.0% | 11.5% | 12.3% | 8.4% |
| 1986 | 6.5% | 4.6% | 5.2% | 7.2% | 7.0% | 8.8% |
| 1987 | 4.2% | 3.3% | 3.9% | 8.4% | 8.1% | 8.5% |
| 1988 | 1.2% | 2.6% | 4.2% | 7.2% | 9.2% | 10.7% |
| 1989 | 4.2% | 4.2% | 5.1% | 11.2% | 9.0% | 11.8% |
| 1990 | 1.3% | 1.7% | 4.3% | 6.5% | 4.6% | 10.8% |
| 1991 | 5.9% | 5.9% | 4.9% | 10.5% | 10.6% | 10.8% |
| 1992 | 1.6% | 4.5% | 3.7% | 2.8% | 8.9% | 8.2% |
| 1993 | 6.8% | 5.8% | 3.9% | 9.6% | 12.3% | 6.4% |
| 1994 | 4.7% | 6.1% | 4.2% | 11.1% | 14.6% | 7.3% |
| 1995 | 8.1% | 7.0% | 5.0% | 19.8% | 17.4% | 8.1% |
| 1996 | 6.2% | 3.9% | 3.8% | 17.2% | 11.0% | 5.6% |
| 1997 | 5.7% | 2.9% | 4.4% | 16.5% | 7.5% | 5.3% |
| 1998 | 3.6% | 2.1% | 4.5% | 7.6% | 0.7% | 3.5% |
| 1999 | −0.4% | 2.3% | 3.3% | −0.2% | 0.4% | −0.6% |
| 2000 | 0.0% | 2.9% | 4.2% | −7.2% | −0.5% | 0.0% |
| 2001 | 3.6% | 3.8% | 5.2% | −0.9% | 0.5% | 1.3% |
| 2002 | 5.7% | 6.0% | 6.3% | 2.4% | 3.2% | 1.9% |
| 2003 | 6.4% | 7.1% | | 7.1% | 6.3% | |
| 2004 | 5.5% | 4.3% | | 4.5% | −1.5% | |
| 2005 | 6.7% | 5.5% | | 3.5% | 0.4% | |
| 2006 | 4.6% | 6.7% | | −4.1% | 2.2% | |
| 2007 | 4.9% | | | −2.2% | | |
| 2008 | 5.8% | | | 0.3% | | |

60/40 and Permanent Portfolio returns generated from Simba spreadsheet with Vanguard data for Total Bond Market and Ibbotson data for other components for comparison.

Figures 3.1 and 3.2 show rolling 10-year returns for the Permanent Portfolio and the 60/40 portfolio. You can see the lumpy real returns of the 60/40 portfolio during some periods compared to the stable and consistent real returns provided by the Permanent Portfolio.

Figure 3.1 shows something very interesting. It is true that a stock-heavy portfolio can do very well when the stock market is performing well. In the 1980s and 1990s, the 60/40 portfolio provided impressive real returns—over 10 percent at times. However, during the high inflation 1970s and volatile 2000s, the 60/40 portfolio was very low on real returns and even negative during some periods.

Figure 3.2 shows lower real returns during the 1980s and 1990s for the Permanent Portfolio. However, it showed near-identical real returns through the very lackluster 1970s and 2000s as well. In other words, no matter what was going on in the markets and overall economy, the portfolio was beating inflation by anywhere from 3 to 6 percent a year.

It's worth taking the time to understand the above because it is not enough to say a portfolio returned a certain percentage over time. We need to know how much it returned *after inflation* has taken its share. An investor may have a career in the 30- to 40-year range before retirement; they can't afford to have long spans of no real growth. Further, someone already in retirement could be even more impacted by protracted periods of no, or negative, growth of their savings.

Fundamentally, a portfolio should be able to generate solid real returns over any extended period and beat inflation. To not do so is a serious failure that is likely to repeat in the future.

## Looking at Total Performance Over Time

In reviewing the historic performance of the Permanent Portfolio, it's useful to compare its performance to other popular investment strategies. In reviewing returns, however, the focus will be on real returns. The portfolios assembled for comparison purposes assume that a U.S. Large Company Stock Market index and a Total Bond Market index are used (both are good choices typically). If these otherwise good and simple index fund portfolios can suffer from these weaknesses, then things only get worse for other strategies. The table below compares the following four portfolios:

1. Permanent Portfolio
2. 75 percent U.S. stocks/25 percent Total Bond Market (75/25)—An Aggressive Allocation
3. 50 percent U.S. stocks/50 percent Total Bond Market (50/50)—A Balanced Allocation
4. 25 percent U.S. stocks/75 percent Total Bond Market (25/75)—A Conservative Allocation

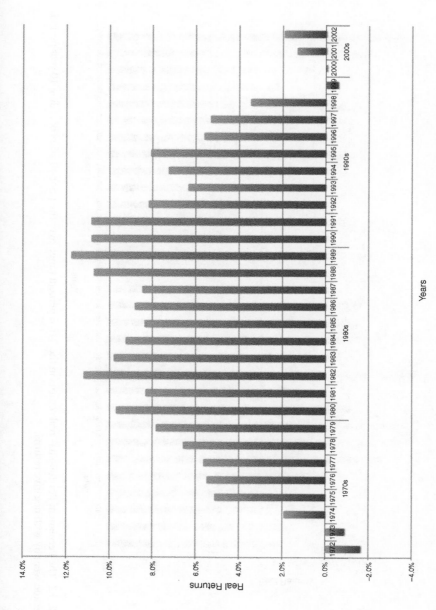

FIGURE 3.1 The 60/40 stock and bond portfolio had a great run in the 1980s–1990s with high rolling real returns. However, in the 1970s and 2000s the 60/40 portfolio lost out to inflation and was negative for extended periods or had very low real returns.

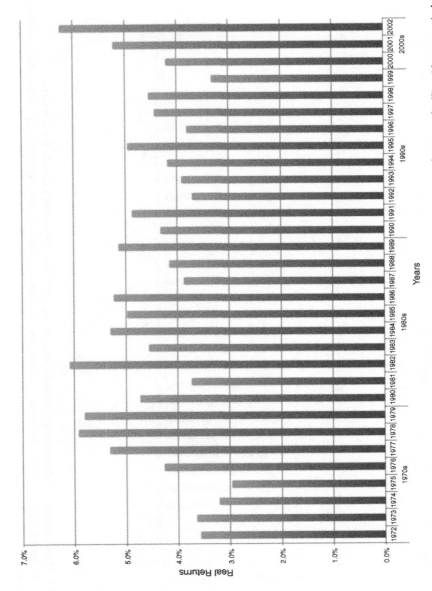

FIGURE 3.2 The Permanent Portfolio has real returns in the 3 to 6 percent range over the prior 40 years of rolling 10-year periods. No decade went by with negative returns.

## 1970s

The 1970s saw an average rate of inflation of around 8.6 percent. During this decade a portfolio would have needed to earn 8.6 percent on average just to maintain purchasing power. Over this time we see that the Permanent Portfolio managed to have real returns of 5.7 percent, while the other portfolios struggled with real returns of −2.0 to −2.3 percent. This means that $1 invested in these strategies at the beginning of the decade was worth around $0.85 10 years later. That's 10 years of negative growth, which could be disastrous to an investor nearing retirement or who was already retired. This doesn't even show the years 1973 and 1974 with terrible stock market losses (−21.5 percent and −34.6 percent in real terms respectively) that the Permanent Portfolio totally shrugged off (5.4 percent and 2.0 percent real *gains*, respectively).

## 1980s

Going into the 1980s we hit the beginning of the biggest and longest sustained bull market for stocks in U.S. history. Stock heavy portfolios did very well, but only if you happened to be investing over this time in a lot of stocks (which had done poorly the previous 10 years). In this period all of the portfolios had respectable real returns, but obviously those that emphasized stocks did the best.

As a point of interest that isn't shown in Table 3.7, in October 1987 there was a single day drop of 22 percent in the stock market known as Black Monday. During that period, the Permanent Portfolio sailed through the event while other portfolios swooned. How many investors dropped out of the market in 1987 in panic, locking in losses only to miss solid gains later? The Permanent Portfolio was up 3.5 percent in real terms that year.

TABLE 3.7 Comparison of Annualized Real Returns by Decade for Four Portfolios

| Decade | Permanent Portfolio | 75/25 Portfolio | 50/50 Portfolio | 25/75 Portfolio |
|---|---|---|---|---|
| 1972–1979* | +5.7% | −2.3% | −2.1% | −2.0% |
| 1980–1989 | +4.7% | +10.5% | +9.1% | +7.6% |
| 1990–1999 | +4.3% | +12.4% | +9.8% | +7.2% |
| 2000–2009 | +4.2% | −1.2% | +0.6% | +2.2% |

*Market data used for equal comparison begins in 1972 after gold standard ends.

## 1990s

The 1990s saw another great time for stocks as the Internet technology bubble grew. As stocks soared, so did the real returns of stock-heavy allocations. By the year 2000 though, the bubble was getting ready to pop and erase a good portion of the previous stock gains. But again the Permanent Portfolio just chugged along with its steady consistent growth. When the Internet bubble was deflating the Permanent Portfolio protected its assets when the high-flyers took a big fall.

## 2000s

When the 2000s came along, for stock investors it felt a lot like the 1970s, with very poor real returns on stocks. The 20-year bull market in stocks had ended. Between the Internet bust from 2000 to 2002, the terrorist attacks of 2001, and the real estate bust that started in 2007, things were very rocky across the whole economy. However, the Permanent Portfolio again just chugged along, turning in another decade of 4.2 percent average real returns with no wild swings in value.

### Steady Growth in Unsteady Markets

When reviewing the portfolio's performances on a decade-by-decade basis, consider all of the events that happened during this period. It included economic booms, recessions, wars, terrorism, stock market crashes, asset bubbles, and turmoil all over the world. But during this time the Permanent Portfolio was able to maintain its smooth steady growth no matter what was going on in the economy and around the world.

# Recap

Total portfolio performance consists of three things:

1. A good growth rate that can expand your money over time without being too risky.
2. Avoiding large losses. Large losses are difficult to recover from without taking a lot of risk (which can make things even worse), being very lucky, or just letting time pass (which may not be an option for someone nearing or in retirement).
3. Real returns matter most. Inflation cannot be ignored when looking at investment returns.

Investors can't afford to have long stretches of poor returns or large losses. Just as compounding can grow money over time, it can also work to reduce your savings significantly when pitted against you. Investors require growth, protection, and real returns. If you don't have all three, your investment plan is going to eventually run into serious problems.

The ability to deliver smooth and consistent real returns over a multi-decade period is a feat that *very* few investment strategies can offer. The Permanent Portfolio, however, has been able to provide smooth and consistent real returns in the 3 to 6 percent range over a 40-year period covering a variety of good and bad markets.

# CHAPTER 4

# Simple, Safe, and Stable

## *Three Factors to Success*

A side from good growth, avoiding large losses, and real returns in portfolio performance, there are three other factors that allow an investment strategy to be successful:

1. Simplicity
2. Safety
3. Stability

The three factors above help an investor avoid bad investments and effectively manage the emotional ups and downs that come with investing.

## Simplicity

Investors should invest as simply as possible. This strategy applies even to very large portfolios. *Complexity kills returns.* Complicated investing strategies and products can conceal many hidden costs and risks that may be hard to see from the outside. These costs and risks will often not be discovered until it's too late.

Complexity kills returns.

Investing does not need to be, nor should it be, complicated. There is a strong relationship between complicated investment products, lower performance, and higher risks—all things you don't want.

Understand that no investment is "risk free." This is an immutable law of investing. Someone claiming that an investment is risk free either does not know what the risks actually are, or is not telling the truth about the investment. All investments have risks and a simple portfolio allows you to *isolate* and *understand* those risks to your life savings so you can diversify against them.

Invariably, the more complicated and opaque an investment product is, the more likely it is to have hidden risks that simpler investments do not have. What investors want to do is identify and diversify against known risks intelligently. What investors do *not* want to do is have any risks come as a surprise. Surprises can be expensive. Unfortunately, complicated investments are often full of surprises. Investors should not go out looking for trouble if it can be easily avoided by keeping things simpler.

Additionally, investment professionals will often try to convince their clients that more complex strategies produce greater returns. The truth, however, is that complex strategies provide more opportunities to conceal fees, commissions, and other expenses that increase investment professionals' income, while reducing their clients' returns.

Lastly, the ability to manage and make adjustments to complicated portfolios is often harder and more expensive than with simpler strategies, which can also result in a greater drain on overall returns.

In sum, portfolios that are simple yet well-designed have the following advantages over those that are complex. This will become clearer as you read through the following chapters in this book. Simple portfolios:

- Have less chance of hidden risks.
- Have lower management fees.
- Are more tax efficient.
- Require a small time commitment on the part of the investor to maintain.
- Are likely to outperform more complicated strategies over time.

These advantages increase the chances that you will have long-term investment success. Keep things simple!

## Safety

A safe portfolio is one that is invested using strong diversification in case things don't go according to plan. The Golden Rules of Financial Safety tell us that it is your career that should be the basis of your wealth, and this wealth may not be replaceable if it is lost. So why gamble your savings on some get-rich-quick investment scheme that can cost you a big chunk of your savings if it goes wrong?

A safe portfolio does not mean tucking money under your mattress (which is actually not safe at all since inflation will silently and steadily erode its value). Safety means risks are taken on a calculated basis and avoided where they add nothing to the bottom line. It also means using a strong diversification strategy to protect against the unexpected and unthinkable. An intelligently allocated portfolio can hold assets that are risky in isolation, but when owned in combination with other assets can actually result in a package that is far safer than any of the assets would be if held individually.

## Stability

A stable portfolio is one that can perform well during good or bad markets, while also protecting against large losses. It will not have wild swings in value. Wild swings in value can exacerbate losses experienced by investors. This is because very few investors are able to withstand large fluctuations in a portfolio's value without eventually abandoning a strategy (often at the worst possible time and locking in those losses).

A stable portfolio allows an investor to avoid panic when the markets are in turmoil. Stability doesn't mean an investor won't ever take a loss; rather, it means that any losses will be small enough that the pain won't drive the investor to make bad investment decisions based upon fear. Once an emotion like fear takes over, an investor can be persuaded to do many things that are very unprofitable or even *riskier* than leaving things alone. The key is *avoiding* these situations, rather than trying to make good decisions once you are in them.

It is fun to think of the fabulous riches we might have if we followed the latest high-flying investment strategy. Who wouldn't want to earn 20 percent a year, for instance? Unfortunately, there is a cost to chasing abnormally high returns and that cost is your portfolio usually becomes very volatile and extremely risky. Sure, you may get lucky and see large gains in some markets, but you're more likely to see large losses.

The ups and downs of the markets make it hard for any investor (even professionals) to stick to a plan. All investors are human and experience the same range of emotions, including the occasional wave of overwhelming fear. As much as market commentators talk about discipline and ignoring short-term market fluctuations, the fact is that most investors will eventually bail out of almost any investment when faced with large enough declines.

> Investors should simply stay out of investment strategies that have the potential for large losses so they can remain a spectator and not an active participant in a market panic.

A market panic is not a situation where only the *other* guy panics—it could sweep *you* up as well. It's unrealistic for investors to think that they will be the ones in a market decline who are thinking clearly. Investors should simply stay out of investment strategies that have the potential for large losses so they can remain a spectator and not an active participant in a market panic. A stable portfolio will allow them to do exactly that.

If you have a sound long-term investment plan there is no reason to reach for huge gains since that always means exposing yourself to potentially large losses and instability. A steady and consistent rate of growth can prove incredibly powerful if just left alone. And, not coincidentally, a stable portfolio means investors *will leave it alone*. Since long-term investment success is related to the ability to stay the course and not try to outguess the markets, a stable portfolio will help you emotionally to stick with the plan.

## Making the Most of Your Investments

A portfolio that is simple, safe, and stable can be achieved by doing the following:

- Using passive investing only.
- Keep costs low.
- Use volatile individual assets to reduce overall portfolio volatility.
- Expect the unexpected and embrace the idea of market uncertainty.

### Passive Investing

Passive investing is the opposite of the active asset management that is typically offered on Wall Street. The Permanent Portfolio is a passive strategy, which means that it does not engage in market timing, actively trading stocks, moving in or out of the market on chart signals, or other similar tactics. All of these activities assume excess profits can be made if just the right trade is made at just the right time. Many investment strategies are based on principles of active management, with the implicit assumption that the future is predictable.

The problem is that the future is *not* predictable. Think about it like this: If the market's next moves were truly predictable by some easy and reliable method, why would anyone be selling *you* this information on the Internet or through a broker's office? Wouldn't you expect the people who possessed such knowledge to jealously guard it and make the fortunes in their own accounts instead of hawking it to you for relative peanuts? What would you do with that knowledge if you had it for absolute certainty? Would you sell it on TV for $19.95 and a free coffee mug while supplies last?

"One of these men dresses in an elaborate costume to make you
think they can predict the future. The other wears a turban."

**THE DISMAL RESULTS OF ACTIVE MANAGEMENT**   Even though investors are
sold the idea that active management is required for success, the actual results show that it simply doesn't work. Actively managed strategies are far
more likely to lose out to passive strategies over time. This result, as counterintuitive as it may sound, has been shown repeatedly by academic and industry research for *decades*. In most cases, actively managed funds are all
fighting for second place behind passive investing strategies.

Standard & Poor's (S&P) has its own S&P Indices Versus Active Funds
(SPIVA) scorecard. S&P is the leading market index creator, known for its
S&P 500 Index (made up of the 500 largest U.S. companies) and many other
benchmarks covering major market sectors across the world (stocks, bonds,
and real estate). In the fund industry active managers will compare their performance to various S&P indices to gauge how well they did compared to the
overall market.

The SPIVA report is S&P's way of reporting on industry performance
compared to their benchmarks. They use a methodology that accounts for
"survivorship bias." Survivorship bias is what happens when the final results
of a data series don't show all of those who dropped out before the end.

> Think of survivorship bias as going into your school records, erasing the courses you took where you received a bad grade, and then recalculating your GPA. It's the same thing, except when you do it you don't make millions a year from unsuspecting investors.

A fund that is performing poorly will often be closed or merged with another fund in order to sweep poor results under the rug. This can make a group of funds look better over the years as the stinkers are quietly buried. The poor results are removed from the industry totals, boosting the overall averages of those that remain. Think of survivorship bias as going into your school records, erasing the courses you took where you received a bad grade, and then recalculating your GPA. It's the same thing, except when you do it you don't make millions a year from unsuspecting investors.

As noted above, however, the results of each year's SPIVA scorecard do not allow for this removal of bad funds from performance data and the results are eye opening. Simply put, actively managed funds (regardless of what strategy they use) overwhelmingly lag their respective indices over any time period analyzed. Here are a few of the observations from the SPIVA report on fund performance:

> *Over the five-year market cycle from 2004 to 2008, S&P 500 outperformed 71.9 percent of actively managed large-cap funds, S&P MidCap 400 outperformed 79.1 percent of mid-cap funds and S&P SmallCap 600 outperformed 85.5 percent of small-cap funds. These results are similar to that of the previous five-year cycle from 1999 to 2003.*
>
> —S&P Indices Versus Active Funds Scorecard 2008

> *The belief that bear markets favor active management is a myth. A majority of active funds in eight of the nine domestic equity style boxes were outperformed by indices in the negative markets of 2008. The bear market of 2000 to 2002 showed similar outcomes.*
>
> —S&P Indices Versus Active Funds Scorecard 2008

> *Over the past three years, which can be characterized by volatile market conditions, 63.96 percent of actively managed large-cap funds were outperformed by the S&P 500, 75.07 percent of mid-cap funds were outperformed by the S&P MidCap 400 and 63.08 percent of the small-cap funds were outperformed by the S&P SmallCap 600.*
>
> —S&P Indices Versus Active Funds Scorecard 2011

> *Indices have outperformed a majority of active managers in nearly all major domestic and international equity categories. In addition, five-year asset-weighted averages suggest that active managers have fallen behind benchmarks in 11 out of 18 domestic fund categories.*
> —S&P Indices Versus Active Funds Scorecard 2011[1]

As the SPIVA reports show, professionals simply do not beat the market as a group. Worse yet, the small percentage of actively managed funds that do beat the market changes over time. For instance, even if you figured out the 20 percent of actively managed funds that actually beat the underlying index last year, there is no guarantee that the same funds are going to beat the index next year.

By constantly moving in and out of markets, or choosing poorly performing actively managed funds, average returns for the typical investor are abysmal. As noted by N. Scott Pritchard in a research study he conducted tracking performance over a nearly 20-year period from 1988 to 2007:

> *[T]he S&P 500 returned an annualized 11.81 percent from 1988 through 2007; yet the average investor's return over that same period was a paltry 4.48 percent—even less than the most conservative of investments, the 30-day Treasury Bill.[2]*

These poor results are likely due to a combination of factors, including not using a portfolio that is simple, safe, and stable. However, one significant factor is certainly relying on actively managed investment portfolios. Whether the investor himself is hopping in and out of hot funds and sectors, or a professional manager is doing it through the funds the investor owns, the results are going to be similarly bad.

Passive investors don't want to beat the market. Instead, they want to sit back and collect gains across multiple asset classes by being widely diversified at all times. Ironically, just trying to get the market average means over time you will beat most investors and investment professionals.

## Keep Costs Low

Wall Street makes a tremendous amount of money from management fees charged on mutual funds and other investment products. A typical actively managed fund charges 1 to 2 percent a year in management and other fees.[3]

---

[1] *S&P Indices Versus Active Funds Scorecard,* www.standardandpoors.com/indices/spiva/en/us.

[2] N. Scott Pritchard, "The Tyranny of Choice," *Journal of Pension Benefits* 6, no. 1 (Autumn 2008).

[3] Various sources on industry average, including Morningstar, which shows a 1.3 percent average fee as of 2011 and it varies each year. Some funds also have front end loads and other fees.

This means, for example, that if the underlying market returns 10 percent a year, an actively managed fund is going to have to make 11 to 12 percent a year *before fees* just to match it (since fund management fees reduce fund performance by the amount of the fees). In other words, actively managed funds have to perform 1 to 2 percent *better* than the index they are being measured against just to pay their management fees and not be beaten by the index. This is almost impossible for any manager to consistently do over the years.

However, if an investor can *eliminate* the 1 to 2 percent in fund management fees (that aren't really buying any performance advantage anyway) this can provide the investor with a tremendous edge. That's 1 to 2 percent more in returns each year and that adds up over time.

Consider Table 4.1, which you'll see again later. This table assumes a market return of 10 percent for illustration purposes. Notice what happens when your fund hits the average, but *then* deducts fund management expenses.

Being cheap pays. This is not just because you avoid paying for something that provides little or no value such as active management, but also because it leaves more money to compound in the portfolio. The second 9.8 percent figure above would be what a passive portfolio management fee of 0.20 percent would be in terms of cost impacts each year. Economist William F. Sharpe, Recipient of the Nobel Memorial Prize in Economic Sciences, said this:

> *Properly measured, the average actively managed dollar must underperform the average passively managed dollar, net of costs. Empirical analyses that appear to refute this principle are guilty of improper measurement.*[4]

**TABLE 4.1** Hypothetical Impacts of Portfolio Management Costs If You Earn 10 Percent a Year for 20 Years

| Starting Value | Expense Ratio | After Expense Return | Years | Final Value | Fee Impact |
|---|---|---|---|---|---|
| **$10,000** | 0% | 10% | 20 | $67,275 | $      0 |
| **$10,000** | 0.1% | 9.9% | 20 | $66,062 | $  1,213 |
| **$10,000** | 0.2% | 9.8% | 20 | $64,870 | $  2,405 |
| **$10,000** | 1% | 9% | 20 | $56,044 | $11,231 |
| **$10,000** | 2% | 8% | 20 | $46,609 | $21,116 |
| **$10,000** | 3% | 7% | 20 | $38,696 | $28,579 |

---

[4] William F. Sharpe, "The Arithmetic of Active Management," *Financial Analyst's Journal*, January/February 1991: 7–9.

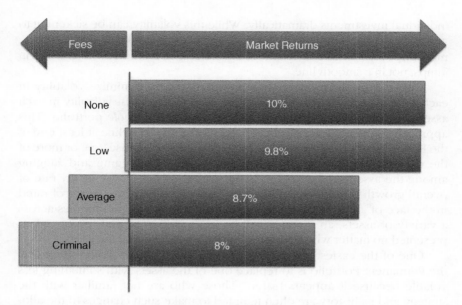

**FIGURE 4.1** Higher fees always equals lower average returns.

Figure 4.1 illustrates Professor Sharpe's observation. In this example, it is assumed that the market returned 10 percent to all participants in a year to illustrate. Therefore, the returns of the average fund must be the market average itself minus the costs to operate the fund. There is no other way for the math to work!

Once you subtract management fees the expensive funds will underperform unless they get lucky and happen to get returns well above average that particular year. And luck has much to do with it. There are other costs besides management fees that also need to be considered. For example, taxes eat up a significant portion of returns with certain types of investments. However, there are ways to control these costs that will be discussed later. But here's a hint: Passive management is the most tax efficient way to invest as well.

The bottom line is this: If you reduce your annual costs, for example, from 1.5 percent a year to 0.20 percent a year you instantly gain a 1.3 percent performance improvement with no effort and no additional risk. It's the closest thing to free money an investor is ever going to get.

## Use Volatility to Avoid Volatility

Markets are often volatile when you look at assets individually. Good or bad things can happen in the markets at any time and these events can affect individual investments dramatically. While this volatility can be sickening to watch as it is happening, it is ironically the volatile days that contribute the most to profits (as well as losses). This is because markets tend to move in jumps, not in a smooth line.

Unlike some investment strategies that seek to minimize volatility in each asset class, the Permanent Portfolio seeks to *increase* volatility in each asset class in order to achieve stability across the *whole* portfolio. This approach sounds counterintuitive, but it works. In fact, while at least one of the Permanent Portfolio's assets is normally in the doghouse, one or more of the other assets are usually doing quite well. This zigging and zagging among the assets typically cancels out and translates into a steady rate of overall growth. This growth allows an investor to maintain peace of mind in the face of all market conditions. By staying invested at all times across a variety of assets, an investor will be in a position to grab profits when presented no matter which asset happens to be generating the gains.

One of the easiest ways to destroy the safety and stability offered by the Permanent Portfolio is to replace one of the assets with something less volatile because it appears "safer." Those who are not familiar with the strategy and its history are often tempted to make such changes to the allocation. Such changes will, however, seriously compromise the protection of the portfolio. The Permanent Portfolio *depends on volatility* in its individual asset classes, and it works as a package. Most attempts to reduce volatility within one of the Permanent Portfolio asset classes will result in greater volatility in the overall portfolio package, which is exactly what the investor was trying to avoid in the first place.

**ASSETS IN ISOLATION**   To understand how the Permanent Portfolio reduces overall volatility you must understand the difference between assets in isolation and total portfolio performance. *Only total portfolio performance matters*.

> It is not necessary to like each Permanent Portfolio asset to be a successful Permanent Portfolio investor.

The Permanent Portfolio holds asset classes that by themselves are very volatile. The volatility of stocks, for instance, needs no explanation. Well-publicized stock market crashes throughout history illustrate how this asset can easily drop 30, 40, 50 percent, or more at any moment and for any reason. Likewise, stocks can post tremendous gains under certain market conditions. Other assets the portfolio holds such as bonds or gold are similarly volatile for their own reasons. Large losses or large gains can happen in *any* of them at any time.

Yet, a loss in one of the portfolio's assets usually doesn't mean the total portfolio performance is impacted. Often the portfolio manages to pull off an annual gain despite even significant losses in one or more asset classes.

One of the largest obstacles for investors to overcome is the tendency to focus on individual assets in isolation within a portfolio instead of looking at the *complete* package. It is not necessary to like each Permanent Portfolio asset to be a successful Permanent Portfolio investor. You simply need to accept that it's the complete package that provides the growth and safety regardless of what you think about any single component.

Unfortunately, the only experience many investors have had with certain asset classes has been unsuccessful speculative plays. For an investor who has been burned by bad trades in an asset like stocks or gold, the idea that these assets could be configured in a way that results in *more* safety and *less* overall risk can be hard to accept. When properly used as part of an overall portfolio, however, the risk involved in individual asset classes can be almost completely neutralized. When the Permanent Portfolio's volatile asset classes come together they generate a surprisingly smooth ride, as shown in Figure 4.2.

When considering the way the Permanent Portfolio combines volatile asset classes, think of the periodic table of the elements. There are a variety of elements that on their own can be toxic, explosive, corrosive, or worse. Yet, when combined in certain ways, these elements form the building

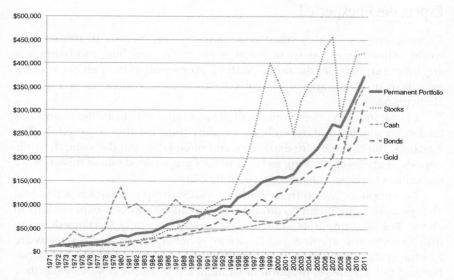

**FIGURE 4.2** Volatile assets, when combined, make for a smoother ride. Growth of $10,000 from 1972 to 2011.

blocks of life, along with products we use every day that may have few characteristics of their raw components.

A key concept for Permanent Portfolio investors to understand is that *only total portfolio value matters*. If one asset has fallen in price, but another has gone up enough to provide the portfolio with an overall gain, then there has been no loss to your savings. Review the performance table and see how even in the worst years for a popular asset like stocks the overall portfolio performed well. No matter which asset is leading or which asset is lagging, the winning asset usually went up enough to either completely absorb the loss, or dampen the losses to the point where it was insignificant across the entire portfolio.

The point above is important because investors can be led astray with their Permanent Portfolios when the markets are in turmoil based on declines in one or more of the individual assets. Investors are often in such a habit of tweaking their investments during market turbulence that the idea of just leaving everything *alone* is hard to accept. The truth is, though, that the Permanent Portfolio has seen it all over the years, and it needs no tweaking in response to market jolts. Just leave the portfolio alone and let it do its thing. An unexpected benefit of this hands-off approach for many Permanent Portfolio investors is a previously unknown sense of calm and peace of mind about their investments.

## Expect the Unexpected

Expectations and reality often don't line up very neatly. In the start-up world, where Craig has spent much of his career, anything can happen at any time. Surprises are the norm. Nothing ever seems to happen as expected in a start-up company, and that's part of what makes them fun and challenging.

In any industry, companies will always have small problems and setbacks. To stay around, though, a company must be able to avoid the big mistakes. Big mistakes are expensive and often fatal, and the same dynamic applies to investors. As long as big mistakes are avoided (small mistakes are sometimes impossible to avoid), you'll be okay.

An important lesson from working with start-up companies is that you always want to maintain an attitude of flexibility and keep expectations in check. For investing, this same advice applies. Basically it comes down to this: Expectations are fine, but flexibility is better. Good start-up teams are flexible and can adapt to new problems and succeed. Bad teams aren't flexible and fail. Likewise, investment strategies that are flexible in what they expect from the markets adapt and prosper. Strategies that expect something in particular to happen tend to get into trouble and fail.

The irony is that something called the Permanent Portfolio is one of the most flexible investment models you can use. This is because it owns assets that can work in any economic environment. No matter what is going on, the Permanent Portfolio has a way to deal with it.

The irony is that something called the Permanent Portfolio is one of the most flexible investment models you can use. This is because it owns assets that can work in any economic environment. No matter what is going on, the Permanent Portfolio has a way to deal with it.

When investing, it's a good idea to get away from expectations about what you think an individual asset may or may not do. People who love stocks, for example, expect that stocks will *always* go up (we call them "stock bugs"). Stock bugs never consider that stocks can have a decade or more of zero real returns or market declines that can wipe out half of their wealth or more. This is believed even though these very things have happened in the United States and many other world stock markets historically. For a truly horrific scenario for stock bugs, consider the Japanese stock market, which as of 2012 was 75 percent below the peak level it was at in 1989!

Gold lovers expect the price of gold to always go up (such people are "gold bugs"). Gold bugs never expect gold to hit a 20-year stretch of bad returns or declines as steep as the stock market, even though the end of the 1970s bull market for gold ushered in exactly such conditions.

Bond lovers ("bond bugs"?) who are expecting to live off of the interest income from their bonds can get hammered if inflation gets bad and eats up their returns for many years, which has happened in many countries over the years. Even owners of bonds that provide inflation-adjusted interest payments can be hurt if their inflation-adjusted interest payments do not actually match their own personal rates of inflation.

Any investment, even your favorite, is not obligated to provide you with some minimum level of return and may not perform on your preferred timeline or based upon your expectations. No matter how much anyone wants to believe that investing can be quantified and reduced to a set of equations, *investing is an inherently uncertain activity*.

Many investment professionals are fond of sweating details over a spreadsheet and complicated financial models to squeeze out every last fraction of a percent of performance. They will use terms like "expected returns" to gloss over the randomness of financial history and how it fails to meet expectations *all the time*. The past is not guaranteed to repeat into the future. Without realizing it, many investors are essentially driving forward by looking in the rearview mirror.

Investors will get burned when they *expect* what cannot be promised: certainty in the markets.

In the real world things happen that a spreadsheet or financial model simply *can't* predict. For instance, a supposedly safe money market fund loses a large part of investors' assets because it was exposed to serious risks behind the scenes. Or a currency may suddenly go down in value, dragging citizens' savings along with it. Finally, as discussed above, sometimes an asset that has a historic expected return can stay flat or even decline in value for years, or even decades, despite what experts thought would happen.

In short, investors will get burned when they *expect* what cannot be promised: certainty in the markets. By being prepared for the full range of unknowns, however, you are positioning yourself to be protected no matter what actually occurs, whether it is good or bad.

## Recap

Three factors that greatly affect portfolio performance are simplicity, safety, and stability. Investing should be simple. Not only does simplicity make portfolio management easier, it will often also make it more profitable. A simple portfolio is easier to maintain, has lower costs, and is less likely to contain hidden risks to your wealth.

A safe portfolio is one that is invested in assets that serve a clear diversification purpose that can grow and protect your life savings against catastrophic loss.

A stable portfolio is one that avoids volatility that can cause an investor to abandon the strategy during market declines.

The average actively managed fund will always underperform the average passively managed fund by the amount of the management fees. Virtually all of the data and research on this subject supports this idea. Passively managed portfolios will capture maximum market returns over time and have repeatedly been shown to outperform actively managed strategies.

When putting together a portfolio, volatile assets can be combined to produce a portfolio that is actually safer than any asset is individually. This principle is part of what makes the Permanent Portfolio deliver such consistent and stable returns.

The markets are inherently uncertain and there is no way of getting around this fact. Once you accept the uncertain nature of the markets, however, you can develop and deploy a strategy to deal with this uncertainty profitably and safely.

# CHAPTER 5

# Investing Based on
# Economic Conditions
## *The Illusion of Diversification*

T he notion that investors should build diversified portfolios is based on the idea that by allocating funds among different investments no single catastrophic event can inflict too much damage on the whole portfolio. The idea itself is simple, but achieving strong diversification in a portfolio actually takes quite a bit of thought to make sure that it will really work when needed.

The financial crisis that occurred in 2008 exposed many cases of what might be called "simulated" diversification, meaning that many portfolio allocations that investors *thought* were diversified were actually exposed to the same basic set of market risks. When a serious crisis hit, the assets all tended to fall in value together, bringing large losses to investors' overall portfolios.

In the wake of these losses (many of which still haven't been recouped as of this writing in mid-2012), many pundits proclaimed that diversification had failed. The truth, however, is that diversification didn't fail, but confusion about what *real* diversification looks like was in many cases cleared up at great expense. Investors in strategies such as the Permanent Portfolio who were *truly* diversified in 2008 did just fine.

The Permanent Portfolio utilizes strong diversification because it approaches the idea of diversification from a very different, and more sensible, perspective than many other investment strategies. Before we discuss the Permanent Portfolio's approach to diversification, however, let's discuss how other diversification strategies can run into problems.

## When Diversification Fails

When diversification fails it is normally related to several key factors:

1. The strategy took too much risk in a single asset class.
2. The portfolio held assets that ultimately were exposed to the same types of risk.
3. The strategy was designed based upon false assumptions about asset class correlations.
4. The portfolio held no hard assets.
5. The portfolio had little or no cash reserves.

In order to understand what solid diversification involves it is important to gain a better understanding of why these factors are allowed to creep into the design of investment strategies in the first place.

### Taking Too Much Risk in One Asset Type

Many investors imagine that their portfolios are diversified, but the reality is that investors often concentrate too much money into one particular type of asset, typically one that they personally favor. Often such portfolios are based on little more than chasing past returns (though the investor may not actually be aware of it, especially if he is acting on the advice of an investment manager). If the bet on the individual asset fails, the portfolio fails.

Remember the idea of expectations that was discussed in Chapter 4. The key point from that discussion is worth repeating here: Any investment, even your favorite, is under no obligation to provide you with any minimum level of return, and it may not perform according to your timeline or expectations. Investors are strongly encouraged to get the idea out of their heads that their favorite asset is always going to perform well going forward, because it may not happen according to their plan (and it may not happen at all).

For instance, one piece of advice often given to investors is that they should take more risks in stocks than in other assets (especially when they are young). While it is true that stocks will periodically have extended periods of great performance, stocks can also have long periods during which returns are very poor (as can happen with *any* asset).

> Just because you've held a stock for 20 years does not mean that a market crash in year 21 is going to grandfather in your previous returns and let you keep them. The stock market doesn't owe you any favors.

A common reason for having a lot of stock exposure is that "stocks grow less risky the longer you hold them," but this is simply not true. Stocks that have been held for many years are just as risky as stocks that were purchased yesterday. Just because you've held a stock for 20 years does not mean that a market crash in year 21 is going to grandfather in your previous returns and let you keep them. The stock market doesn't owe you any favors.

This idea that stocks become less risky the longer you own them is what is called the "Fallacy of Time Diversification." This idea was thoroughly debunked in a paper by John Norstad:

> . . . *consider the 15 years from 1968 through 1982, when after adjusting for inflation the S&P 500 lost a total of 4.62 percent. . . . Are you really prepared to say beyond a shadow of a doubt that a period of high inflation and low stock returns like 1968–1982 can't happen again within your lifetime, or something even worse? Some older people in the United States remember this period, which wasn't all that long ago, and they'll tell you that it was a very unpleasant time indeed to be a stock investor. If you'd like another example, consider the near total collapse of the German financial markets between the two world wars, or the recent experience of the Japanese markets, or the markets in other countries during prolonged bad periods in their histories, which in many cases lasted much longer than 15 years. Do you really feel that it's a 100 percent certainty that something like this couldn't happen here in the United States? If we're going to take this notion of "risk" seriously, don't we have to deal with these possibilities, even if they have low probabilities? That in a nutshell is what our argument is all about. It's not just the theory and the abstract math models which teach us that risk is real over long time horizons. History teaches the same lesson.*[1]

Interestingly, Norstad's paper was written in April 2000. From 2000–2011 the S&P 500 index cited in his example has returned 0.54 and −1.88 percent after inflation. In other words, $10,000 invested in 2000 is worth only about $7,950 today. To make matters worse, if an investor had put his money in very safe and stable Treasury Bills he would have $9,806 today after adjusting for inflation, handily beating the much riskier stock market (even if it resulted in a net loss after adjusting for inflation).

Even if an investor got lucky and missed the 2000–2002 tech bust and invested in stocks from 2002–2011, he would have only seen a 2.9 percent annual return before inflation and a 0.43 percent annual return after

---

[1] John Norstad, "The Fallacy of Time Diversification," www.norstad.org/finance/risk-and-time.html.

inflation. In other words, after adjusting for inflation the investor's $10,000 would have grown to only $10,433 over that 10-year period for a paltry profit of $433 over a decade of investing in risky assets that may have caused many sleepless nights along the way.

As of 2011, many investors had experienced over a decade of negative real returns, even though the models on which their investment decisions were frequently based suggested that the U.S. stock market should have been delivering around 10 percent a year on average. What investors expect and what really happen are frequently quite different. For the record, the Permanent Portfolio returned 7.8 percent (5.2 percent after inflation) from 2000 to 2011, which would have turned the investor's $10,000 into $18,337 after inflation over this time period with a fraction of the risk and volatility of a 100 percent stock portfolio.

Again, while the stock market may have impressive gains over certain periods of time, there is no guarantee that the stock market is going to perform well on *your* particular timetable.

The point above applies to other assets as well, whether it is gold, bonds, real estate, or anything else an investor may purchase. Any one of them can go into a bad market for extended periods and stay there for years or even decades. And yes, at different points in time all of these assets have done exactly that. When it comes to investing, there are just no guarantees. A strongly diversified portfolio should not overweight *any* particular asset. Instead, it should assume that the future might not resemble the past and hold a *balanced* allocation that will position the portfolio well for whatever the future may bring. The purpose of a balanced allocation is so that when one asset unexpectedly begins performing poorly there will be other assets to take up the slack and protect against serious losses. Taking too much risk in one asset class is gambling, not investing.

## Assets Sharing Similar Risks

Another common problem in many portfolios is that asset classes that appear to be diversified can be subject to the same risks under certain market conditions. In particular, many portfolios concentrate risks into one particular asset type (usually stocks). But, because the portfolio holds different stock asset classes or sectors such as international, emerging markets, large company, small company, technology, etc. an investor may think that he has a diversified portfolio. However, such portfolios are really only providing the *illusion* of diversification. When a serious problem comes along affecting an asset class like stocks, an investor often finds that *all* stocks may drop in value at *once*, including stock funds focusing on different segments of the economy and investments in stock markets around the world.

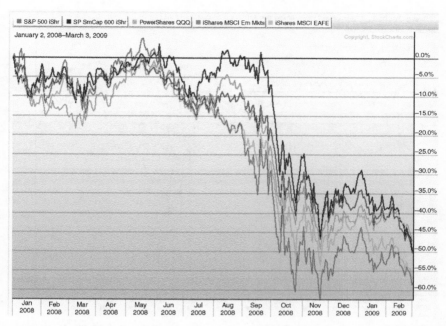

FIGURE 5.1 In 2008 to early 2009 no stock asset class was spared. Losses ranged from very bad to horrendous.

Chart courtesy of stockcharts.com.

As shown in Figure 5.1, in the market crash of 2008 large company stocks, small company value stocks, technology stocks, international stocks, and emerging market stocks all fell sharply in value. The diversification investors thought they had by owning different classes of stock turned out to be illusory.

The same type of risk can show up in bond investments as well. Many bonds (especially low-quality bonds) share stock-like risks in terms of how they respond to market panics. The 2008 to early 2009 period covered in Figure 5.2 shows the performance for the Total Bond Market, Corporate Bond Index, High-Yield (Junk) Bonds, and the popular American Century International Bond Fund during the market crash.

At the bottom of the 2008 crash high-yield junk bonds and corporate bonds suffered losses of 30 percent and 20 percent, respectively. The other funds slightly lagged or remained relatively flat during this period. But simply avoiding losses in a bond fund was not helpful to investors who were experiencing large stock market losses as well. Strong diversification means that when one asset falls in value, another one will *rise*. If one of the assets merely treads water, then the overall portfolio may still see large losses.

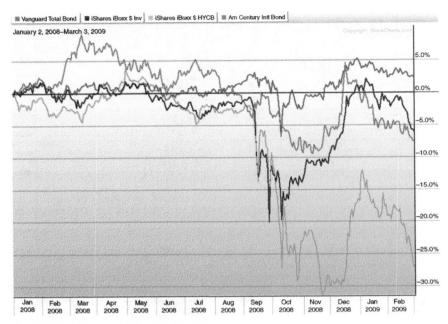

**FIGURE 5.2  In 2008 and early 2009 low-quality bonds exhibited stock-like losses.**
Other bonds did not move enough to offer solid diversification.

**Chart courtesy of stockcharts.com.**

## Relying on Asset Class Correlations

In the investing world there is a lot written about asset class correlations. A
high positive correlation between assets means that the assets tend to move
up or down together. A negative correlation means those assets tend to
move opposite to one other (e.g., one goes up when the other is declining).
The idea is that an asset class like stocks is not correlated with an asset class
like bonds, or that large company stocks are not correlated with small company stocks.

Simply relying upon historical asset class correlations, however, is dangerous. The reason it is dangerous is that many asset class correlations do
not explain *why* the correlations exist, and what might cause them to change
in the future. Just because two asset classes have behaved a certain way in
relation to one another in the past does not mean they are going to necessarily do that going *forward*. In statistics you'd simply say: "Correlation does
not equal causation." Without an explanation for what caused these asset
classes to move, the correlation information may lead to wrong conclusions.
In fact, depending on what time period is selected, the correlation numbers

TABLE 5.1 U.S. Stock and U.S. Long-term Bond Correlations Over Time

| Asset Class | Correlation 1972-2011 | Correlation 1972-1979 | Correlation 1980-1989 | Correlation 1990-1999 | Correlation 2000-2009 |
|---|---|---|---|---|---|
| Stocks/Bonds | 0.06 | 0.51 | 0.32 | 0.54 | −0.83 |

can be radically different. Unfortunately, a lot of investment literature discussing portfolio construction and diversification is based upon the incorrect belief that historical asset correlations are somehow not subject to change, and this oversight often results in the failure of diversification strategies.

Table 5.1 illustrates this idea. The correlation of the U.S. stock market to U.S. Treasury long-term bonds is provided as an example of two assets with very different risk profiles. In terms of correlation, understand that a correlation of 1.0 between two assets is considered a perfect positive correlation; when one goes up, the other one will go up as well. When, however, a correlation between two assets is 0.0, it means that the assets are moving randomly in relation to one another and no correlation exists. When a correlation is −1.0 it means that the assets are negatively correlated, meaning that when one goes up, the other asset will go down and vice versa. It is unusual to see perfect 1.0 or −1.0 correlations. Correlations will normally be somewhere in the middle. A correlation of 0.50 means a medium positive correlation relationship exists between two assets and the assets will usually move up together. A correlation hovering around 0.0 means no real correlation is present and the assets do not move in a predictable way in relation to one another. A correlation around −0.50 means a medium negative correlation exists and one asset will likely move *down* as the other moves up.

So what does Table 5.1 show? In the testing period of 1972–2011, the 0.06 correlation means that U.S. stocks and U.S. bonds do not show any meaningful correlation to each other. Someone designing a portfolio looking over this time period might make the incorrect assumption that stocks and bonds are not going to provide good diversification in a portfolio. But what happens when the dates are moved around? Here is where the asset class correlation theory of portfolio design starts to fall apart.

From 1972–1979 the correlation of U.S. stocks and U.S. bonds shows a medium positive correlation of 0.51. Someone back then might have concluded that stocks and bonds move together so they are not good for diversification. And of course they would have been right based upon the correlation that existed between U.S. stocks and U.S. bonds at that time and over that period.

From 1980–1989 the correlation between U.S. stocks and U.S. bonds drops to 0.32, which is not very strong, but still shows that bonds tend to move with stocks, though the correlation is weaker than in the 1970s.

Over the 1990–1999 period, the correlation moves back to 0.54, which shows a medium positive correlation similar to the 1970s. Based on this data, it was assumed through the late 1990s that U.S. long-term bonds would tend to move up along with stocks (you can't argue with the data, right?). In fact, common advice given to investors when building their portfolios was not to buy U.S. long-term bonds to diversify against U.S. stocks because the two assets were positively correlated.

But now look at the 2000–2009 time period. The correlation goes from a medium positive correlation to a *very strong negative correlation* of −0.83. That means that the price of U.S. long-term bonds over this period was showing very strong movements away from the price of stocks. This is the exact *opposite* conclusion people had reached over the previous 30 years! As a result of the 1972–1999 correlation data, investors were told to avoid U.S. long-term bonds because these bonds were "positively correlated" to U.S. stocks. Investors who followed this advice missed out on the diversification power of U.S. long-term bonds during the poor stock market performance from 2000 to 2009. The notion that asset class correlations are a good indicator of portfolio diversification had simply failed.

The lesson from this review of asset correlation data is that stocks and bonds move for very specific reasons having to do with what is going on in the overall economy and not what each other is doing as asset class correlations assume. Stocks do not go up because bonds are going down, and stocks do not go down because bonds are going up. These assets move in price for very specific reasons in the economy. To make a conclusion based upon asset class correlations alone is going to eventually lead to a bad outcome when that correlation variable suddenly shifts.

> Strong diversification is not built by looking at asset class correlation data, but rather through an understanding of how certain assets respond to changing economic conditions.

Strong diversification is not built by looking at asset class correlation data, but rather through an understanding of how certain assets respond to changing economic conditions. *Hold onto this thought—it's important and we're going to be covering it in much more detail.*

## Neglecting Hard Assets

Most assets held by investors are so-called "paper assets." A paper asset is essentially someone else's promise to pay back a debt in the future (as with bonds) or in recognition of some ownership interest in assets under someone else's control (as with stocks). In contrast to paper assets, "hard assets" are physical objects or property that can be held in one's own possession and retain value independent of what the value of a currency or other paper may be doing. A hard asset can be something as simple as gold or silver bullion coins tucked away in a safe deposit box, or something more involved like real estate that an investor can also use to generate income.

An important thing to understand about hard assets is that they are subject to *different market forces* than stocks, bonds and other paper assets, and thus they do not share the same risks that can impact paper assets. In some economic conditions hard assets are the only component of a portfolio that can provide protection from serious losses when currencies, stocks, and bonds are all performing poorly.

## Not Enough Cash

Cash is similar to hard assets in that many investors don't view it as an asset that has a vital role in their investment strategies. "Cash is trash" is the attitude that many investment managers have toward a cash allocation (not coincidently, these managers don't make fees if you have money in cash). Yet, when the markets are doing poorly cash can provide needed stability and liquidity to support your living expenses, cover emergencies, cope with the loss of a job or any number of other contingencies. A cash allocation is also a handy place to park profits from gains generated by more volatile assets within a portfolio. Finally, during a market crash a cash allocation can provide a source of funds that can be used to purchase assets at deep discounts when everyone else is fleeing those assets in panic.

In other words, cash is not trash. When the markets are in turmoil, the person with cash on hand is the one who can pick through the rubble and buy assets cheaply. During such periods, "cash is trash" becomes "cash is king."

## A Different Way to Diversify

Given the problems with conventional beliefs about diversification discussed above, there is a better way to look at the challenge of achieving strong diversification within a portfolio.

A diversified portfolio only works when the assets you own are not all moving in lockstep. A portfolio where everything is going up at the same time can also turn into a portfolio where everything is going *down* at the same time.

A diversified portfolio only works when the assets you own are not all moving in lockstep. A portfolio where everything is going up at the same time can also turn into a portfolio where everything is going *down* at the same time. That's not diversification.

Therefore, when thinking about the problem of developing a truly all-weather portfolio it becomes necessary to think about market conditions that may seem farfetched at a given point in time. When the economy is doing well, for example, it can be hard to conceive of experiencing a second Great Depression. And during periods of high inflation, the idea that runaway price increases will completely disappear might seem naïve.

What history teaches, however, is that one economic condition is frequently followed by a very different kind of economic condition, often to the surprise of almost everyone. In the Roaring Twenties, for example, no one could have imagined that the United States was on the verge of a terrible decade-long economic depression. In the 1970s, few would have believed that the high inflation they were witnessing would end shortly and be followed by two decades of the greatest bull market for stocks in U.S. history. And in 1999, it was hard to believe that the double-digit stock market returns of the past 20 years were about to end and be followed by over a decade of poor stock market performance.

More recently, the financial crisis of 2008 caught most investors by surprise. In fact, at the beginning of 2008 investors seemed most concerned about rising inflation and interest rates, but by the end of the year those same investors were talking about a deflationary depression being a very real possibility. When it comes to economic matters, the future is simply unpredictable.

The future is always uncertain and investors need to develop a strategy to deal with it. It's important to fully understand once and for all that no economist, investing system, or expert can tell you what the markets are going to do next. This realization forms the foundation for an investment strategy that can actually work no matter what is happening in the world. In other words, we can develop a *strategy* that takes uncertainty about the future as a given and builds a portfolio based upon that core assumption.

Once you internalize the idea that the future is unpredictable, the second thing that you must do is define the scope of all potential economic environments, even if some of them may seem *impossible* to you right now. This is required so your investment strategy can be prepared to deal with any economic environment at all times. This is not as hard to do as it may sound.

The economy is a bit like the weather—although it is driven by an almost infinitely complex set of processes, it manifests itself in the form of climatic conditions in which it is always either hot or cold and wet or dry.

The entire universe of potential future economic environments is actually quite small. The economy is a bit like the weather—although it is driven by an almost infinitely complex set of processes, it manifests itself in the form of climatic conditions in which it is always either hot or cold and wet or dry.

Rather than attempting to overcome uncertainty through predictions, market analysis, and punditry, the Permanent Portfolio strategy embraces the concept of uncertainty in all human affairs and assumes that uncertainty will always be present, and that this uncertainty will manifest itself through changes in the *economy*. This aspect of the Permanent Portfolio is one of the features that most distinguishes it from other approaches to investing.

The Permanent Portfolio strategy assumes nothing is impossible or that some particular outcome has to happen. It assumes the future is not predictable and holds assets that are designed to provide safety and stability in a wide variety of economic conditions.

## Four Economic Conditions

The Permanent Portfolio approaches diversification by selecting assets that are correlated to the economy and pays *no attention* to how asset classes are correlated to each other. This is an unusual approach in the investing world and provides a simple and powerful model for achieving strong protection in many different market environments.

While there are seemingly many different economic climates, there are actually only four basic configurations of an economy at any given time, and those are:

1. Prosperity
2. Deflation
3. Recession
4. Inflation

At any point in time the economy will be experiencing some combination of these four economic environments. Once having identified the way these economic conditions interact with one another, it is possible to begin thinking about what kind of investment strategy would be responsive no matter when or how a certain set of economic conditions came about. First, though, it will be useful to provide more detail about these four economic conditions.

1. **Prosperity**—Periods of prosperity are characterized by rising productivity and profits, low unemployment, and stable or falling interest rates. Optimism is widespread and stocks normally perform very well. The United States experienced such a period from 1982 to 2000, for instance.

2. **Deflation**—Deflation is an economic environment in which some economic shock, such as a credit crisis or market panic, sets off a cycle of declining prices, falling interest rates, and rising currency value. Under deflationary conditions, interest rates normally fall as demand for loans dries up or it becomes hard to get loans due to tighter lending requirements. Prices also may start to fall across the economy as people reduce their spending.

Although a period of falling prices may sound appealing, the problem it presents is that businesses often have inventory they bought for a higher price than consumers are now willing to pay. This makes it difficult for businesses to sell their goods at a profit. In response to these conditions, businesses are forced to cut prices, take losses to clear out their inventories, lay off employees, and, hopefully, be able to stay in business until economic conditions improve.

3. **Recession**—The word recession has become a blanket description of any economic condition outside of prosperity. However, for the Permanent Portfolio it has a particular meaning, and it involves what Harry Browne called a "tight money" recession. In a tight money recession, the central bank elects to raise interest rates to help tame high inflation in an economy that is already weak. The unfortunate side effect of repeatedly raising interest rates, however, is a recession. The Federal Reserve adopted such a policy in the early 1980s, which tipped the economy into recession, though it did succeed in reducing a decade of high inflation from the 1970s.

The important thing to remember when thinking about recession as an economic condition is that it is by definition temporary. A typical recession only lasts until consumers begin spending again or the economy adjusts to a lower level of overall demand (which usually takes 12 to 24 months).

4. **Inflation**—Periods of inflation are the result of too much money circulating in an economy relative to the available supply of goods and services. This means prices go up, sometimes rapidly. Periods of high inflation are also accompanied by rising interest rates. This is a response of bondholders and other lenders who demand higher returns on borrowed money to compensate for the reduced purchasing power of future dollars.

One of the features of inflationary periods that can be difficult to control is the effect that increases in prices and wages can trigger. A falling currency makes it more expensive for businesses to acquire raw materials, pay employees, and produce their products. These costs are passed onto the consumer in the form of price increases, which lead workers to demand higher wages to keep up with rising prices, and the cycle repeats. This aspect of a sustained period of inflation is called a "wage-price spiral" and is illustrated in Figure 5.3.

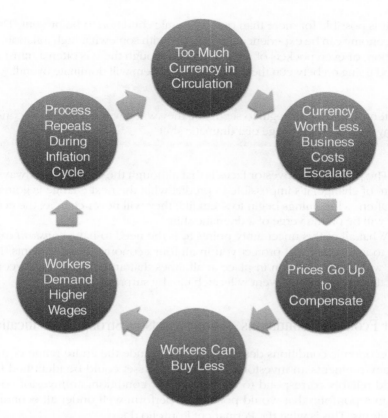

FIGURE 5.3  Wage-price spiral. Just one effect of inflation in an economy.

If inflation is 5 percent a year that means your money will be worth 5 percent less each and every year, no matter what you do. As discussed in Chapter 3, if the investment returns in your portfolio do not beat inflation then you are losing money in real terms. Over time, inflation can be thought of as a hole in the bottom of a boat. If the boat isn't bailed out fast enough, eventually it will sink. If inflation gets too bad, there is a serious risk of losing a large part of one's life savings if adequate protection isn't built into a portfolio.

The four economic conditions (or some combination of them) are the only ones that can exist in a modern economy. In other words, at any point in time, the economy is either expanding (prosperity) or contracting (recession) and the money supply relative to the supply of goods and services is either expanding (inflation) or contracting (deflation).

It is possible for more than one economic condition to be present. Thus, an economy can be experiencing prosperity with somewhat high inflation, no inflation, or even pockets of deflation. Even though there is often a transition period going on between these states, one of them will dominate overall.

> Often, when things begin to seem like they will never change, the economy will be on the verge of a dramatic shift.

The problem an investor faces is that although the economy is always in a state of change, it's impossible to predict what the next change is going to be. Often, when things begin to seem like they will never change, the economy will be on the verge of a dramatic shift.

What all of this uncertainty points to is the need to have *constant exposure* to assets that will protect you in all four economic environments. It is only with this protection in place at all times that an investor can be confident that no economic event will catch him by surprise.

## Four Economic Conditions + Four Assets = Strong Diversification

The economic conditions described earlier include the entire range of market environments an investor will face. If an asset could be identified that would reliably correspond to *each* economic condition, an investor could design a portfolio that would potentially perform well under all economic conditions. This is what the Permanent Portfolio does.

### Prosperity—Good for Stocks and Bonds

During times of general prosperity when the economy is expanding, corporate profits are rising, and unemployment is low, the stock market will generally be experiencing rising stock prices. Also, bonds typically perform reasonably well during prosperity (but not as good as stocks) and provide a good revenue stream from their interest payments.

While prosperity is normally good for stocks, an asset like gold would not be expected to perform well during such periods. In such conditions, investors would rather have their money exposed to the higher potential returns of stocks than gold, which pays no interest or dividends.

### Deflation—Good for Bonds and Cash

Periods of deflation are characterized by falling interest rates. Falling interest rates are very good for high-quality, long-term bonds. Deflationary conditions also typically involve a strengthening currency, which manifests in the form of falling prices. During such periods cash-like assets do well because the purchasing power of cash is increasing.

During periods of deflation, stocks would be expected to perform very poorly as falling prices lead to a decline in corporate profits and excess inventory that is worth less than when purchased. Gold would also be expected to perform poorly during a period of deflation because a smaller amount of cash can be used to buy the same amount of gold as purchasing power increases.

There is, however, an interesting wrinkle when thinking about gold and deflation. When negative real interest rates are present (as they have been in recent years in the United States and many other countries) gold can do well even in a period of deflation. This will be touched on in Chapter 9 on Gold. But mostly, serious deflation is not going to be good for gold, as real interest rates are often *not* negative under this economic condition.

## Recession—Good for Cash

During periods of recession the economy is contracting, and when the economy is contracting stocks are going to perform poorly. Gold also tends to perform poorly because deliberate tight-money recessions have the effect of slowing down or stopping inflation. Lastly, in a recession that includes rising interest rates, bonds would be expected to perform poorly, since rising interest rates make existing bonds less attractive.

The only asset that can be relied upon during a recession is cash. In an environment where stocks, bonds, and gold are all falling in value, you want to own enough cash to help dampen the losses in other parts of your portfolio and provide you with stable liquid assets. Cash can be used to purchase other assets at depressed prices during these periods.

Even though cash is the asset of choice during recessionary conditions, cash doesn't provide the potential for powerful price moves like the other assets in the portfolio. Although cash can help buffer a portfolio during a recession, the reality is that it serves more as a portfolio anchor during such periods. Luckily, a period of recession is normally short-lived and one of the other three assets (stocks, bonds, or gold) will quickly take up the slack as the economy decides which direction it wants to go (e.g., a return to prosperity, inflation or a descent into a full blown deflationary depression).

## Inflation—Good for Gold

When an economy is locked in a cycle of rising prices and falling currency value, gold is the only asset that can be relied upon to perform well. Gold performs this function most effectively when an economy is experiencing high inflation (more than 5 percent a year) and/or expectations of higher inflation in the future. In these cases, gold can experience explosive increases in value.

It is important to remember, too, that when people say gold is doing well, what they often mean is that gold is simply maintaining its value while the value of their currency or other assets are falling. Gold should not necessarily be thought of as a long-term investment, but as a long-term insurance policy protecting against bad economic events. It is a fact of modern life that central banks have inflation targets that are greater than 0 percent (the Federal Reserve, for example, targets 2 percent inflation but it's been over 4 percent since the early 1970s). This inflation causes your money to lose value. Over time, all paper currencies will lose value; it's just a question of whether a paper currency loses value quickly or slowly. Gold protects you when a currency is losing value quickly in a period of rising inflation.

Unlike gold, which can protect purchasing power during periods of high inflation, other assets, such as bonds, perform poorly during periods of high inflation because interest rates are normally rising as well. Rising interest rates are very bad for bonds. Stocks may or may not perform well during inflationary periods on an after-inflation basis. Often stocks are only able to tread water during periods of high inflation. Stocks may appear to be rising during such periods, but it is often at roughly the same rate as inflation across the entire economy (e.g., stock returns rise 10 percent in a year but inflation that year is also 10 percent resulting in zero net gain). Lastly, cash in an interest bearing account tends to also tread water during inflation as rates are rising. Sometimes it may slightly lag inflation. But overall cash is not a good asset to own during periods of high inflation because the purchasing power is being rapidly destroyed.

## How the Portfolio Works with Economic Conditions

What the Permanent Portfolio does is place an *equal bet* on each economic condition by owning 25 percent each of stocks, bonds, cash and gold. Further, it holds these assets at all times no matter what the investor thinks is going to happen in the future.

One of the assumptions built into this approach is that some of these bets will be losers and some will be winners, but it's impossible to know which ones will be winners and losers in advance. The good news is that the winners will routinely provide gains far in excess of the losses incurred by the losers. For example, when an asset is rising in value it will routinely see gains far in excess of 100 percent, while the losers can never lose more than 100 percent (and usually not more than 50 percent except under unusual circumstances). Over time this process of the winners providing gains in excess of the losses elsewhere in the portfolio translates into a steady positive inflation-adjusted return on the whole.

This idea of putting winners and losers in the same portfolio at the same time seems counterintuitive, but it works. The winners will have enough power on the upside to absorb the losses of the underperformers.

The key difference between the Permanent Portfolio and many other investment strategies is that other approaches are normally tilted toward one economic environment over the others. For instance, a portfolio that heavily favors stocks inherently tilts toward prosperity. However, if the bet on prosperity doesn't pan out, such investment strategies can produce long periods of disappointing returns or even real losses. Similarly, a portfolio that bets on high inflation might overweight gold, foreign currencies, and similar inflation hedging bets. But if the inflation doesn't materialize, or doesn't continue rising as expected, then these assets could generate large losses.

The Permanent Portfolio seeks to take a neutral stance toward all economic conditions. The potential for prosperity, inflation, deflation, and recession are equally weighted for the most part. This equal weighting allows the portfolio to provide real returns in any market without having to rely on correct bets about a particular economic scenario or the need to ride out huge market declines while hoping for the best. The equal weightings also prevent you from being overexposed to any one asset, which protects your life savings against a serious loss that could occur in any one investment.

Figure 5.4, shown here from Chapter 4, illustrates the smooth ride of the Permanent Portfolio from 1972 to 2011 as the solid line. No matter what the economy was doing, the Permanent Portfolio was able to keep growing without experiencing any serious losses while providing real returns over inflation. And before you get too excited about that stock market line (which covers the biggest stock bull market in U.S. history), just remember that

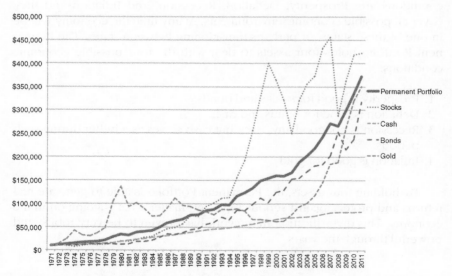

**FIGURE 5.4** Permanent Portfolio (solid line) versus stocks, bonds, cash, and gold from 1972 to 2011.

those high peaks were sandwiched by two-decade-long periods of poor returns and two massive asset bubbles that eventually led to huge market declines. The steady line of the Permanent Portfolio, however, means your savings were able to grow safely and smoothly the entire time.

The Permanent Portfolio assumes the future is uncertain and the strategy it employs leverages this uncertainty to drive profits. The diversification of the Permanent Portfolio also protects against catastrophic losses from a world that is always full of surprises. By investing based on economic conditions, the portfolio has a strategy to deal with uncertain markets no matter what is happening.

# Recap

Many diversification strategies fail because investors:

- Take too much risk in a single asset class.
- Hold assets that are exposed to the same types of risk.
- Use false assumptions about asset class correlations.
- Hold no hard assets.
- Have little or no cash reserves.

The Permanent Portfolio is different because it derives its diversification from investing based on changing economic conditions. The four economic conditions are: Prosperity, Deflation, Recession, and Inflation and they cover all possible economic environments. At any time the economy will be in one of these states, or perhaps transitioning between states. The Permanent Portfolio holds four assets to deal with the four possible economic conditions:

1. Prosperity is good for stocks and bonds.
2. Deflation is good for bonds and cash.
3. Recession is not good any asset, but cash serves as a buffer during such periods.
4. Inflation is good for gold.

By holding four assets, the Permanent Portfolio is able to generate real returns and protect against serious losses no matter what is going on in the economy. This diversification framework has proven to be very robust and powerful through the years.

# CHAPTER 6

# Stocks

## *The Power of the Stock Market*

The stock market is the best asset to own during times of prosperity. In periods of prosperity the following conditions, which are all good for stocks, are present:

- The economy is growing and inflation is not seriously eroding purchasing power.
- Interest rates will normally be low and stable or perhaps slightly falling.
- Unemployment is low and the economy is expanding at a good rate to support new businesses and production.

During these conditions it is not uncommon to see stock prices increase sharply as corporate profits grow along with the broader economy. Annual stock returns can be in the 10 percent and higher range. Owning stocks is the best way for investors to have ownership in the productive capacity of a prosperous economy.

However stocks do have a dark side, and that is they can experience large losses or no real gains for years at a time. Additionally, many stock opportunities that are presented to investors are poorly managed in terms of risks and costs. This chapter will lay out the case for stocks and the best way to invest in them, as well as what investments to avoid.

## Benefits of Stocks

The Permanent Portfolio holds an allocation to stocks at all times because they can add tremendous gains to a portfolio during a good year or series of good years. Sometimes even during a seemingly bad economy stocks can

TABLE 6.1   Asset Class Returns—Stock Boom Years—1980–1999

| Asset | Annualized Return | Real Return | Growth of $10K in Real Dollars |
|-------|-------------------|-------------|-------------------------------|
| **Stocks** | 17.9% | 13.3% | $122,400 |
| **Bonds** | 10.7% | 6.4% | $ 34,700 |
| **Cash** | 6.9% | 2.8% | $ 17,300 |
| **Gold** | −2.3% | −6.1% | $  2,800 |

Rounded to nearest hundred in this and other tables.

turn in tremendous gains offsetting losses in the bonds, gold, and cash portions of the Permanent Portfolio.

Let's consider the golden days for stocks as a best-case scenario. During the 20-year period of 1980 to 1999 we saw the biggest sustained bull market for stocks in U.S. history. Over this time stocks saw compound annual growth rates of 17.9 percent a year (13.3 percent in real return terms). That means a $10,000 investment in stocks in 1980 grew to over $268,000 by 1999 (or $122,000 in real terms). This tremendous growth overshadowed every other asset in the Permanent Portfolio by a wide margin. Table 6.1 breaks down the returns for the various assets over this 1980 to 1999 time frame.

Over this time period stocks were very profitable and a portfolio that held stocks performed well. At the same time, any portfolio that avoided stocks did relatively poorly. The big loser over this time frame was gold, which does badly under prosperous economies when inflation is not a threat. Any portfolio that concentrated its bet in an asset like gold and owned no stocks took large losses in real terms.

## Risks of Stocks

You'll read advice sometimes that says stocks always win over time. However, contrary to what some advocate, stocks are not the best asset to own under all economic conditions. They may not perform on your particular timetable either as has been covered. Stocks can experience very long periods in which they provide investors with little or no return. They also go through volatile periods that can inflict large losses quickly.

Table 6.2 shows a snapshot of the high-inflation 1970s, where stocks showed decent annual returns, but after inflation took its share they were below water the entire time. Bonds and cash also did very poorly under this condition. In fact the period of bad returns for stocks actually started around 1966 and ended in the early 1980s. Inflation over this time removed so much

TABLE 6.2  Asset Class Returns—Stock Bust Years—1972 to 1979

| Asset | Annualized Return | Real Return | Growth of $10K in Real Dollars |
|---|---|---|---|
| **Stocks** | 5.1% | −2.8% | $ 8,000 |
| **Bonds** | 3.8% | −4.0% | $ 7,200 |
| **Cash** | 6.5% | −1.5% | $ 8,900 |
| **Gold** | 34.1% | 24.1% | $56,000 |

Market data used for equal comparison begins in 1972 after gold standard ends.

TABLE 6.3  Asset Class Returns—Stock Bust Years—2000 to 2009

| Asset | Annualized Return | Real Return | Growth of $10K in Real Dollars |
|---|---|---|---|
| **Stocks** | −1.0% | −3.4% | $ 7,100 |
| **Bonds** | 7.7% | 5.0% | $16,400 |
| **Cash** | 2.8% | 0.2% | $10,200 |
| **Gold** | 14.9% | 12.1% | $31,200 |

purchasing power that the stock gains just couldn't offset it. Inflation is not good for stocks.

From 2000 to 2009 stocks experienced very bad market crashes: the 2000 to 2002 tech bust and the 2008 real estate bust. The real returns over this decade were negative for stockowners and $10,000 invested in 2000 was worth only $7,100 real dollars in 2009 as shown in Table 6.3. Yet over this time period, gold and bonds did well. Stock investors who ignored gold and bonds took a beating.

## Volatility

As with bonds and gold, stocks are extremely volatile on their own. This volatility can show up as large losses or large gains depending on what is happening in the economy. The worst sustained losses were over −89 percent from the period of 1929 to 1932 at the beginning of the Great Depression.

Then again, there have been years where +30 percent gains were happening. Sometimes these boom years happen right in the middle of what seems like a horrible economy. For instance, in 1973 and 1974 the market saw losses of −14.7 percent and −26.5 percent respectively. Then in 1975 and 1976 there were gains of +37.2 percent and +23.9 percent! In 2008 there were market losses of −37 percent. Yet in 2009 the market gave +26.5 percent returns back to patient investors. This kind of up and down price movement is very trying.

Stocks, just like the other components of the Permanent Portfolio, are volatile. But this volatility can help at times as much as it can hurt. The important point is that a portfolio that avoids stocks may miss market declines, but it also can miss market gains, and those gains can prove to be very valuable when bonds and gold are doing poorly. For this reason the Permanent Portfolio holds stocks *at all times* regardless of what an investor may personally feel is going to happen.

## Owning Stocks

To profit during times of prosperity you should own a broad-based stock index fund that captures the returns offered by the stock market without trying to *beat* the market. A broad-based stock index fund is able to capture the maximum gains available to all investors.

There are many stock index funds available today. Some are great, some are mediocre, and some are downright bad. Unfortunately, the term "index fund" has also been used in recent years to describe all kinds of investment products, some of which bear little resemblance to a true index fund. These products are easily avoided if you follow the advice laid out in this chapter.

For purposes of the Permanent Portfolio stock allocation, you want to own the cheapest and most broadly based stock fund available. In selecting a stock index fund, consider ones that:

- Track a Total Stock Market Index or S&P 500 Index.
- Have an expense ratio below 0.50 percent a year.
- Are passively managed (no active management of the fund).
- Are from well-established companies with a track record for index investing.
- Are 100 percent invested in stocks at all times.

### S&P 500 Index

The S&P 500 is an index of stocks compiled by Standard and Poor's that comprise the 500 largest publicly traded companies in the United States by market capitalization. These are the companies that are household names—General Electric, Walmart, 3M, Microsoft, Johnson and Johnson, Google, Coca-Cola, IBM, Home Depot, McDonald's, and so on.

You can see the current list of companies in the index by searching for the S&P 500 index online. The S&P 500 represents around 70 percent of the total value of the U.S. stock market.

## Total Stock Market Index

The Total Stock Market (TSM) index includes not only all the companies of the S&P 500, but also all of the other publicly traded companies that aren't quite large enough to make it into the S&P 500 list. These are called "mid-cap" and "small-cap" companies, which means they have a market capitalization (size) that is smaller compared to the large-cap companies.

The total stock market index is also called other names, such as the Wilshire 5000 or Russell 3000. A total stock market index commonly holds thousands of companies (3000 or more) in its composition as opposed to the 500 in the S&P 500. The total stock market index easily covers 98 percent or more of the entire United States' publicly traded stock market. This is why it's called the Total Stock Market Index. It owns just about everything except the stocks of very small companies that aren't liquid enough to trade easily or penny stocks (stocks trading less than $5 a share that you don't want anyway because they are usually on the verge of bankruptcy).

# Recommended Stock Index Funds

The following funds meet the criteria above for stock allocation in the Permanent Portfolio.

### S&P 500 Index

- Vanguard S&P 500 Index Mutual Fund (Ticker: VFINX)
- State Street S&P 500 SPDR Exchange Traded Fund (Ticker: SPY)
- iShares S&P 500 Exchange Traded Fund (Ticker: IVV)
- Fidelity Spartan 500 Index Mutual Fund (Ticker: FSMKX)
- Schwab S&P 500 Index Mutual Fund (Ticker: SWPPX)

### Total Stock Market Index (TSM)

- Vanguard Total Stock Market Mutual Fund (Ticker: VTSMX)
- Vanguard Total Stock Market Exchange Traded Fund (Ticker: VTI)
- iShares Russell 3000 Index Exchange Traded Fund (Ticker: IWV)
- Fidelity Spartan Total Stock Market (Ticker: FSTMX)
- Schwab Total Stock Market (Ticker: SWTSX)

This list is far from exhaustive, as many fund companies offer some type of index fund in their investment lineup. If you are at a brokerage or mutual fund company that offers its own index fund then you can use that as long as it meets the criteria outlined in this chapter.

# Which Type of Index Fund to Use?

Given the choice between the two types of index funds described above, a total stock market fund offers wider diversification and tax efficiency when compared to S&P 500 index funds. A typical total stock market fund will hold thousands of stocks compared to the 500 stocks in the S&P 500 index. Total stock market funds also provide slightly better long-term performance. If, however, you only have access to an S&P 500 index fund, this will still work great for purposes of the Permanent Portfolio.

# Why Use an Index Fund?

An index fund is a way of passively tracking a predefined basket of stocks. Index funds usually own stocks in proportion to the size of the company in the overall index. For example, an index fund tracking the U.S. stock market will typically own a larger number of shares of General Electric than a regional publicly traded utility company.

The advantage of stock indexing is that an index fund doesn't need to engage in expensive activities associated with actively traded investment funds, such as research, analysts, advisors, and so on. Because an index fund owns the entire market, it is simply expected to earn the average performance of the market in any one year minus its management fees.

> Because an index fund owns the entire market, it is expected to earn the average performance of the market in any one year minus its management fees.

## Low Expense Ratios

Indexing is the best and most efficient way to invest in stocks. Not only does it guarantee you maximum possible returns because you own all of the companies all of the time, it's also cheap. A typical index fund may have an expense ratio of less than 0.20 percent per year. This means for every $10,000 you have invested in the index the fund management company is going to take just $20 for managing the fund. Many of these funds are now at 0.10 percent a year or less in fees. That means for a mere $10 a year the fund company will manage all stock operations for each $10,000 you have invested with them. Jack Bogle, founder of The Vanguard Group (one of the largest mutual fund companies in the world), stated it best when he said: "The shortest route to top quartile performance is to be in the bottom quartile of expenses."

TABLE 6.4  Hypothetical Impacts of Expense Ratio Costs if Your Fund Earns 10 Percent a Year

| Starting Value | Expense Ratio | After Expense Return | Years | Final Value | Fees |
|---|---|---|---|---|---|
| **$10,000** | 0% | 10% | 20 | $67,275 | $    0 |
| **$10,000** | 0.1% | 9.9% | 20 | $66,062 | $  1,213 |
| **$10,000** | 0.2% | 9.8% | 20 | $64,870 | $  2,405 |
| **$10,000** | 1% | 9% | 20 | $56,044 | $11,231 |
| **$10,000** | 2% | 8% | 20 | $46,609 | $21,116 |
| **$10,000** | 3% | 7% | 20 | $38,696 | $28,579 |

Compare the low expenses of most index funds to a non-index fund that can charge 1 percent, 2 percent, or more each year. It may not sound like that much, but for each $10,000 invested with such an actively managed fund, you're paying $100, $200, or more every year to the fund's managers. Over the years, fees at this level start to really add up and hurt performance. A high expense fund is like driving a car dragging an anchor behind it. Table 6.4 shows the impact of a fund with a 0.1 percent expense ratio and ones that are much higher, assuming a 10 percent return on stock investments.

## Maximum Diversification

In addition to the benefits of index fund investing outlined above, an index fund approach automatically insulates you from anything that may go wrong at an individual company. The idea of holding only a few stocks, or concentrating your bets into a single sector, opens your portfolio up to risks associated with factors other than just how the entire economy is performing. For example, consider the Vanguard Total Stock Market index fund, one of the largest such funds in the world. The current top 10 holdings as of late 2011 are shown in Table 6.5.

Looking at Table 6.5, even if an investor woke up tomorrow to find Microsoft had gone completely bankrupt, the impact to the whole fund would only be −1.50 percent in total value.

Suppose that the same investor instead chose a few stocks (perhaps his own employer's stock) and concentrated his bet. If there were a large problem in one of those stocks, instead of a 1 to 2 percent loss, he could be looking at a much larger impact on his stock portfolio.

Investors seeking safe and stable returns shouldn't have to worry about the headlines they are going to read in tomorrow's paper about their favorite company.

TABLE 6.5  Top 10 Holdings of Vanguard Total Stock Market Index

| Company | Percent of Assets |
|---|---|
| Exxon Mobil | 2.84% |
| Apple Computer | 2.80% |
| IBM | 1.68% |
| Microsoft | 1.50% |
| Chevron | 1.48% |
| Proctor & Gamble | 1.39% |
| Johnson & Johnson | 1.39% |
| AT&T | 1.34% |
| General Electric | 1.28% |
| Pfizer | 1.11% |

*Data source:* Vanguard Group, December 2011.

In recent years investors have been surprised to see many companies that were considered safe disappear almost overnight (Enron in 2001, Lehman Brothers in 2008, etc.). Investors seeking safe and stable returns shouldn't have to worry about the headlines they are going to read in tomorrow's paper about their favorite company. A broadly based index fund protects you from disaster.

## Tax Efficiency

For investors with significant holdings in taxable accounts, tax efficiency is an important consideration. A fund that is tax efficient is managed so that it generates as little taxable income as possible for its shareholders each year. As with all expenses, tax costs add up over time, and thus tax efficiency should be a consideration when designing an investment strategy. As it happens, index funds are the most tax-efficient stock fund you can own. They do not have managers actively trading stocks and generating unnecessary taxes behind the scenes.

Table 6.6 shows how index funds have fewer taxes by comparing two leading index funds with the Fidelity Magellan fund (Ticker: FMAGX). The

TABLE 6.6  Current Pre and Post-Tax Returns of the S&P 500 versus Total Stock Market, Winter 2011

| Fund Name | 15-Year Pre-Tax | 15-Year After-Tax Returns | Tax Impacts |
|---|---|---|---|
| **Vanguard Total Stock Market** | 5.38% | 4.91% | −0.47% |
| **Vanguard S&P 500** | 5.15% | 4.69% | −0.46% |
| **Fidelity Magellan** | 3.31% | 2.27% | −1.04% |

*Data source:* Morningstar Tax Analysis.

Fidelity Magellan fund is a popular, actively managed fund that largely mirrors the S&P 500 and Total Stock Market funds due to its size, but actively trades stocks in a (failed) attempt to beat these indexes.

Over the past 15 years the Total Stock Market fund had slightly higher annual returns, but also higher after-tax returns than the S&P 500 fund. When compared to the Fidelity Magellan fund, however, both index funds easily beat the Fidelity Magellan fund both in pre and post-tax returns. Due to its active management, the Fidelity Magellan fund had over twice the tax impacts of a typical index fund. This translates into lower returns and higher taxes for investors with taxable accounts compared to those who owned a basic index fund.

## Warning

Tax Efficiency and Time—A Warning

A short time period is not enough to judge a fund's tax efficiency. It is important to look for a fund that has been through at least one good bull market and one bad bear market (at least 10 years), as many funds come and go over time. When a fund is forced to go through a bull and bear market it tests the ability of the managers to handle the fund's tax efficiency. If

"Him? That's one of our fund managers."

the managers are not conscientious about tax efficiency (and most aren't), then they will simply dump the tax costs onto the fund holders and this lowers returns. Index funds are inherently more tax efficient due to how they are constructed and operated and are one reason why they are recommended above all others when assembling a Permanent Portfolio.

## Avoid Actively Managed Stock Funds

Unfortunately, most stock funds you see advertised are not passive index funds, but actively managed. For purposes of the Permanent Portfolio's stock allocation, you should avoid actively managed stock funds regardless of their past performance or any other reason that might make an actively managed fund seem like a good idea.

Among other reasons for avoiding actively managed stock funds, the portfolio requires that the 25 percent stock allocation be fully invested in stocks *all the time*. With an actively managed stock fund, sometimes the fund manager may choose to hold a significant portion of the fund's assets in things other than stocks. The manager may feel that bonds are a better deal, or sitting on cash is. Who knows? You don't need a fund manager making decisions to move between stocks, bonds, cash, commodities, and so on and disturbing the balances that are already present in the Permanent Portfolio. The Permanent Portfolio holds an asset mix that will grow and protect your life savings already. You don't need a stock fund manager trying to outguess the markets.

> The Permanent Portfolio holds an asset mix that will grow and protect your life-savings already. You don't need a stock fund manager trying to out-guess the markets.

Morningstar (www.morningstar.com) is a great resource for investors to find information about funds they are considering, including how much they charge and their turnover, which are two critical pieces of information about fund performance. Morningstar shows that the Vanguard Total Stock Market is an excellent example of an index fund. This fund has a current expense ratio of 0.18 percent a year, which is very low (the exchange-traded fund version of this fund is even lower at 0.07 percent!). This fund also has a low turnover of 5 percent. The turnover figure means that only 5 percent of the fund is traded each year on average. High turnover almost always means higher costs and active management. Both are things you don't want. It also has no front-end load, which is a purchase fee to buy the fund.

TABLE 6.7  Vanguard Total Stock Market Index Fund versus a Typical Actively Managed Stock Fund

| Fund Name | Load | Expense Ratio | Turnover | 15-Year Performance |
|---|---|---|---|---|
| Vanguard Total Stock Market | 0% | 0.07–0.18% | 5% | 6.35% |
| Guggenheim Large Cap Core | 5% | 2.10% | 92% | 1.89% |

*Source:* www.morningstar.com.

> High turnover almost always means higher costs and active management. Both are things you don't want.

For comparison, the Guggenheim Large Cap Core fund (Ticker: SEQBX) is an example of a fund you don't want. This fund is inappropriate because it has high costs (2.10 percent a year), a load (you are charged up to 5.00 percent just to own it!) and it has a very high turnover of 92 percent (a sure sign of active management).

When you see a fund like the one from Guggenheim, you may ask, "What am I getting for the high load, high fees, and huge turnover?" How about bad performance? Table 6.7 shows the breakdown of both of these funds and the past 15 years of performance *before* inflation. Inflation over this time was around 2.3 percent a year. That means after inflation, the Guggenheim fund has had negative real returns for 15 very long years! For all the fees you got nothing in return.

> Morningstar is one of the best resources on the web for digging into investment options. They offer a free portfolio tracking service and provide valuable information relating to fees and tax impacts of funds. However, skip the idea of using Morningstar's rating stars to buy funds. The ratings do not predict future performance, just how the fund has done in the past. Simply buy a broad-based index fund with the lowest expense ratio you can find. The funds listed in this chapter are the top picks.

## Actively Managed Funds Hurt Performance

Do actively managed stock funds offer any advantages to a Permanent Portfolio investor? In a word: No. Using actively managed funds can, however, hurt the portfolio's overall performance in several ways.

First, the Permanent Portfolio has a fixed allocation to stocks, bonds, cash, and gold. You don't want to own a fund for your stock allocation and have the fund manager suddenly decide he doesn't want to own stocks and go to 100 percent cash or bonds.

Second, as discussed more fully below, active fund managers are the market. This means that they are frequently competing against themselves and charging investors a fee just to watch the show. Studies on this topic have shown repeatedly that index funds will beat the vast majority of their comparable actively managed funds over time. The results are so striking that it is amazing actively managed funds have remained so popular. This is a tribute to how effective good sales and marketing can be. A February 2011 study by the Wharton Business School came to this conclusion:

> *Over the 23 years ending in 2009, actively managed funds trailed their benchmarks by an average of one percentage point a year. If a benchmark like the Standard & Poor's 500 returned 10 percent, the average managed fund investing in similar stocks would therefore have returned 9 percent, while an index fund would have returned 9.8 to 9.9 percent, giving up only a small amount for fees . . .*
>
> *. . . When all the active managers are taken together, their holdings are so large that they reflect the entire market, and their performance will therefore match the market's. But the expenses they incur in their search for hot stocks and bonds undermine their results. The average actively managed stock fund, for example, incurs annual expenses of about 1.3 percent, or $1.30 for every $100 an investor has in the fund.*
>
> —Knowledge@Wharton[1]

## Fund Managers Are the Market

The goal of each of the Permanent Portfolio's assets is not to beat the market, it's simply to own the market, while capturing any gains the market is providing as cheaply as possible each year. In the quest to achieve this simple goal in the portfolio's stock allocation, an investor should stick with index funds simply because active fund managers as a group can't provide better returns than the overall market is offering, since these managers *are the market*.

In 1960 professional trades (pensions, mutual funds, etc.) accounted for 30 percent of all transactions. By 1979 that figure had increased to

---

[1] *If Index Funds Perform Better, Why Are Actively Managed Funds More Popular?*, Knowledge@Wharton, February 2, 2011.

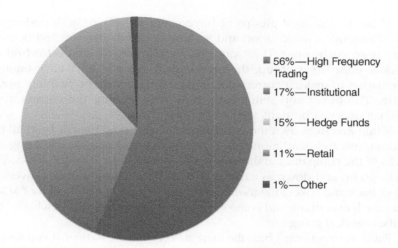

**FIGURE 6.1** Percentage of daily trades by group.

60 percent.[2] By 1989 the figure went up to 70 percent.[3] By 2010 that figure had reached 88 percent according to a recent analysis from Tabb Group. Only 11 percent of all stock transactions today are individual retail investors.[4] See Figure 6.1.

What this means is that nearly 9 out of 10 trades happening each day on Wall Street are between professionals. These groups are largely all trading against each other. Each has access to the same information, the same real-time news, the same hot tips, the same high speed trading systems, and so on. Yet, in every trade one party has decided to buy a stock and one has decided to sell that same stock.

> These professional groups of buyers and sellers are both trading on virtually identical information and making decisions that are 180 degrees away from each other. How can that be? Simple: *They are trading on random noise.*

[2] Michael E. Porter, *Cases in Competitive Strategy* (New York: Free Press, 1983), 212.
[3] Josef Lakonishok, Andrei Shleifer, and Robert W. Vishny, "The Impact of Institutional Trading on Stock Prices," *Journal of Financial Economics* 32 (1992): 23–43.
[4] Bob Pisani. *Man Vs. Machine: Pros and Cons of High-Speed Trading.* CNBC, September 13, 2011, www.cnbc.com/id/39041598/Man_Vs_Machine_Pros_and_Cons_of_High_Speed_Trading.

These professional groups of buyers and sellers are both trading on virtually identical information and making decisions that are 180 degrees away from each other. How can that be? Simple: *They are trading on random noise.* As a group, the professionals simply don't have enough information to make a correct decision about a trade's profitability in the future. The buyer and seller both think they making the correct decision, yet one will be right and one will be wrong.

When investors own the entire stock market they benefit from all the wisdom, research, and money these other firms have spent analyzing the stocks of the companies in the index. The index holds all of the stocks. The stocks go up and down as earning outlooks are adjusted. Index investors can sit back and collect the money without having to pay a bunch of MBAs to research everything and come to opposite conclusions about what to do. It's the best deal going.

Fund managers can't beat the market. *They are the market.* If you simply work to attain the market average you eventually will bubble up to the top in ultimate performance.

## Indexing Is a Marathon

Some people don't like indexing because they don't want to be "average." In fact, a lot of Wall Street marketing touts their funds for precisely this reason. Yet the truth is that by trying to be average you end up winning over time.

Let's say you're a marathon runner in a group of 10 people. You're not the fastest, but you have consistent performance and finish in the top half of all participants each time you race. Sometimes you're fifth, sometimes third, sometimes fourth, and so on. *You're average.* Pity you! Now you enter a series of races against your nine competitors and you race annually for 20 years.

Now if you follow the results you'll probably find something like this happens:

- One year the fastest runner goes on to be the slowest runner in the following year.
- The second best runner becomes the best runner the next year.
- The third year the best runner hurts his knee and drops out of racing entirely due to the injury.
- The fourth year the slowest runner goes on a steroid bender and comes in first, but soon after the drug affects their health and they, too, are forced to retire.

The years go by and you never win a race, but you're *consistent.* You're so consistent that you've racked up many fifth place, fourth place, third place, and maybe even a couple of second place finishes. You've never won a race, but you've also never done poorly. In fact, you've managed to show up for each and every race and never missed one yet. You're consistent, reliable, and always finish with respectable average results.

After 20 years of this consistent performance you will probably find that you've *won the marathon series.* Your rivals have either dropped out, burned out, or were never consistent enough to be in the top five. Your supposedly average performance pushed you into an elite category because you were so consistent and reliable year in and year out.

> The indexing paradox is that by trying to be average you end up well above average in long-term returns.

That's indexing. You're not going to be the best each year, but over time you may be surprised to see that you've won. You kept costs low, were consistent, and were always in the market when profits were being handed out when others may not have done so. The indexing paradox is that by trying to be average you end up well above average in long-term returns.

## Beware of Trading Costs

The acronym ETF stands for Exchange Traded Fund. This is a type of fund that can be traded like any stock on the market. You can buy an ETF in the morning and sell it at lunch then buy it back again before you go home from work (although this wouldn't be a good idea).

A typical mutual fund, however, allows redemptions and deposits on a fixed basis (at the end of the trading day). This means when you buy a fund you get the price of the fund after the market closes. You can't trade in and out of it multiple times a day. Some companies (like Vanguard) won't even let you buy back into a fund you have just sold for 60 days. Some funds may also charge you an early sale redemption fee as a penalty. This sort of policy is in place to keep the market timers and performance chasers from hurting the long-term holders of the fund and keep down costs.

The difference here doesn't matter much for a buy-and-hold investment strategy like the Permanent Portfolio. The hourly or even daily fluctuations in price are irrelevant. However there is one major difference between ETFs and mutual funds: *trading costs.*

When you buy a mutual fund you send your money to your broker or fund custodian and make the purchase. Many times if the mutual fund is with the same company there is no transaction fee for this. You would, for example, send your money into Vanguard and tell them "Buy as many shares of the Total Stock Market Index as my deposit allows." The sale is made, and the shares deposited into your account with no other fees involved.

With an ETF you need to deal with a brokerage. You have to place a market order, perhaps worry about a bid/ask spread, then pay a commission on the whole transaction. The commissions can be free for a limited number of trades a year, less than $10 at a discount broker, or be hundreds of dollars at a full-service brokerage for each trade. Costs vary.

The problem is, if you are making many small trades then the ETF can get expensive. If you are, for instance, depositing $100 a month into your portfolio you may spend $10 just to purchase the ETF. In other words, 10 percent of your savings that month went into transaction costs! Not good.

However, if you sent that same $100 into a mutual fund company they simply buy the fund without charging you a commission. Your $100 is used to buy the full $100 worth of mutual fund shares. You are able to buy more shares of the fund because you avoided the sales commission. That's much better.

Now there are times where ETFs make sense and many brokerages now offer a certain number of free trades. But the important thing to remember is that you would need to do the transactions in bulk and not through a bunch of small trades. For instance, if you are using ETFs, pool up your money to do a bulk purchase once a quarter or bi-annually from your cash allocation. If you follow that rule you can limit the commission charges that can really add up over time.

## Large-Cap and Small Cap-Stocks

In the markets there are segments for stocks depending on the size of the company. The S&P 500 index, for instance, tracks very large companies like General Electric. These companies have values in the billions of dollars and a worldwide presence. These stocks are called "large capitalization stocks," or large caps, and represent most of the value of the U.S. stock market.

At the opposite end are small-capitalization stocks, or small caps. These companies may be valued in the millions and can be quite localized in terms of their presence (such as a regional grocery chain or utility). There are thousands of companies that represent the small-cap market in the United States and they are a smaller part of the total value of the U.S. stock market when compared to large-cap stocks. The top 500 companies represent 70 percent of the value of the U.S. stock market. The thousands of other smaller companies represent the remaining 30 percent.

Some academic research suggests that there is an advantage in shifting (or tilting) a portfolio to favor small-cap stocks (specifically what are called "small-cap value stocks"). For purposes of the Permanent Portfolio, it's probably not worth the added trouble, expense, and complexity of slicing your stock exposure in this way. If you simply own a total stock market fund you will own large-cap stocks, small-cap stocks, and everything in between, providing you with exposure to everything.

Do small caps really outperform? Academics have said "Yes," while reality says: "It depends." There are periods of time when large-cap stocks provide the best returns and other times when small-cap companies provide the best returns. It is unpredictable.

Let's look at a portion of the last long-term bull market for stocks to make this point. From 1980 to 1999 small-cap stocks (specifically "small cap value") returned 14.9 percent annualized but large-cap stocks returned 17.6 percent annualized. So for nearly 20 years the higher returns of small-cap stocks over large-cap stocks didn't exist. How many people would have been able to stick with a small-cap-only stock strategy for almost two decades as large-cap stocks consistently provided superior returns? Not many.

While it is true that in the 2000s, small-cap stocks did outperform large cap-stocks, this was only observable *after the fact*. The next 20 years could again see large caps outperforming small caps. No one knows. In addition to this, since the small cap value effect was popularized there are now many funds that attempt to take advantage of this situation. So many people are now able to invest in small-cap value funds it is likely that the return bonus (if present) will have been arbitraged away by the market trying to exploit it. The markets are very efficient and these kinds of free lunches just don't exist for very long.

Craig once had a broker at Merrill Lynch lean over and discretely tell him that the secret to success for Merrill Lynch's advisory services was that they used small-cap value strategies. Wonderful! So in other words the secret of market outperformance is now being shared with perhaps millions of clients of a major broker like Merrill Lynch? How good must that secret information really be now that so many people are doing it?

So this debate of small versus large will rage on for years and both sides will have points to their argument. However, the beauty of the total stock market index is that you will own *everything* with simplicity and no regrets.

## International Stock Funds

In addition to the stock funds that invest in different segments of the U.S. stock market, international stock funds are another option available to investors. For purposes of the Permanent Portfolio, however, international stock exposure is not that important to U.S. investors, in part because the U.S. stock market includes companies already responsible for about half of the world's economic output.

In other words, an investor who owns an index fund that holds the largest American companies already has exposure to international economic activity already. Think about it: you can travel to many foreign countries and never be far from a McDonald's or Starbucks. Microsoft and Apple Computer sell their products everywhere, as do Coca-Cola, Caterpillar, and Boeing. Need some running shoes? There is a store down the street that sells Nike. So even if you think you have 0 percent international exposure by only owning American companies you actually don't. It's almost certain that the profits you receive from these stocks are generated from all over the world and not just from the United States.

If you decide to make an international stock fund part of your investment strategy, bear in mind that ownership of international stocks introduces an element of currency risk into the equation. Currency risk is the idea that even though a group of companies are very profitable, those profits may be in another currency that is losing value compared to your home currency. Thus, the foreign profits may not translate into significant gains where you live if the U.S. dollar is strong and other currencies are weak.

An investor who wants more international stock exposure within the Permanent Portfolio should consider limiting the exposure to perhaps 5 to 10 percent or so of the overall portfolio (e.g., 15 to 20 percent U.S. stocks market and 5 to 10 percent international). Any greater allocation to international stocks within the Permanent Portfolio begins to weaken the connection in the portfolio's stock allocation to the economic condition of domestic prosperity. If you have too much exposure to international markets it can hurt performance of the portfolio under some conditions. Just because U.S. markets are doing great doesn't mean those in Japan or Europe are, for instance.

This idea is country-dependent and discussed in Chapter 12, Implementing the Permanent Portfolio Internationally, more fully. Just realize that overweighting a lot of stock outside of your home economy you can be impacted by events that otherwise would have had no effect on you. For non-U.S investors it may be more of a factor, and this will be covered in Chapter 12 as well.

## Recommended International Stock Index Funds

If you want international exposure, use an index fund as well. An international index fund should be broad-based and inexpensive just like a domestic stock fund for the same reasons. The EAFE international index, FTSE international ex-U.S. index, or what is sometimes called a "Total International Index," are good choices:

- Vanguard FTSE ex-U.S. Index ETF (Ticker: VEU)
- Vanguard FTSE ex-U.S. Index Mutual Fund (Ticker: VFWIX)
- Vanguard Total International Index Mutual Fund (Ticker: VGTSX)
- iShares EAFE Index ETF (Ticker: EFA)
- Fidelity Spartan International Index Mutual Fund (Ticker: FSIIX)

International index funds have higher fees when compared to domestic index funds because of the added expense of trading on foreign stock exchanges. Look for the typical international stock index fund's expense ratio to be around 0.75 percent or less. Lower is always better.

## Vanguard Total World

If you want international exposure weighted to the world markets, then Vanguard has a relatively new fund called the Vanguard Total World index. This fund mirrors the relative weightings of all stock markets on the planet. The current 2012 breakdown of the markets it holds is shown in Figure 6.2.

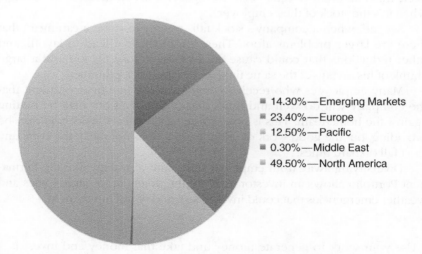

- 14.30%—Emerging Markets
- 23.40%—Europe
- 12.50%—Pacific
- 0.30%—Middle East
- 49.50%—North America

**FIGURE 6.2** Vanguard Total World Index: A one-stop shop for domestic and international stock exposure.

*Source:* Portfolio breakdown according to Vanguard's website, early 2012.

This fund, like all Vanguard funds, has a low expense ratio (but not as low as the Vanguard Total Stock Market due to the international costs).

- Vanguard Total World Index Mutual Fund (Ticker: VTWSX)
- Vanguard Total World Index ETF (Ticker: VT)

This fund is an option to consider for a Permanent Portfolio investor that wants to have international stock exposure, but wants the simplest most broadly diversified fund possible to do it. It is also a possible option for international investors that can purchase the fund and are running their own Permanent Portfolio in their home country. The breakdown in Figure 6.2 shows that the U.S. markets dominate even in this fund.

## A Warning About Company Stock

As a result of stock options, stock in retirement plans, and other opportunities for an employee to accumulate the stock, many investors find themselves with large holdings of the stock of their employer. There are at least two reasons to be cautious about allowing too much of your portfolio to consist of the stock of your employer.

First, if you own too much of a single stock and it falls steeply you will obviously take a huge loss. This would be true of any individual stock. However, this fact often doesn't seem to register with an investor as strongly when it is the stock of their employer.

Second, when a company's stock falls steeply in value it can mean that there are larger problems afoot. These problems can lead to layoffs and other reductions that could cause an investor to lose his job and a large chunk of his savings at the same time during the stock plummet.

Many employees who receive company stock feel overconfident that the company will do well and think that diversifying out may be betting against the home team. This is not to disparage the hard work you may be providing, but the good work of an individual does not mean the company can't fall on hard times.

Diversifying away from employer stock into a strategy like the Permanent Portfolio allows an investor to avoid the potential for large losses and weather emergencies that could involve a period of unemployment.

Use your work to generate money and take that money and invest it elsewhere. Failing to do so risks the loss of both your job and stock profits at the same time.

It is a better strategy to separate your work from your retirement savings. Use your work to generate money and take that money and invest it elsewhere. Failing to do so risks the loss of both your job and stock profits at the same time.

Craig states: "Although I have never been laid off, I did learn the value of diversification after being caught owning too much company stock. I was giving a presentation in Monterey, California in the spring of 2000 and was watching the news during a huge market decline. At that time I owned too much stock of the company where I was working. In the morning the news of the market crash was underway and I saw the ticker go by with my company stock below my stop-limit I had set. The stop-limit is a way to limit downside risk if a price drops too low. Once the limit is hit, a sale is executed automatically.

"I thought to myself: 'Well that's that.' I knew the stop-limit would kick in and at least limit my losses, but I never would have thought the stock would have fallen as far as it had in the first place. I never concentrated my stock holdings again after that. I was foolish and got really burned by not diversifying my investments."

## No Index Funds—What to Do?

If you find yourself in a situation where an index fund simply isn't available to you (for whatever reason), then look for the following in the funds that you can choose from:

- Lowest expense ratio possible.
- Should track the broadest part of the U.S. market as possible.
- Should be 100 percent invested in stocks at all times and not be moving in and out of the market based on fund manager judgments.
- Should have low portfolio turnover.
- The fund should not be buying and selling stocks trying to beat the market.

## Recap

Investors must own a 25 percent allocation to stocks at all times with the Permanent Portfolio. The future is unpredictable and a bad stock market can turn into a good one at any moment. By staying in the market at all times, you will always be able to fully profit from whatever gains the stock market is offering, and from whatever sectors of the stock market are offering those gains. Here is a list of what stock funds to own and why:

- Use an index fund, such as a total stock market fund or an S&P 500 fund. These funds own the stock market at the lowest possible cost and in a broadly diversified way.
- Funds with the lowest expense ratio and lowest turnover will result in higher performance.
- The average actively managed fund will lose to the market by the amount of their management fee.
- Never purchase an actively traded stock fund unless you have absolutely no other choice available to you. If forced to do so, make sure it stays 100 percent invested in stocks at all times.
- Do not try to beat the market with your stock fund. Your market protection is already built into the other asset classes you own in the Permanent Portfolio.
- The stock asset class serves a specific purpose and you don't want to tamper with it by trying to outguess the market or having a manager trying to outguess the market.
- If you want to own some international exposure you should limit it to about 5 to 10 percent (5 to 10 percent international + 15 to 20 percent domestic = 25 percent total in stock).
- Don't concentrate your savings in your employer's stock. Diversify out in case of problems at your company that jeopardizes the stock and your job at the same time.

# CHAPTER 7

# Bonds

## *Bonds for Safety and Income*

D uring periods of prosperity when the economy is healthy and expanding, bonds provide a steady stream of income while also dampening the volatility of the stock market. There are, however, periods when the entire economy goes through a period of deflation, serious financial crisis, or some combination of destabilizing events. It is during these periods that bonds can be one of the few assets that actually go up in value.

A bond is a loan. The borrower makes periodic interest payments over a certain amount of time before returning the initial loan to the lender. Just like risks of a loan you'd make for someone to buy a car or a home, a bond also has risks that affect whether or not it will be repaid and how it will be repaid.

The bond market is probably one of the most complex pieces of the investing world to understand. The main problem is that there are many types of bonds and many types of overt or very subtle risks in bonds. For reasons that will become clear, the only bonds that are appropriate for the Permanent Portfolio are 25- to 30-year U.S. Treasury long-term bonds. These bonds provide the strongest protection during deflationary events and also robust returns when times are good. They also avoid a lot of risks that are present in other kinds of bonds you can buy.

## Benefits of Bonds

Just like the other assets in the Permanent Portfolio, bonds are held *at all times* regardless of what an investor may think is going to happen in the economy. Even when the outlook for bonds is bleak, history has shown that they can seemingly come out of nowhere to defend against severe losses to a portfolio.

In the Fall of 2008 when the stock market lost 37 percent of its value, the bonds the Permanent Portfolio held saw price appreciation of over 30 percent, wiping out virtually all losses in the overall portfolio (gains in gold for the year allowed the portfolio to finish 2008 with minimal losses).

And in 2011, bonds pulled in another strong year with gains of over 33 percent when the U.S. stock market posted a paltry 1 percent gain and international markets lost anywhere from −14 percent to −19 percent due to problems in the euro. In both 2008 and 2011, few (if any) market experts were predicting such a result from bonds. Meanwhile, Permanent Portfolio investors have simply enjoyed the overall returns of the portfolio, which have in part been the result of large but unanticipated gains in the bonds. Previous years have seen similar movements in bonds when the stock market has done poorly.

As discussed in Chapter 6, Stocks, the financial media is fond of claiming that over time stocks will outperform bonds. Yet, over relatively long periods of time this is not always true. For example, the past decade has been so bad for stocks that some bonds (like the ones the Permanent Portfolio holds) have easily beaten them. In fact, at a low point of the stock market, bonds managed to exceed stocks in total returns for the past 30 years. That's a startling thing to consider and something that many investors would never think could happen.

> The truth, however, is that markets are simply not predictable and popular storylines such as "stocks always beat bonds" often yield to the more sobering reality.

The truth, however, is that markets are simply not predictable and popular storylines such as "stocks always beat bonds" often yield to the more sobering reality. That reality is that bonds *can* outperform stocks over some periods, and sometimes those periods can be very long (a decade plus). The problem is you simply won't know ahead of time when this can happen, which is why you need to always hold bonds no matter what someone else is advising. Jeremy Siegel, author of *Stocks for the Long Run*, said in a phone interview for Bloomberg News on October 31, 2011:

> *The bond market posted its first 30-year gain over the stock market in more than a century during the period ended Sept. 30. The last time was in 1861, leading into the Civil War, when the U.S. was moving from farm to factory.*

In addition to providing security during times of crisis, bonds can also provide strong gains with a stock market that is performing well. In other

TABLE 7.1  Asset Class Returns—Bond and Stocks Both Do Well—1980 to 1999

| Asset | Annualized Return | Real Return | Growth of $10K in Real Dollars |
|---|---|---|---|
| **Stocks** | 17.9% | 13.3% | $122,400 |
| **Bonds** | 10.7% | 6.4% | $ 34,700 |
| **Cash** | 6.9% | 2.8% | $ 17,300 |
| **Gold** | −2.3% | −6.1% | $  2,800 |

TABLE 7.2  Asset Class Returns—Bonds Beat Stocks—2000 to 2009

| Asset | Annualized Return | Real Return | Growth of $10K in Real Dollars |
|---|---|---|---|
| **Stocks** | −1.0% | −3.4% | $ 7,100 |
| **Bonds** | 7.7% | 5.0% | $16,400 |
| **Cash** | 2.8% | 0.2% | $10,200 |
| **Gold** | 14.9% | 12.1% | $31,200 |

words, an economy that is prosperous for stocks is often prosperous for bonds. From 1980 to 1999 stocks turned in excellent performance, but bonds also performed respectably in the Permanent Portfolio.

In 2000, however, stocks entered what turned into a decade-long period of negative real returns. Yet, bonds kept on providing a steady stream of income and capital appreciation, resulting in solid gains. Tables 7.1 and 7.2 illustrate the performance of bonds during these times.

## Risks of Bonds

All investments have risks, and the main risk to the bond allocation in the Permanent Portfolio is *inflation*. It is more commonly called "interest rate risk." Interest rate risk means that when interest rates rise, bond prices fall, and when interest rates fall, bond prices rise. In other words, *bond prices move opposite to interest rates.*

> Bond prices move opposite to interest rates.

Interest rate risk becomes a real danger during inflation. In periods of inflation, interest rates are often rising (sometimes rapidly). Bond prices move opposite to interest rates, which means the bond prices will *fall*. Rising

TABLE 7.3  Asset Class Returns—Bonds Hurt by Inflation—1972 to 1979

| Asset | Annualized Return | Real Return | Growth of $10K in Real Dollars |
|---|---|---|---|
| **Stocks** | 5.1% | −2.8% | $8,000 |
| **Bonds** | 3.8% | −4.0% | $7,200 |
| **Cash** | 6.5% | −1.5% | $8,900 |
| **Gold** | 34.1% | 24.1% | $56,000 |

Market data used for equal comparison begins in 1972 after gold standard ends.

inflation can not only cause the value of bonds to fall, but the money bonds are *paying* in the form of interest payments will also be able to buy less.

Rising inflation is therefore a double blow to bond holders in terms of real returns. First you get falling bond prices as interest rates rise and secondly your interest payments can't buy as much. As a result, real returns are often going to be negative under high inflation for bonds, and investors will want very high interest to compensate them for the risk inflation is posing.

Table 7.3 illustrates how during the high-inflation 1970s bonds had a real return loss of −4.0 percent a year. By the end of the decade, the real purchasing power was nearly cut by 30 percent. Ten thousand dollars invested in bonds in 1972 was worth only $7,200 by 1980.

Notice, however, that during the 1972 to 1979 period when bonds performed poorly, gold went up sharply in price and easily offset the losses. The assets in the Permanent Portfolio are designed to offset each other's risks. Economic conditions that hurt bonds (like inflation) are very good for assets like gold.

Besides interest rate risks, there are many other risks to non-Treasury bonds as well which will be covered. Just understand that interest rate risk is perhaps the biggest risk to bonds.

## Volatility

Like stocks and gold, the Permanent Portfolio holds long-term bonds because they can provide strong returns in certain economic conditions. But also like stocks and gold, long-term bonds are volatile.

In 2008, for example, rapidly falling interest rates resulted in bond gains of over 30 percent at the peak as the stock market sank, as shown in Figure 7.1. The top line is the bond allocation of the Permanent Portfolio, while the bottom line is the U.S. Total Stock Market index. The bond gains offset most of the losses in the stock market. The volatility in the long-term bonds offset the volatility of the stocks during this time.

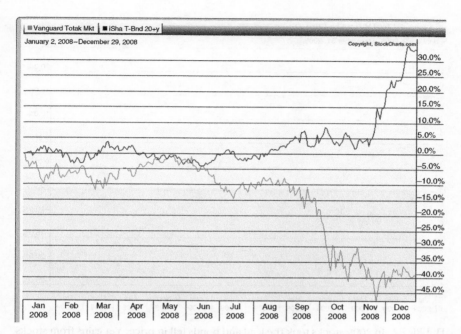

**FIGURE 7.1  Bond volatility in 2008 offset most stock losses. Volatility is not a bad thing for the Permanent Portfolio.**

Chart courtesy of stockcharts.com.

During periods of rising interest rates, however, the bond allocation will also generate losses. After the large gains in 2008 for instance, bonds lost 20 percent in value in 2009 as stocks posted 25 percent gains. Figure 7.2 shows this reversal of trends with stocks on top and bonds below.

However, the overall gains of the portfolio in the stocks and gold allocation still produced a total portfolio profit of +12.7 percent (+9.7 percent real returns) in 2009. In other words, the loss in the bonds was completely absorbed in the stock and gold gains and produced a net profit, even though the bonds lost −20 percent this year at the worst. The volatility of the bonds was offset by the volatility of the other components. When looked at individually it may seem that the bond loss would be bad. But when you look at *the total portfolio value* (all that really matters), an investor walked away with great gains in the entire portfolio.

The portfolio harvests these gains and losses and the profits are locked in to keep the portfolio moving forward. The important point is that investors *need the volatility* of the bonds, just as with the other assets, to make the portfolio work. Just like the other assets in the Permanent Portfolio, the assets in isolation may appear to be volatile. But when combined together

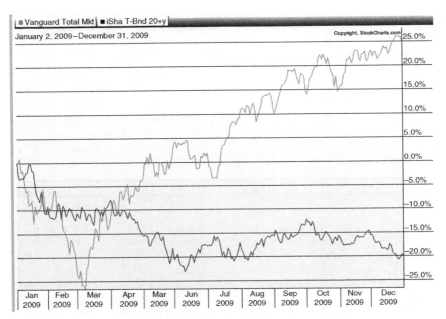

**FIGURE 7.2** In 2009 stocks took the lead and bonds fell in price. Yet gains from stocks and gold prices this year still produced returns in excess of 12.7 percent (+9.7 percent real returns) even with the bond losses in the Portfolio.

**Chart courtesy of stockcharts.com.**

the volatility is essentially neutralized and the result is a smooth and stable ride upwards under all economic environments.

## Bonds and Deflation

During a period of deflation, interest rates are dropping. A decline in interest rates causes existing bonds to rise in value.

For example, if an investor owns a bond paying 5 percent a year for 30 years, and the new market rate for bonds falls to 3 percent a year for 30-year bonds, then the 5 percent bond will be more valuable because it pays more interest over the same period. After all, if you were buying a bond, which would you rather own: A bond paying 5 percent for 30 years or a bond paying 3 percent for 30 years? Table 7.4 illustrates.

If the bonds were the same price you would of course want the 5 percent bond. However, the market would never let this price disparity exist. What happens is that your 5 percent bond price goes up in value until the effective payout matches the 3 percent bonds in the market over 30 years.

TABLE 7.4  A 5 Percent Bond is Much More Valuable Over Longer Periods and Commands a Premium in Falling Interest Rate Environments

| Interest Rate | Simple Interest Earned on $10,000 over 30 Years |
| --- | --- |
| 3% | $ 9,000 |
| 5% | $15,000 |

The rule with bonds is that if rates go up, bond prices go down, and if rates go down, bond prices go up. The longer the time until the bond matures, the stronger these price movements will be. Thus, a change in interest rates from 5 to 3 percent would translate into a larger price movement on a 30-year bond than on a 10-year bond. Thirty years' worth of higher interest payments is simply more valuable than 10 years' worth of those same payments.

If the above is confusing, don't worry. The only rule you need to remember is that bond prices move opposite to interest rates. The bond market adjusts prices instantly to reflect these changes. The kind of bonds you own is also going to influence the price movements as well and this will be explained.

## Owning Bonds

Although there are many types of bonds available, only one type is appropriate for the Permanent Portfolio, and it is the 25- to 30-year nominal long-term U.S. Treasury Bond.

> Although there are many types of bonds available, only one type is appropriate for the Permanent Portfolio, and it is the 25- to 30-year nominal long-term U.S. Treasury Bond.

Long-term Treasury Bonds are appropriate for the Permanent Portfolio for the following reasons:

- They have no default risk.
- Their long maturity provides maximum volatility to profit from periods of deflation.
- They are nominal (fixed rate) bonds, meaning they do not have inflation adjustments built-in.
- They avoid other bond problems such as credit risk, political risk, and currency risk.

## Bonds to Buy

Any long-term nominal U.S. Treasury bond with 25 to 30 years to maturity is appropriate for the Permanent Portfolio. Investors will not be holding them for 25 to 30 years, though. To maintain the desired volatility within the Permanent Portfolio's bond allocation, investors will sell a treasury bond when it reaches 20 years to maturity, and then purchase a new 25- to 30-year bond to replace it. This is a simple process that any broker can handle for you in a matter of minutes (or seconds). The bond markets buy and sell bonds of all different maturities constantly and you aren't obligated to hold a bond until it matures.

> The bond markets buy and sell bonds of all different maturities constantly and you aren't obligated to hold a bond until it matures.

The important point is that investors want average bond maturity in the portfolio to be *greater than 20 years*. Any bond with less than 20 years' maturity is cycled out of the portfolio and replaced with one that has a longer maturity.

Here is a step-by-step description of the process above:

1. Buy a U.S. Treasury long-term bond with 25 to 30 years maturity.
2. Hold the bond until it has 20 years to maturity remaining (meaning it sits in your account for 5 to 10 years paying you interest).
3. Sell the 20-year maturity bond and use the proceeds to buy a new 25- to 30-year bond to replace it, if needed.
4. Repeat the process as appropriate to maintain your asset allocation.

If the above intimidates you, don't worry. There are a few long-term Treasury bond funds that are appropriate for use with the Permanent Portfolio, if you desire. These funds maintain a constant average years to maturity and require no action on your part other than to periodically rebalance the entire portfolio.

## Buying Bonds

There are three basic ways to buy U.S. Treasury long-term bonds:

1. At auction from the Treasury.
2. On the secondary market.
3. Through a bond fund.

## At Auction or on Secondary Markets

Buying and holding bonds directly is the best and *safest* way to have exposure to Treasury bonds. This can be done at a bond auction or on the secondary market.

> Buying and holding bonds directly is the best and safest way to have exposure to Treasury bonds.

Buying bonds at auction from the Treasury can be done in two primary ways:

1. Open an account at Treasury Direct (www.treasurydirect.gov) to make the purchase.
2. Use your mutual fund company or broker to make the purchase.

Treasury Direct is a service of the U.S. Treasury that allows individuals to participate in the auction and buying process of Treasury bonds of all types. Treasury Direct accounts can be set up like any brokerage account and your bond purchases will be held in custody for you. This service has limitations in terms of flexibility as it only hold bonds for you. This can make it somewhat harder to move money among the assets in your portfolio.

Brokerages can also purchase bonds at auction. Investors should check their brokerage or speak to a representative to find out the process used by their broker to participate in Treasury bond auctions. Investors can call the broker's bond desk for help as well.

The secondary market is for bonds that have already been issued. Bonds on the secondary market are sold like stocks every day and are an easy way to get bond exposure without waiting for Treasury auctions. Bonds purchased on the secondary market may not have exactly 30 years to maturity (could be 27 years, for instance), but any Treasury bond with 25 to 30 years to maturity is perfectly fine.

> Using the secondary market to buy bonds and store them at your brokerage or mutual fund provider is probably the easiest way to own bonds directly.

Again, a bond desk at your brokerage or mutual fund provider can normally be used to purchase long-term Treasury bonds in this way. Using the secondary market to buy bonds and store them at your brokerage or mutual fund provider is probably the easiest way to own bonds directly. Many brokers have online services that make buying bonds directly easy. For instance, TDAmeritrade and Fidelity have services that make buying bonds at auction or the secondary market as easy as ordering a book and they can offer assistance for first-time users.

## Long-Term U.S. Treasury Bond Funds

If you do not wish to purchase bonds directly, there are some funds available that make owning this asset easier. Recognize that doing this is *not* as good as direct ownership, but for investors that want the convenience or have no other options, they are a solution.

**iSHARES LONG-TERM TREASURY ETFs**   Unfortunately, many bond funds hold a mix of bonds that are not appropriate for the Permanent Portfolio or use a manager to move bonds around trying to beat the market. However the ETF below will hold mostly Treasuries:

- iShares Treasury Long-Term Bond ETF (Ticker: TLT)

    This fund fits the primary criteria for bonds in the Permanent Portfolio:

- It holds 100 percent U.S. Treasury nominal long-term bonds.
- It holds bonds with maturities over 20 years.

    This fund also has a low expense ratio. This is a mandatory requirement in any bond fund because the returns from interest can be low and you don't want your profits being eaten up by high management fees.

    Although this ETF ostensibly is 100 percent in Treasury bonds, in recent times they have been in the business of securities lending. The activity of lending securities can introduce new risks into the fund (if the person they are lending them to can't return them for instance). It also introduces new tax risks (the mix of government and non-government interest has different tax treatment). Although this Treasury ETF is convenient, it again is not as good as owning the bonds directly.

**LONG-TERM TREASURY FUNDS OFFERED BY VANGUARD AND FIDELITY**   Vanguard and Fidelity both offer the following mutual funds with some caveats as well:

- Fidelity Spartan Treasury Long-Term Bond Fund (Ticker: FLBIX)
- Vanguard Long-Term Treasury Bond Fund (Ticker: VUSTX)

    Unfortunately, these funds do not meet the criteria set out above, primarily because the bonds these funds hold may not be of long enough maturity. Also they can hold as little as 80 percent in Treasuries and can hold 20 percent in various other government-backed bonds which do not serve any benefit to Permanent Portfolio investors—all at the discretion of the fund managers.

However if you have no other choice available, they are a better option than most other long-term Treasury bond funds you'll find. The Fidelity fund tends to be more pure Treasury than the Vanguard fund and is the first choice of the two. The Vanguard fund unfortunately often mixes in too much cash or other types of bonds (like mortgages) that can affect performance and safety.

**BOND FUND COMPOSITION** Morningstar's tools come in handy again to view how bond funds break out in terms of what they hold. The iShares and Fidelity Funds are nearly 100 percent in bonds. But more importantly they are nearly 100 percent in *Treasury* bonds. The small amount of cash they hold (for fund operations) is not meaningful.

The Vanguard fund however is roughly 76 percent in Treasury bonds, 16.7 percent in government agency bonds (mainly mortgages) and 7.2 percent in cash (or equivalent) as of this writing (and it frequently changes). This is an example where the bond fund managers are trying to guess what the markets may do and this can hurt performance in the Permanent Portfolio. Table 7.5 breaks out the bond funds and relevant data on their composition.

> An important note about passively managed bond funds like those in this chapter is that they will show a high turnover. Normally, high turnover in a stock fund is bad because it usually means a fund manager is actively trading. However in a bond fund, high turnover is common because as bonds mature they are cycled out of the fund and replaced with new bonds of longer maturity. So if you see high turnover in these bond (and cash) funds, it is perfectly normal.

**TABLE 7.5** iShares, Fidelity, and Vanguard Treasury Bond Fund Holdings

| Bond Fund | Expense Ratio | Treasury Bonds Holdings | Other Bond Holdings | Cash Holdings |
|-----------|--------------|------------------------|---------------------|---------------|
| iShares   | 0.15%        | 99.98%                 | 0%                  | 0.02%         |
| Fidelity  | 0.10%        | 100%                   | 0%                  | 0%            |
| Vanguard  | 0.22%        | 76.0%                  | 16.7%               | 7.2%          |

*Data source:* Morningstar as of early 2012.

With all of the above said, the prospectus of all of these funds give them a range of options they can use to adjust the holdings at the manager's discretion within limits. And, as mentioned above, even the iShares fund has its warts with securities lending going on behind the scenes. Again, bond funds are convenient but not as safe as direct ownership. However, if they are what you can use easily for your situation, then take advantage of them.

## Other Bond Risks—The Case for Treasury Bonds

There are other risks that bond investors must consider besides interest rate changes as discussed. Many of these risks are present in non-Treasury bonds, while Treasury bond holders needn't worry about many of them. Below is a discussion of some of these risks.

### Default Risk

Default risk is the probability that investors won't get paid back. Default risk is very real in corporate and other types of non-Treasury bonds. Bonds issued by governments are often considered safer than bonds issued by corporations, but there are some governments that have defaulted on their promises to bondholders so even that is no guarantee.

Since the U.S. government issues U.S. Treasury bonds, it can raise taxes to make payments in a crisis. Also, in a pinch, it can always print money to pay bondholders if necessary. This would not be the preferred approach, of course, and would probably result in bad inflation. However, a government defaulting because of a lack of funds is not likely if it can print its own currency to pay bondholders. In other words, with U.S. Treasury bonds you may get paid back with inflated dollars that are worth less, but you won't find yourself in a situation where you get nothing back as you can with other bond types (such as a company bankruptcy).

### Credit Risk

Bond credit risk is very similar to an individual's own credit rating. A lower personal credit rating means more risk of creditors not being paid back. As a result, people looking to do business with you will want more interest to compensate for the risk. Just like your own credit rating, there are agencies that rate bond issuer's credit as well.

Credit ratings on the bond markets are determined by an agency such as Standard & Poor's (S&P) or Fitch Group. Often when an agency downgrades a bond issuer it will translate into higher interest rates for their bonds. A credit downgrade can make interest rates skyrocket and, since bond prices move opposite to interest rates, the prices will fall. If you are holding a bond that has a credit downgrade, chances are the price will decline.[1]

## Call Risk

Call risk is a special kind of provision in some bonds that allows the issuer to elect to pay off the bond early (normally when interest rates are falling and the debt can be refinanced at lower rates). The problem is that when the refinancing occurs the owners of the existing bonds that have been called miss out on the gains in the bonds' value. This gain would have occurred if they were allowed to keep the higher-yielding bonds.

Many municipal bonds, for example, have call provisions. What this means is that if you were to hold a callable bond paying 6 percent and interest rates dropped to 4 percent, the issuer could call the bond and re-issue a new bond paying 4 percent. This deprives bondholders of the higher interest payments they were expecting and a higher bond price that they could use for additional profit. Of course, if interest rates are rising the bond issuer is more than happy to leave bondholders with the lower interest paying bond.

You probably are already aware of call privileges if you own a home. Mortgages in fact have a similar call provision. Basically, when interest rates are falling homeowners can refinance their homes for a lower rate. In essence they are calling back the mortgage bond on their home by paying it off with a new lower interest rate mortgage. The more interest rates fall, the more incentive there is for homeowners to refinance. And of course if interest rates rise, homeowners will keep the lower interest payment mortgages and would never think of refinancing to something more expensive.

Call risk, therefore, is asymmetric and strongly favors the bond issuer, not the buyer. They are a classic case of heads they win, tails you lose.

> Callable bonds offer no advantages to investors seeking protection from falling interest rates and should be avoided.

Therefore, callable bonds offer no advantages to investors seeking protection from falling interest rates and should be avoided.

---

[1] In 2011, however, the U.S. government was downgraded from AAA to AA+ and nothing happened at all. In fact, interest rates continued to fall and the bond prices *increased* ! The markets are not predictable. Normally however, credit downgrades are very bad for bondholders.

## Currency Risk

Currency risk only applies to bonds issued in a foreign currency. Whereas U.S. Treasury bonds pay you in U.S. dollars, Japanese bonds pay in yen, British bonds in pounds, and so on.

The problem with bonds issued in another currency is that if you live in the United States, you spend your money in dollars, not yen (or pounds). Holding bonds denominated in foreign currencies means that, in addition to the other risks bondholders face (credit, default, etc.), you would also be subject to the risk of fluctuations in the value of the currency in which the bonds are denominated.

For instance, high inflation in the British pound would be very bad for British bonds. The value of the currency in this case is going down and can purchase less and less. This would mean the value of your British bonds (and the pounds they pay you in) could fall in value even though the economy in the United States may be perfectly fine and have negligible inflation. In effect, the inflation happening in London, England, is bled over to a holder of British pounds in Hometown, USA. While the British government may appreciate your patronage in this situation (by imposing their inflation on you), your portfolio will not.

Since the Permanent Portfolio relies on being coupled to your local economy for protection in all situations, for a U.S. investor only U.S. Treasury bonds are appropriate for the bond allocation.

## Political Risk

Political risk is the idea that the government issuing the bonds may implement changes that put bondholders (*especially* foreign bondholders) at a disadvantage. As a foreign holder of a nation's debt, an investor will often pay taxes on bond dividends to the government issuing the bond, which subjects the investor to potentially unfavorable changes in the issuing country's domestic tax policy. In other cases, to prevent capital flight in a crisis, the government may simply prevent foreign investors from removing their money from the country.

> Some countries may decide it is a good idea to implement an extra tax on foreign bondholders or to simply not pay foreign bondholders during a crisis.

Finally, some countries may decide it is a good idea to implement an extra tax on foreign bondholders or to simply not pay foreign bondholders during a crisis.[2] In all cases, foreign investors often face the realization that, as non-voting members of the countries they are investing in, it is easier for the politicians to take advantage of *them* than it is to take advantage of their *own* citizens.

## Tax Risks

Bond interest in the United States is normally taxable income for bondholders. The type of bond you own determines the kind of taxes you will pay. Paying as little in taxes as possible is important, but tax considerations should not lead an investor to assemble a portfolio that is not adequately diversified just to save on taxes exclusively.

Some kinds of bonds, such as municipal bonds, receive favorable tax treatment (usually tax free at the state and federal level). However, they are not appropriate for the Permanent Portfolio due to the credit and call risks discussed above. These risks outweigh the higher taxes of U.S. Treasury bonds.

> Although the interest income from U.S. Treasury bonds is taxed at the Federal level, they are not taxed at the state and local level.

Although the interest income from U.S. Treasury bonds is taxed at the Federal level, they are not taxed at the state and local level. This makes them less tax efficient than municipal bonds, but more efficient than many other types of bonds, such as those issued by corporations and foreign countries that are often subject to multiple tax jurisdictions.

The bottom line concerning tax efficiency and U.S. Treasury bonds is that they do enjoy the benefit of being free from state and local taxes, but their tax efficiency (or lack thereof compared to another bond) should not be a determining factor in whether or not to purchase them as part of a diversified portfolio. What is far more important is to make sure that the bonds you own provide you with the kind of safety you need when required. For purposes of the Permanent Portfolio, only U.S. Treasury bonds provide this kind of safety, taxes or not.

[2] Ana Nicolaci da Costa and Samantha Pearson. "Brazil Doubles Tax on Foreign Bond Buys to Curb Real," *Reuters*, www.reuters.com/article/2010/10/05/brazil-economy-forex-idUSN0413289020101005.

## Bond Fund Manager Risks

Another great feature of government treasury bonds is they are easy and safe to hold directly and not with a fund. With most other bond types you are safer using a fund for the diversification, and this means you need a fund manager, and that means manager risk. Manager risk is the risk when the human behind the fund makes a bad market call that costs their investor's money. Even previously well-performing bond fund managers can lose out when their decisions go against them:

> *Bond market guru Bill Gross is telling his investors what many of them already know: He made the wrong call on U.S. Treasury bond interest rates this year, and that has cost him dearly in his renowned Pimco Total Return bond fund.*
>
> *Gross told the Financial Times on Monday that the U.S. economy has grown more slowly in 2011 than he had expected, which has pushed Treasury bond yields lower as investors have rushed for relative safety. [Editor: Causing prices to go up sharply]*
>
> *Because he kept the $245-billion Pimco fund largely out of Treasuries until recently, Gross missed out on the rising market value of older fixed-rate Treasuries as rates on new bonds fell.*
>
> *"Do I wish I had more Treasuries? Yeah, that's pretty obvious," Gross told the FT.*[3]

The Permanent Portfolio strategy requires the investor to hold a fixed allocation of long-term U.S. Treasury bonds at all times. You don't need a fund manager actively trading a bond portfolio with the objectives of either trying to dampen volatility or squeeze out slightly higher returns. When fund manager decisions go wrong, it can compromise safety.

Again, in the 2008 financial crisis, there were actively managed bond funds that suffered losses in excess of 35 percent due to manager mistakes. For instance, investors in some bond funds used in popular college savings plans were badly burned:

> *The Oppenheimer Core Bond fund, (Ticker: OPIGX) offered by 529 plans in Oregon, Texas, Maine, and New Mexico, fell 36% last year, vs. a loss of about 5% for the average intermediate-term bond fund, according to Morningstar, an investment research firm. The losses stemmed*

---

[3] "How Bill Gross' Wrong Call on Bonds Has Cost His Pimco Investors," *Los Angeles Times*, August 29, 2011, http://latimesblogs.latimes.com/money_co/2011/08/bill-gross-pimco-total-return-bond-fund-returns-2011-treasury-bet-recession.html.

*from the management team's decision to take big bets on mortgage-backed securities and credit default swaps, Morningstar said.*[4]

Investors in these funds were forced to absorb losses that they never even considered were possible. But here's the good news:

*If you own your Treasury bonds directly you need not worry about any of these issues with bond fund management.*

Owning Treasury bonds directly means you are in control and aren't going to be taking unnecessary risks with your bond holdings. You're going to be holding 100 percent long-term Treasury bonds in your own account and you won't have to worry if a manager is doing something risky with your money. As a bonus, you won't pay annual management fees for someone to hold Treasury bonds for you (which is extremely low risk).

If you do choose to use a bond fund for your Permanent Portfolio bond allocation, do your own careful research before investing in any fund that claims to own Treasuries. The preference should always be for a fund that only holds 100 percent long-term Treasury bonds and is not shifting around maturities or bond types through active fund management. The funds listed in this chapter are decent options, but manager risk is always a threat so just be aware of it.

## Bonds to Avoid

Given the above risks, the following kinds of bonds are *not appropriate* for the Permanent Portfolio's bond allocation:

- Treasury Inflation Protected (TIPS) Bonds
- Municipal Bonds
- Mortgages
- Corporate Bonds
- Junk Bonds
- International Bonds

### Treasury Inflation-Protected Securities

Treasury Inflation-Protected Securities (TIPS) are bonds issued by the U.S. Treasury that are designed to provide investors with an inflation-adjusted stream of interest payments over the life of the bond. TIPS have low default risk like other Treasury bonds, but are not suitable for the Permanent

---

[4] "Oppenheimer Bond Fund Losses Hit College 529 Savings Plans," *USA Today*, January 4, 2009, www.usatoday.com/money/perfi/college/2009-01-01-oppenheimer-bond-fund-529-plans_N.htm.

Portfolio. The main problem is that TIPS are designed to respond to *infla-tion*. They will not provide the price spike that nominal long-term Treasury bonds will provide during periods of *deflation*.

> TIPS provide almost no protection against economic conditions involv-ing *deflation*, which is the main risk that the bond portion of the Perma-nent Portfolio is designed to protect the investor against.

The 2008 financial crisis was deflationary. This crisis saw TIPS not only have a liquidity problem on the market that affected their prices (which nobody thought could happen), but their interest payment meth-odology affected how much they went up in value for investors. In this year long-term Treasury bond funds went up at least 30 percent in value, while a popular TIPS bond fund *fell* 7 percent in value. TIPS simply did not provide the protection under deflationary conditions that nominal Treasury bonds did (see Figure 7.4 for a comparison chart of bond types and how they performed that year).

TIPS are frequently advocated in the investing industry for a bond hold-ing. But, again, do not buy TIPS for the bond portion of the Permanent Port-folio (nor in place of the gold portion as will be discussed later). They serve no purpose for the strategy and can damage the protection of the portfolio if used in place of nominal U.S. Treasury bonds (or gold).

## Municipal Bonds

The attraction to municipal bonds is they are tax-free in some cases at the local, state, and federal levels. It should be reiterated that while tax consider-ations are important, it is more important not to compromise on total portfo-lio protection and municipal bonds, unfortunately, do exactly that.

Since state and local governments cannot tax Treasury bond interest payments, the tax savings provided by municipal bonds are not as great upon closer inspection. Also, the yields on these bonds tend to be signifi-cantly lower than Treasury bonds of comparable maturity. This is the result of the market arbitraging away much of the tax savings municipal bonds are supposed to provide. The difference in yields between U.S. Treasury and Municipal bonds is often the tax advantage.

Further, municipal bonds may have credit, default, and call risks. In the case of severe deflation, many municipal bonds paying a higher interest rate can be called by the issuing agency, depriving bondholders of the price appreciation that results from falling interest rates. Thus, the bonds you thought you held to offset portfolio losses due to deflation might no longer be available to you. You'll have to look for new bonds to replace those that have been called along with everyone else. Usually this is the *exact moment* that you don't want to be buying non-callable Treasury bonds, as their prices will have gone way up in price. Consider it like a backup generator your neighbor loaned you. Then when a hurricane comes along, they ask for it back and force you to go to the store during the rush to buy a new one at premium prices. That's call risk.

Credit and default risks also exist for municipal bonds as well. In 2008, municipal bonds suddenly looked very risky as the market realized that it was easy to imagine a world where municipalities could have trouble meeting their financial obligations. This was at the same time that large insurance companies guaranteeing the municipalities' bonds were also on the verge of insolvency. Municipal bond holders that thought they were getting a good deal by avoiding some taxes had many sleepless nights.

## Mortgages

Like municipal bonds, mortgages have a call provision because the holders of the mortgages (homeowners) can refinance in a falling interest rate environment to get a better deal. Therefore in a situation like deflation, when interest rates are falling, mortgage bonds tend to not appreciate as much in value because investors know that the homeowners behind them are likely to pay them off early with a lower rate loan. Not just this, but mortgage interest payments are often taxable at all levels and some mortgages that aren't backed by a U.S. government agency also have credit and default risks.

## Corporate Bonds

Corporate bonds are not especially well suited for the Permanent Portfolio. Even high-quality corporate bonds can have call features, and top-rated companies can see their fortunes turn very quickly (as investors have been reminded often in the past).

> If you have moral objections to loaning money to the U.S. government, then your primary option is to own a high-quality, long-term corporate bond fund.

Ignoring the weaknesses in corporate bonds when compared to U.S. Treasury bonds, if you have moral objections to loaning money to the U.S. government, then your primary option is to own a high-quality, long-term corporate bond fund. Since default risk is a primary concern with owning corporate bonds, you want to make sure your fund only owns the highest rated bonds and owns the bonds of many companies to diversify against the risk of bankruptcy from a single issuer. Using a fund in this case to diversify across many companies is going to be safer than trying to buy corporate bonds on your own.

The Vanguard Long-Term Investment Grade bond fund (Ticker: VWESX) is a good choice for an inexpensive, long-term corporate bond index fund if you simply do not want to own U.S. Treasury bonds.

Investors who opt for this approach should realize that they are sacrificing deflation protection by making the decision to avoid U.S. Treasury bonds. A serious economic crisis could see widespread defaults in corporate bonds, including those previously considered very safe.

## Junk Bonds

High-yield bonds (also known as junk bonds) are a type of bond with an enticingly high yield but lots of risk. Don't let the high interest rates convince you to buy them for the Permanent Portfolio, as they are totally unsuitable for this application. Bonds are for safety and not speculation. Buying higher risk bonds means you are chasing yield and it can be dangerous because higher rewards always mean higher risk.

> Bonds are for safety and not speculation.

If you need your bonds to protect you during an economic crisis you don't want them to be subject to credit or default risk, but that's exactly what junk bonds give you—in spades. In a sense, they are one of the worst investments you can own—you get all of the volatility and risk of stocks but little of the upside potential. Junk bonds can also generate very poor tax treatment if not held in a tax-deferred account as they are taxed at all levels.

During 2008 in the midst of the financial crisis, many junk bond funds lost 30 percent or more in value. Figure 7.3 shows the performance of junk bonds versus long-term U.S. Treasury bonds.

Imagine owning high-yield bonds thinking they would protect you in a bad market only to see the fund sink by 30 percent right along with your stocks. That's not the kind of diversification you need in the Permanent Portfolio. Stick with U.S. Treasury bonds.

## International Bonds

International bonds offer currency and political risks to investors. Not only will these bonds fluctuate in value due to the ups and downs of the currency

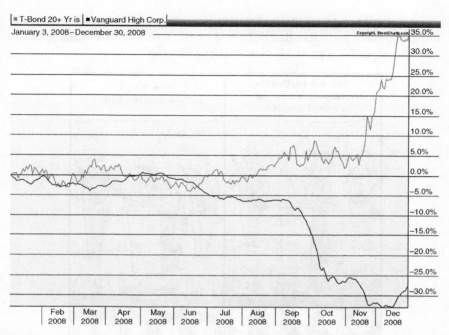

**FIGURE 7.3** 2008 performance of long-term U.S. Treasury bonds versus junk bonds. U.S. Treasury bonds were up over 30 percent and junk bonds sunk by 30 percent providing no diversification benefit and compounding losses.

Chart courtesy of stockcharts.com.

markets, there is also the risk that some foreign countries may simply decide to not pay you back at all.

Emerging market bonds in particular offer an easy way for an investor to be separated from his money. Here is how Ecuador decided to treat their bondholders in 2008 according to the *Wall Street Journal*:

> *Ecuador's President Rafael Correa said his nation is defaulting on its foreign debt, in a hardball move prompted as much by leftist ideology as economic distress. Mr. Correa said Ecuador will skip a $30.6 million payment to bondholders due Monday, asserting that there are irregularities in how the debt had been contracted by an earlier administration. Mr. Correa, an economist who is close to [Editor: communist dictator] Venezuelan president Hugo Chávez, lashed out at foreign creditors as "real monsters."*[5]

---

[5] http://online.wsj.com/article/SB122911515875502569.html.

As of 2011, it looks like Ecuador is going to issue foreign bonds again under the same president that defaulted on them in 2008 after calling investors "monsters."[6] It's probably best to skip their offer.

## Flight to Safety

When investors panic in a market crisis they'll shun anything with risk. If they think the stock market has too much risk, they will often see the corporate bond market as also having too much risk. Likewise, municipal bonds will cease to have appeal when it becomes obvious that issuers will be exercising call options in the face of falling interest rates or possibly have problems making bond payments.

The scenario described above is what happened in late 2008 when the stock market crashed. Fearing a full-scale international financial crisis, investors sold everything and bought U.S. Treasury bonds for protection. But since Permanent Portfolio investors already owned these bonds before the

---

[6] www.bloomberg.com/news/2011-08-04/ecuador-plans-international-bond-sale-to -test-market-demand-after-default.html.

crisis hit, they were able to profit from this so-called flight to safety. Indeed, 2011 saw a repeat of this performance when the euro was facing trouble with a possible default by Greece and domestic markets started to sink. U.S. Treasuries again soared in value as investors sought their relative safety. The seemingly higher yields of other bonds were dwarfed by the capital appreciation of high-quality U.S. Treasury long-term bonds.

Figure 7.4 shows the year 2008 and a Long-Term Treasury Bond Fund versus Vanguard's Long-Term Corporate Bond Fund versus Vanguard's High-Yield Corporate Bond Fund versus Vanguard Long-Term Tax Exempt Bond Fund versus Vanguard Treasury Inflation Protected Securities (TIPS) Fund.

You can see that when the stock market was crashing and fears of deflation were taking hold, long-term U.S. Treasury bonds went up nearly 35 percent in value while long-term corporate bonds lost 5 percent (down 20 percent at the low), high-yield (junk) bonds dropped 30 percent in value, long-term tax-exempt bonds sank 10 percent, and TIPS were down 7 percent by the end of the year.

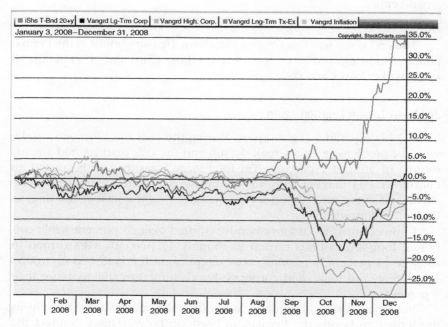

**FIGURE 7.4** 2008 Crash—U.S. Treasury long-term bonds outperformed every other kind of bond.

Chart courtesy of stockcharts.com.

## 2008—The Long-Term Bonds Cinderella Story

In the first half of 2008 long-term U.S. Treasury bonds as an asset class were almost universally scorned due to the conventional wisdom that interest rates were about to start rising rapidly. In reality, just the opposite was about to happen. It came as a great surprise to many investors at the end of 2008 to find that long-term U.S. Treasury bonds were easily the best performing asset class of the year.

When credit and call risk showed up in the Fall 2008, people were paying premium prices for nominal Treasury bonds over corporate bonds, junk bonds, and municipal bonds. TIPS, which respond only to inflation and not deflation, provided no diversification benefit under this scenario either.

> When credit and call risk showed up in Fall 2008, people were paying premium prices for nominal U.S. Treasury bonds over corporate bonds, junk bonds, and municipal bonds. TIPS, which respond only to inflation and not deflation, provided no diversification benefit under this scenario either.

The end result was that owning long-term Treasury bonds in the Permanent Portfolio allowed investors to harvest those gains and offset almost all stock market losses in 2008.

## 2011—A Lesson Learned Again

In 2011 history had a slight repeat. During the year the Euro was on the verge of problems with a Greek default and the U.S. markets had anemic returns of around 1 percent. Yet long-term Treasury bonds posted an enormous +33 percent gain, mostly in the last quarter. This gain overshadowed every other bond a U.S. investor would consider holding, as Figure 7.5 illustrates.

In this chart U.S. Treasury bonds returned over 33 percent while corporate long-term bonds turned in roughly 17 percent, TIPS turned in roughly 13 percent, long-term, tax-exempt bond funds turned in around 11 percent, and high-yield corporate bonds turned in slightly more than 7 percent.

In fairness, these other funds do not have the same average maturity as the long-term bonds the Permanent Portfolio holds. This will affect the upside movement when rates go down. However, these funds represent the *best in class* for these kinds of bonds, so they are likely what investors will be able to purchase to obtain exposure to these assets easily and safely.

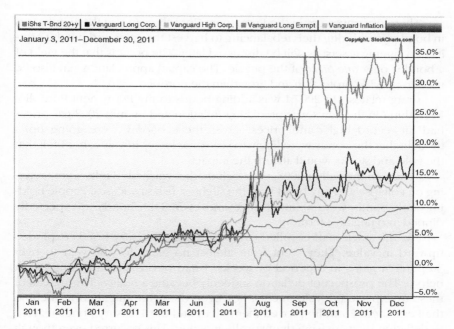

**FIGURE 7.5** Long-term Treasury bonds dominate again in 2011.

Chart courtesy of stockcharts.com.

Additionally, other funds may have chosen to start the year with short-term bonds to limit interest rate risk. But in this year that was a bad bet and those funds lagged the long-term bonds considerably.

## Earning Money Multiple Ways

One of the most common misconceptions about bonds is that they are only profitable for their interest payments. But this is not *completely* true. Bonds can profit you both in interest payments and also in capital gains when interest rates decline.

The potential for large capital gains in bonds has been demonstrated repeatedly in recent years. To take 2007 to 2008, for example, long-term U.S. Treasury bonds started off 2007 with yields around 5 percent, but by the end of 2008 their yields had fallen below 3 percent. Now a 2 percent decline doesn't sound all that exciting. But, when you look at the price swing from this movement you will find that they generated capital gains of over 30 percent. Then again, in 2011, interest rates fell after rising in 2009 and bonds posted 33 percent gains in capital gains as well.

Therefore, investors in the Permanent Portfolio can use these increases in bond prices during their rebalancing to harvest the gains and put the profits into lagging assets, as will be discussed later. The point is that the yield of a bond is only *one piece* of the puzzle. The capital appreciation can also be used to provide protection and growth in the portfolio.

Craig relates: "In 2007 I was adding bonds to my Permanent Portfolio. Everything in the news was predicting inflation and by mid-2008 gas prices had hit record highs and prices across the economy were going up. I thought that the bonds were likely to see some losses in value, but I felt that the gold and stocks would absorb the impact.

"Then, in the Fall of 2008, the stock market crashed. Banks were teetering on collapse and any bond with the slightest risk saw losses. People holding junk bonds were skinned alive and even TIPS bonds unexpectedly dipped into negative territory.

"As the stock market rolled over, long-term Treasury bonds exploded upward in value. They went from almost no gains for the year to over 30 percent gains in a period of weeks. I had never seen anything like it before. The prospect of deflation suddenly became a reality. Through all of these unexpected developments, however, the economic theories behind the Permanent Portfolio proved themselves and the Treasury bonds reacted to deflation by increasing dramatically in value. This occurred even though virtually no one went into 2008 expecting Treasury bonds to be the year's best performing asset.

"Instead of having to sit through the 2008 crisis worrying about my life savings, I was able to watch the events unfold with a detached curiosity. I didn't need to worry about credit risk because my Treasury bonds had none. I didn't need to worry about call risks when interest rates fell because my bonds were non-callable. I didn't need to worry about bond fund managers doing risky things because I owned my bonds directly. Finally, I didn't need to worry about the stock market losses because my bond profits almost completely offset them.

"By the end of the year I was able to take my Treasury bond profits and rebalance into stocks, which had fallen to a decade-low price. I never would have guessed it would all work out that way, but that was part of Harry Browne's basic investing philosophy—we need to be prepared for all possible economic conditions because you just never know what's going to happen next."

## Bond Risk Matrix

As discussed earlier, bonds have some mixture of credit risk, default risk, call risk, political risk, currency risk, and tax risk. These risks are priced into a bond in the form of the interest rate that the bond pays. More risks associated with a bond translate into higher interest rates to compensate investors. Simply, the bonds of the U.S. Treasury pay less interest than those from Fly-By-Night, Inc. But the U.S. Treasury also has a much higher chance of actually paying the investor back.

> Simply, the bonds of the U.S. Treasury pay less interest than those from Fly-By-Night, Inc. But the U.S. Treasury also has a much higher chance of actually paying the investor back.

Despite all of the bad press that U.S. Treasury bonds sometimes get, long-term debt issued by the U.S. government enjoys almost complete immunity to all of the bond risks outlined in this chapter. Because U.S. Treasury bonds do not have risks associated with most other bonds, they are the safest to own for U.S. Permanent Portfolio investors.

Table 7.6 shows that U.S. Treasury bonds look the best when all of the risks to bonds are taken into consideration. Note that private companies may insure some municipal bonds and some mortgages are guaranteed by the government. However, in 2008 some very large insurers were put under pressure and if they had gone bankrupt this could have reverberated all through the municipal bond market. Additionally, prior to 2008, mortgages owned by government-sponsored enterprises like Freddie Mac had an implied backing by the U.S. government, but it was not as absolute as Treasury bonds. This caused a lot of problems as well. The only bonds that were truly safe were Treasury bonds when the markets were in panic.

As the table shows, U.S. Treasury bonds pose the least risk to investors when all the factors are considered.

**TABLE 7.6  Bond risk matrix—U.S. Treasuries Score Best**

|  | U.S. Treasury | Municipal | Mortgages | Corporate | Junk | International |
|---|---|---|---|---|---|---|
| Default Risk | *No* | Yes | Maybe | Yes | Yes | Yes |
| Credit Risk | *No* | Yes | Maybe | Yes | Yes | Yes |
| Call Risk | *No*\* | Yes | Yes | Yes | Yes | Yes\*\* |
| Political Risk | *No* | No | No | No | No | Yes |
| Currency Risk | *No* | No | No | No | No | Yes |
| Manager Risk | *No* | Yes | Yes | Yes | Yes | Yes |
| International Taxes | *No* | No | No | No\*\*\* | No | Yes |
| State/Local Taxes | *No* | No | Yes | Yes | Yes | Yes |
| Federal Taxes | *Yes* | No | Yes | Yes | Yes | Yes |

\*Some U.S. Treasury long-term bonds issued in the high-inflation, early 1980s had call terms but they are no longer in circulation.
\*\*Different governments will have varying policies on callable bonds.
\*\*\*Only if they are domestic corporations.

## Bond Funds and Retirement Plans

For investors with a significant amount of their funds in tax-qualified retirement plans, such as 401(k) plans, there is normally not a suitable long-term U.S. Treasury fund in the plan's fund lineup. Most of these bond fund offers are of limited use to a Permanent Portfolio investor.

If you find yourself with a large 401(k) plan balance relative to your other investments and no suitable long-term Treasury bond fund in the plan, you still may have a few choices:

- Ask your 401(k) plan administrator to include a long-term Treasury bond fund to the plan's fund lineup. Be sure that any such fund that is added actually is a 100 percent long-term U.S. Treasury bond fund (fund names can be deceptive).
- Ask your 401(k) plan administrator if the plan offers a brokerage window. A brokerage window may allow you to either buy bonds directly from the secondary market or buy a suitable long-term Treasury bond fund outside of the plan, such as those listed in this chapter.
- Use the funds that you have to the best of your ability.

If you are forced into the last option, then try to look for the following in your funds that you do have:

- Lowest expense ratio possible.
- Uses U.S. Treasury Bonds only, or at least mostly U.S. Treasury bonds.
- Has the longest maturity U.S. Treasury Bonds available.
- Won't be actively managed with someone shifting around bond maturities as they feel is appropriate. You want static maturity targets in the bond fund.
- Uses nominal bonds and not TIPS or mortgages.

## Recap

The Permanent Portfolio holds long-term Treasury bonds to protect against deflation and provide additional income during prosperity. Remember these dos and don'ts when dealing in bonds:

- You should purchase bonds with a maturity of 25 to 30 years.
- You should hold the bonds until they have 20 years left of maturity and then sell them to buy new 25- to 30-year bonds.
- Credit risks, default risks, call risks, and political risks should be avoided with the bonds in your Permanent Portfolio.

- Bonds should be used for safety, not speculation.
- Do not purchase TIPS, municipal bonds, mortgage bonds, international bonds, corporate bonds, or junk bonds.
- If you have objections to owning U.S. government bonds, then choose a high-quality, long-term corporate bond index fund (while realizing the vulnerabilities that this approach may create for the overall portfolio).
- If possible, bonds should be purchased and held directly to avoid bond fund manager risk.
- If you do use a fund, make sure it is as close to 100 percent Treasuries as possible.
- If you choose to use a bond fund, never use an actively managed fund. Only passive index funds should be considered.
- If your retirement plan doesn't offer a suitable long-term Treasury bond fund, see if one can be added. Or, utilize a brokerage window if one is available to make your purchases of bond directly.

# CHAPTER 8

# Cash

## *Cash, the Forgotten Asset*

Most financial advisors recommend that investors keep some cash reserves on hand, but almost no investment strategies work these cash holdings into an overall investment strategy. However, the Permanent Portfolio is unique in that it calls for a 25 percent allocation to cash and these cash holdings are a fundamental building block of the overall strategy.

Unlike the other Permanent Portfolio assets, which are designed to be volatile, cash is designed to act as a stabilizer to the portfolio during market volatility. The cash allocation also provides an investor with a place to store interest, dividends, and capital gains from the other assets, and provides "dry powder" for rebalancing purposes during market declines. Cash also occasionally serves as the leading asset in the portfolio when the stocks, bonds, and gold are all having a bad year.

In addition to the functions described above, cash also acts as an emergency reserve for life's unexpected events, such as periods of unemployment or health emergencies. For those in retirement, the cash portion of the portfolio can be tapped for living expenses. Overall, the cash allocation in the Permanent Portfolio performs several important functions.

Because the safety and stability of cash is so important, the Permanent Portfolio holds its cash in ultra-safe U.S. Treasury Bills (T-Bills) with maturity of 12 months or less. The reasons why T-Bills are preferred over other options will be discussed in this chapter.

## Benefits of Cash

Cash dampens volatility in the Permanent Portfolio during market fluctuations and can provide surprising benefits under almost all economic conditions. There is, however, one particular economic condition during which a significant allocation to cash can be crucial.

## Tight Money Recessions

The economic environment in which cash holdings are most essential is during what Harry Browne called a "tight money" recession. A tight money recession is a recession that is deliberately induced by a central bank raising interest rates in an economy that is already very weak. This is done in the hopes of reducing inflation as part of their monetary policy.

One of the effects of a tight money recession is that almost *every* asset loses value as a result of significant increases in interest rates. Thus, while at least one of the Permanent Portfolio's stock, gold, or bond assets are normally rising under prosperity, inflation, or deflation, during a recession all three of these assets could fall in value for a short period.

The good news is that a recession of this type is by definition a relatively brief period (usually 18 months or less). A central bank can only raise interest rates so much before either inflation ceases to be a concern or the high interest rate policy tips the economy into a depression (in which case long-term bonds would be expected to perform well).

The U.S. economy encountered this environment during the early 1980s when the Federal Reserve repeatedly raised interest rates to stop the inflation they had caused in the 1970s. During this period the Permanent Portfolio's T-Bill holdings carried the portfolio.

Table 8.1 illustrates the recession induced by the Federal Reserve in 1981 in the hope of taming runaway inflation. Before this episode was over, the prime interest rate (the short-term rate banks charge to their best and most creditworthy customers) topped out at over 20 percent and mortgage rates were in the mid-teens.

In this case the markets, not being able to get an idea what was going to happen, showed unpredictable results. Stocks, bonds, and gold all dropped in value in real terms as inflation continued to erode the dollar's purchasing

TABLE 8.1  Cash Performed Best During the 1981 Recession

| Asset | 1981 Return | 1981 Real Return | Growth of $10K in Real Dollars |
|---|---|---|---|
| **Stocks** | −4.9% | −12.7% | $ 8,729 |
| **Bonds** | 1.9% | −6.5% | $ 9,352 |
| **Cash** | 14.7% | 5.3% | $10,531 |
| **Gold** | −31.1% | −36.7% | $ 6,329 |

power. Cash, an asset that many think is a loser all the time, actually posted the highest returns in 1981. This was the worst year the Permanent Portfolio ever had. It lost only −4.9 percent (−12.6 percent in real terms) when other strategies did much worse.

> Cash, an asset that many think is a loser all the time, actually posted the highest returns in 1981.

Investors who had a cash buffer in their portfolios not only were able to ride out the market gyrations in 1981, but by having cash on hand they could also rebalance into assets that had fallen to very attractive levels. Table 8.2 shows what happened the very next year in 1982 once the markets calmed down. The small loss in the portfolio in 1981 turned into a very nice 20.2 percent gain (15.8 percent real) in 1982. Stocks and bonds went up sharply that year and gold and cash also recovered. Investors who waited out the storm (with the help of their cash anchor) profited very nicely.

Even though the Wall Street phrase "Cash is trash" sounds catchy, the reality is that during market swings cash is a very powerful asset for diversification. Cash is an asset a lot of people dislike right up until the point things go haywire. Then, it's the belle of the ball.

"...but I heard **cash** was **trash**."

TABLE 8.2  All Four Assets in the 1982 Recession Recovery

| Asset | 1982 Return | 1982 Real Return | Growth of $10K in Real Dollars |
|---|---|---|---|
| **Stocks** | 21.6% | 17.1% | $11,707 |
| **Bonds** | 40.4% | 35.2% | $13,518 |
| **Cash** | 10.5% | 6.5% | $10,646 |
| **Gold** | 8.3% | 4.3% | $11,694 |

## Risks of Cash

Because cash is a low-risk asset, it is not surprising that it also has relatively low inflation-adjusted returns. Because its real returns are low, cash is very vulnerable to inflation and over time inflation can erode any real return cash may be earning.

The 1970s were characterized by high inflation, and cash lost −1.5 percent a year in real terms. Over the eight-year period of 1972 to 1979, a $10,000 investment would have been reduced to $8,900 in actual purchasing power as shown in Table 8.3. Cash performed better than bonds and stocks, but overall cash is not a good performer during inflation. In the case of the 1970s, however, good investment performance for most investors consisted of having *small* losses rather than *large* losses.

During times of prosperity a large cash allocation is often seen as a lost opportunity. The sense is often that the cash could have been used to purchase another asset like stocks or bonds that would have provided higher returns. This perspective assumes, of course, that an investor could have known which assets would outperform cash ahead of time.

> With the benefit of hindsight it's always easy to pick winners, but hindsight tells us nothing about what will happen going forward.

TABLE 8.3  Cash During High Inflation—1972 to1979

| Asset | Annualized Return | Real Return | Growth of $10K in Real Dollars |
|---|---|---|---|
| **Stocks** | 5.1% | −2.8% | $ 8,000 |
| **Bonds** | 3.8% | −4.0% | $ 7,200 |
| **Cash** | 6.5% | −1.5% | $ 8,900 |
| **Gold** | 34.1% | 24.1% | $56,000 |

Market data used for equal comparison begins in 1972 after the gold standard ends.

TABLE 8.4  Asset Class Returns—Cash During a Period of Prosperity Was a Lost Opportunity—1980 to 1999

| Asset | Annualized Return | Real Return | Growth of $10K in Real Dollars |
|---|---|---|---|
| **Stocks** | 17.9% | 13.3% | $122,400 |
| **Bonds** | 10.7% | 6.4% | $ 34,700 |
| **Cash** | 6.9% | 2.8% | $ 17,300 |
| **Gold** | −2.3% | −6.1% | $  2,800 |

Table 8.4 shows the lost opportunity that resulted from holding cash from 1980 to 1999, which was a very good time for stocks and bonds. During this period, cash performed much better than gold, but cash was unimpressive when compared to the winners over this period.

With the benefit of hindsight it's always easy to pick winners, but hindsight tells us nothing about what will happen going forward. In other words, an investor in 1980 didn't have the luxury of knowing that stocks and bonds were about to begin a period of outstanding performance. All the investor in 1980 knew for sure was that stocks and bonds had performed very poorly for many years up to that point and could very well have continued doing just that.

## Volatility

Because cash acts as a buffer during periods of economic uncertainty, it needs to be held in a form that is *very stable* and *very safe*. Unlike stocks, bonds, and gold, cash is the only part of the Permanent Portfolio that should have virtually no volatility.

Among other reasons for avoiding risk of any kind with cash holdings is that under some market conditions it is essential to have access to cash to buy other assets that have fallen in value. In other cases, an investor may need to use his or her cash to provide living expenses or reserves to cover unexpected expenses. When such situations arise, cash can be indispensible and it must be stable and safe.

The goal with the Permanent Portfolio's cash is to make sure that it is always there when you need it.

As a result of the need for absolute safety and stability, the Permanent Portfolio has a narrow view of holding cash. The portfolio is not seeking risky high returns from its cash allocation, though cash will occasionally be the portfolio's best performing asset. In normal times, however, stocks, bonds, or gold will be the best performing assets in the portfolio. The goal with the Permanent Portfolio's cash is to make sure that it is always there when you need it.

## Interest Rate Risk and Volatility

As described in Chapter 7 on Bonds, interest rate risk is the danger a fixed income investment such as bonds face when interest rates are rising. Like bonds, cash can be vulnerable to rising interest rates depending on how it is invested. Avoiding the potential for interest rate risk is one of the goals of the Permanent Portfolio's cash allocation.

One way of viewing the Permanent Portfolio's cash allocation is that it represents the opposite end of the interest rate risk spectrum from long-term bonds. Long-term bonds will rise in value when interest rates fall, and fall in value when interest rates rise. The amount of gain or loss in each case is determined by the maturity of the bond. If cash is invested in a 12-month T-Bill, however, the period of time until the T-Bill matures (i.e., always less than one year) is so short that the investment is largely immune to fluctuations in value based on interest rate changes.

Investors want their cash to be as nonvolatile as possible. This is the exact *opposite* of the bond allocation. Bonds are very volatile to interest rates because the length of time it takes until they mature is so long. Because T-Bills have such a short time to maturity, they do not move very much when interest rates are changing.

Table 8.5 shows the years 2008 and 2009 as an example. In 2008 long-term rates fell from a January start of 4.35 percent to 2.6 percent by the end of the year, for a total fall of −1.75 percent. But look at the result. Bonds went up by 25.9 percent and T-Bills hardly moved at all, going up only 1.5 percent.

Yet in 2009 long-term rates went back up by a seemingly small 2 percent. This 2 percent increase caused the bonds to fall in value −14.9 percent while

TABLE 8.5  Cash and Bonds Returns in 2008 versus 2009 Bonds are volatile but the cash was very stable in value

| Asset | 2008 Returns | 2009 Returns |
| --- | --- | --- |
| **Bonds** | 25.9% | −14.9% |
| **T-Bills Cash** | 1.5% | 0.10% |

T-Bills barely budged, posting a slight 0.10 percent gain.[1] Remember that bond prices move *opposite* to interest rates and this also applies to T-Bills. The T-Bills were very stable in value through these big swings in interest rates. That's exactly what is needed for the cash allocation.

# Owning Cash

The term cash suggests something you might carry in your wallet or put under your mattress. What cash means in the context of the Permanent Portfolio, however, is a cash equivalent investment. This is an investment that can be converted at any time into currency that an investor can use immediately.

The criteria for the Permanent Portfolio's cash are:

- Be very liquid (can be bought and sold instantly at any time).
- Have no interest rate risk.
- Have no default, credit, call, currency, counterparty, or other common types of fixed income risk.

## Suitable Investment Options for Cash

For a U.S. investor the primary asset that meets these criteria is very short-term debt issued by the United States government in the form of T-Bills with 12 months or less to maturity.

There are three primary ways to purchase T-Bills:

1. At auction from the Treasury
2. On the secondary market
3. Through a Treasury Money Market Fund

**TREASURY AUCTION AND SECONDARY MARKET**   One way of purchasing T-Bills is to get them directly from the Treasury. When T-Bills are purchased in this manner, they are typically held to maturity, at which time the funds are rolled into fresh T-Bills. This approach is called "laddering" and there are two basic ways to do it:

1. Open an account at Treasury Direct to make the purchases (www .treasurydirect.gov) and build the ladder yourself.
2. Use your mutual fund company or broker to make the T-Bill purchases and maintain the ladder for you.

---

[1] www.treasury.gov/resource-center/data-chart-center/interest-rates/Pages/TextView .aspx?data=yield.

Treasury Direct is a service of the U.S. Treasury Department that allows individuals to participate in the auction and purchase of T-Bills in the same manner as with long-term bond purchases described in Chapter 7, Bonds. Treasury Direct can be tied in with your bank account to add and remove funds directly.

Brokerages can also purchase T-Bills at auction or on the secondary market. You can call your broker and speak to the bond desk for help with T-Bill purchases (each broker has slightly different T-Bill purchase procedures). Many brokerages also have online forms to automate this process for you.

> Buying T-Bills and rolling them over is the safest way to hold them, but often it is not as convenient. Luckily, there are a number of funds that manage T-Bill portfolios for very low fees and still offer a high degree of safety.

Buying T-Bills and rolling them over is the safest way to hold them, but often it is not as convenient. Luckily, there are a number of funds that will manage a portfolio of T-Bills for you for very low fees and still offer a high degree of safety.

**TREASURY MONEY MARKET FUNDS**   Treasury Money Market Funds offer an easy way to own T-Bills. The basic criteria for suitable Treasury Money Market Funds is similar to the bond portion of the portfolio in many ways:

- Only owns 100 percent U.S. Treasury bills.
- Has a low expense ratio (preferably below 0.20 percent a year.)[2]
- Is passively managed to track the market, rather than being actively managed to try to beat the market.

In light of the criteria above, the following funds are suitable choices for the cash portion of the Permanent Portfolio:

iShares Short Treasury ETF (Ticker: SHV)
Fidelity Treasury Money Market (Ticker: FDLXX)
SPDR Treasury Bill ETF (Ticker: BIL)
Gabelli U.S. Treasury Money Market (Ticker: GABXX)

---

[2] Many Treasury Money Market funds have high expense ratios and should be avoided. With current yields near 0 percent, a high expense ratio can mean that an investor is actually losing money in many of these funds. Always check the expense ratio before investing in any fund.

The Vanguard fund is tentatively mentioned even though it can hold as little as 80 percent in Treasuries at times:

Vanguard Treasury Money Market (Ticker: VUSXX)—This fund is not pure Treasuries unfortunately, though it is widely available.[3]

Other funds exist that may be suitable for your cash allocation as well. When evaluating them consider the guidelines outlined above. If a Treasury bill fund follows these guidelines, it is probably a good option for the Permanent Portfolio cash allocation.

**U.S. SAVINGS BONDS** Among the types of debt that the U.S. Treasury issues, Series EE and Series I savings bonds have long been popular among small investors. While savings bonds are not popular among many because of their low rates and stodgy reputation, in recent years it has become possible to obtain larger returns on savings bonds than on the currently available T-Bills being issued by the Treasury Department.

Series EE savings bonds pay a fixed interest rate for the life of the bond and Series I savings bonds pay an inflation-adjusted interest rate for the life of the bond. Savings bonds earn interest for up to 30 years and no income tax is due on accumulated interest on a bond until redemption, which make them a useful tax deferral tool as well as a good choice for a portion of the Permanent Portfolio's cash allocation.

The caveat is that redeeming savings bonds is not as easy as selling a T-Bill held in a brokerage account (although they are only electronic now as of 2012 so this dynamic may change), and sales of savings bonds that have been held for fewer than five years will incur a three-month interest penalty. Lastly, there is also an annual limit on an individual's savings bond purchases.

Savings bond holdings as part of a Permanent Portfolio should probably be limited to no more than 30 percent of the entire cash allocation if an investor goes this route (a 25 percent cash allocation means your portfolio will hold no more than about 7.5 percent in savings bonds). Limiting savings bonds will ensure there will always be plenty of cash for rebalancing purposes or to tap in a time of need. At the same time the overall cash allocation will often be able to earn slightly higher yields than a 100 percent T-Bill allocation without assuming any additional risk (since the entire cash allocation is still held in debt issued by the U.S. Treasury).

---

[3] Vanguard can hold as little as 80 percent in Treasuries in this fund and sometimes mixes in mortgages and other assets that offer no advantages to Permanent Portfolio investors. This fund is also closed to new investors as of early 2012.

**SHORT-TERM TREASURIES**   Another optional modification to the cash holdings in the Permanent Portfolio is to replace a portion of the T-Bill allocation with short-term Treasury notes that mature in one to three years. The difference between a T-Bill and a short-term Treasury note is that a Treasury note has maturity greater than 12 months (but less than 10 years), while T-Bills are 12 months and under. Holding Treasury notes of one to three years in maturity can provide slightly higher returns than holding 100 percent T-Bills, though this approach does involve a slightly higher interest rate risk than holding all T-Bills.

> If an investor is in a position where they have at least a year's worth of living expenses in T-Bills for their cash, they may want to consider parking the rest in a short-term Treasury fund.

However, if an investor is in a position where they have at least a year's worth of living expenses in T-Bills for their cash, they may want to consider parking the rest in a short-term Treasury fund.

Consider three similar Permanent Portfolios in Table 8.6. One is set up with 100 percent in T-Bills as cash. The other is set up with a split of 50 percent each in T-Bills and a short-term Treasury note fund. The last one has all of its cash invested in a short-term Treasury note fund.

The portfolios with the short-term Treasury notes had higher returns, but that doesn't tell the whole story. Table 8.7 lists the worst years for the Permanent Portfolio and how each variant performed.

Interestingly, the short-term Treasury notes not only did the best in total performance over this time, but in three of the four down years they also tended to have smaller losses.

Even during the years of high inflation in the 1970s, which was a bad time for cash, the portfolios with short-term Treasury notes did as well as the T-Bill versions. Table 8.8 shows how, during the high inflation period of

**TABLE 8.6**  Permanent Portfolio Returns—T-Bills versus 50/50 Split versus 100 Percent Short-Term Treasury Notes—1972–2011

| Cash Type | Annualized Return | Real Return | Growth of $10K in Real Dollars |
|---|---|---|---|
| **100% T-Bills** | 9.5% | 4.9% | $67,800 |
| **50% T-Bills/Short-Term Treasury Notes** | 9.7% | 5.1% | $73,200 |
| **100% Short-Term Treasury Notes** | 9.9% | 5.3% | $79,000 |

TABLE 8.7 Permanent Portfolio Losing Year Performance with Different Cash Types

| Losing Year | 100% T-Bills | 50% T-Bills/Short-Term Treasuries | 100% Short-Term Treasuries |
|---|---|---|---|
| 1981 | −4.9% | −4.4% | −3.9% |
| 1994 | −0.9% | −1.5% | −2.0% |
| 2001 | −0.7% | −0.2% | +0.3% |
| 2008 | −2.0% | −1.4% | −0.7% |

TABLE 8.8 Permanent Portfolio Returns—T-Bills versus 50/50 Split versus 100 Percent Short-Term Treasuries during the High Inflation Period 1972 to 1979

| Cash Type | Annualized Return | Real Return | Growth of $10K in Real Dollars |
|---|---|---|---|
| 100% T-Bills | 14.3% | 5.7% | $15,600 |
| 50% T-Bills/Short-Term Treasuries | 14.3% | 5.7% | $15,600 |
| 100% Short-Term Treasuries | 14.3% | 5.7% | $15,600 |

1972 to 1979, the short-term Treasury note portfolio modifications actually showed no impact during the rising interest rate environment.

## Short-Term Treasuries Are Optional Only

Using one- to three-year Treasury notes in lieu of shorter duration T-Bills in the Permanent Portfolio is noted here as an optional modification to the strategy that has worked well historically. However, all Permanent Portfolio investors should build a position in T-Bills within the portfolio's cash allocation before experimenting with longer maturity Treasury notes. One of the functions of the Permanent Portfolio's cash allocation is to provide a source of emergency funds should they be needed, and thus the safety and stability of T-Bills should not be completely abandoned, even if short-term Treasury notes may be able to provide slightly higher returns. If interest rates were to suddenly start rising, short-term Treasury notes could see moderate losses, while the value of T-Bills would barely move.

For investors seeking a short-term Treasury fund to combine with their T-Bills for the possibility of slightly higher returns, the following funds are suitable options:

- iShares Short-Term Treasury ETF (Ticker: SHY)
- Fidelity Spartan Short-Term Treasury Bond (Ticker: FSBIX)
- SPDR Short-Term Treasury ETF (Ticker: SST)[4]
- Vanguard Short-Term Treasury Fund (Ticker: VFISX)—Like their Treasury Money Market, this fund is the least recommended on this list due to how they can modify the allocation down to only 80 percent Treasuries.[5]

An alternative to a short-term Treasury note fund is to purchase Treasury notes directly, and a Treasury note ladder can be set up in the same manner as a T-Bill ladder, as discussed earlier.

Again, the above is an *optional* consideration. Holding 100 percent of your cash in very safe T-Bills is also an excellent decision if you do not care about taking on the risk.

## Cash Risks—The Case for Treasury Bills

### Default Risk

Just like Treasury bonds, T-Bills issued by the U.S. Treasury are free from default risk. In the event of any kind of budgetary crisis, the interest on Treasuries will be paid because not doing so would completely halt the operations of the U.S. government.

Further, the ability to control the currency in which its debt is denominated places the U.S. government in a much different position than corporations, banks, municipalities, or even state governments. Unlike the U.S. government, these entities cannot print their own money to pay their obligations, which creates a degree of default risk. The U.S. government printing money to pay off debt will cause bad inflation if done, but at least you will be paid something.

In addition to the low default risk of T-Bills, in a financial crisis investors tend to flock to the safety and liquidity of U.S. T-Bills. No matter how extreme financial and economic conditions become, there are normally plenty of buyers and sellers of T-Bills. To an investor, that means that they

---

[4] This fund is brand new as of Fall 2011. Generally it is best to avoid new funds and let them build up their net asset value to ensure they survive. However, State Street, the company that issues the SPDR series, has a great reputation for running ETFs and this will likely be a good choice to consider along with the others listed.

[5] Vanguard can hold as little as 80 percent in Treasuries in this fund and sometimes mixes in mortgages and other assets that offer no advantages to Permanent Portfolio investors.

can convert a T-Bill into cash at any time, which can be a very appealing feature when the markets for many other assets simply dry up.

## Credit Risk

Along with low default risk, there is very low credit risk with T-Bills. Contrary to what many market pundits say about U.S. Treasuries, every financial crisis seems to prove that in an emergency U.S. Treasuries are viewed as one of the safest place to be. This could always change in the future, but for now the alternatives to T-Bills are all riskier.

> Woe to the investor that held a large amount of Enron or WorldCom debt when news broke of their fraud. Once the credit downgrades began the debt issued by these companies fell in value very quickly. The higher yields weren't the great deal originally thought.

When it comes to credit risk, owning T-Bills is much different than owning short-term debt of a state, municipality, bank, or corporation. Any of these entities can receive a credit downgrade that will lead to a quick markdown in the value and, in some cases, an inability to sell it at all.

Woe to the investor that held a large amount of Enron or WorldCom debt when news broke of their fraud. Once the credit downgrades began the debt issued by these companies fell in value very quickly. The higher yields weren't the great deal originally thought.

## Currency and Political Risk

Just like with bonds, there is no need for investors to hold cash outside of the country where they reside. In the United States, investors spend and save in the form of dollars and have no need to hold a currency like the European Union's euro, the British pound, or the Japanese yen.

One reason to avoid holding foreign currencies in the Permanent Portfolio is that, just like foreign bond holdings, a political decision in another country can put foreign currency holders at great risk. In a crisis, it is not uncommon for countries to implement capital controls in an attempt to control the situation by limiting the flows of money into or out of the country. These policies will adversely affect holders of that currency.

Even the currencies perceived to be the safest in the world are not immune to political risk. In the summer of 2011, the Swiss National Bank surprised the markets by taking steps to control the value of the Swiss franc, which proceeded to lose almost 10 percent in comparison to the U.S. dollar in one week. Prior to this event, many investors had considered the Swiss franc a good way of diversifying out of U.S. dollars for safety. The *Guardian* newspaper reports the effects of this policy:

> *The Swiss National Bank [SNB] in effect devalued the franc, pledging to buy "unlimited quantities" of foreign currencies to force down its value . . .*
>
> *. . . The move stunned currency traders, and sent the Swiss franc tumbling against other currencies. Jeremy Cook, chief economist at currency brokers World First, said it was "intervention on a grand scale," and the start of a "new battle in the currency wars."*
>
> *. . . "That was the single largest foreign exchange move I have ever seen. . . . The Swiss franc has lost close on 9% in the past 15 minutes. This dwarfs moves seen post-Lehman brothers, 7/7 [London Subway Bombings], and other major geo-political events in the past decade," Cook said.*[6]

By holding T-Bills, U.S. investors do not have to worry about currency or political risk in their portfolio. Investors that live in other countries should likewise only own their own country's currency and avoid speculating in foreign currencies for the same reasons.

## Counterparty Risk

When it comes to investing cash it is important to understand counterparty risk. Counterparty risk is the notion that the party you give your money to won't be able to give it back when you ask for it. Counterparty risk is hard to manage, in part, because the periods when an investor most needs access to their funds are often the periods when the parties holding the funds are the least able to return them (usually because they need them for their own emergency). Emergencies cause cascading effects. A common counterparty risk is a bank run. This is when a large number of depositors want their money at the same time and the bank doesn't have enough funds on hand. The result could be the bank simply goes out of business and then, hopefully, government insurance takes over. That's counterparty risk.

In order to meet the requirement of absolute safety, Permanent Portfolio investors shouldn't have to evaluate the creditworthiness of the party to whom they are entrusting their wealth. In other words, a Permanent Portfolio investor wants *zero* counterparty risk for his cash, and the only way to have zero counterparty risk is to invest with the entity that has the power, if

---

[6] Graeme Wearden, "Swiss Bid to Peg 'Safe Haven' Franc to the Euro Stuns Currency Traders," *Guardian UK*, September 6, 2011, www.guardian.co.uk/business/2011/sep/06/switzerland-pegs-swiss-franc-euro.

necessary, to print or borrow in near unlimited quantities. In the United States that entity is the United States Treasury.

## Call Risk

Call risk is the risk that an issuer will take advantage of falling interest rates to recall previously issued debt and refinance it at a lower rate, just like with bonds. Treasury Bills, just like other Treasury securities, do not have call risk.

Call risk is often present in short-maturity municipal bonds and mortgages, just as it is with the long-maturity bonds of these types. And just like the longer maturity bonds, call risk puts investors in a compromised position. The issuer has the power to allow their low-interest loans to remain in the market when rates are favorable to them, but can call the loans back early and pay them off when rates fall to their advantage. Investors lose both ways.

## Tax Risk

Interest from T-Bills is subject to federal income taxes, but is not taxed at the state and local level. This tax treatment offers advantages to investors in states with high taxes.

Although T-Bills do enjoy the favorable tax treatment described above, there are other short-term debt instruments, such as municipal bonds, that are completely tax-free at all levels. As discussed in Chapter 7, Bonds, however, the risks to a Permanent Portfolio investor with such an approach are not justified. The appeal of tax-free bonds often doesn't lead to much of a gain in terms of total portfolio performance, plus you pick up additional default and call risk which will be present at the worst possible time. This topic is discussed more fully shortly.

In other risks, if the political risk associated with owning foreign currencies is not enough to make them unappealing, the prospect of having to deal with both your tax authorities and the tax authorities of a foreign country ought to be enough to keep you away. The high yield that a foreign country's equivalent may offer might be a lot less exciting if you have to pay a lot of their taxes before the funds can leave the country.

Finally, other kinds of higher-yielding cash from corporations or bank savings vehicles (like CDs) are taxed at local, state, and federal levels. Investors owning these assets in taxable accounts will likely find that a good part of the higher interest they are getting for taking on more risk is going to Uncle Sam at the end of the year as taxes.

Taxes *are* important, as has been discussed repeatedly, but investors also want to make sure they don't sacrifice safety for a slight chance of saving some money short-term in taxes. By owning T-Bills you not only get the ability to avoid some taxes at the local and state level, you also avoid other serious risks to your cash allocation.

# Cash to Avoid

While it may seem like finding a safe place to hold cash ought to be easy, the reality is that sometimes very risky things are happening behind the scenes hoping to achieve a higher return. These risks can remain hidden for years until a market emergency happens that causes them to become a reality.

Below are specific kinds of cash investments that should be avoided in a Permanent Portfolio to avoid hidden risks.

## Chasing Yield with Non-Treasury Funds

Chasing yield is a term used to describe efforts by investors to achieve slightly higher returns by moving cash from one investment to another based on small differences in the interest they pay. Chasing yield often leads investors to take on additional risk that easily outweighs the tiny amount of additional interest that may be earned.

Treasury money market funds currently yield around 0 percent. Many investors believe that these low returns justify chasing after a higher yield with their cash. Don't. Cash should be kept very safe. The rest of the portfolio will earn enough that you don't need to take risks with your cash allocation.

> Cash should be kept very safe. The rest of the portfolio will earn enough that you don't need to take risks with your cash allocation.

During the financial crisis of 2008, it was the high-yield assets in many money market funds that faced problems, not T-Bills. Some of these funds even "broke the buck," meaning that they fell below the $1 a share price that money market funds maintain.

In fact, the first money market fund ever created, The Reserve Fund, broke the buck and locked up investor's assets for years. The higher returns it was paying ended up being wiped out entirely when the risks associated with the higher yields finally showed up. One commenter on Craig's blog wrote about cash risks:

*Everyone should follow Craig's advice. I always took cash safety for granted until 2008 when I lost a substantial sum as part of The Reserve*

*Fund fiasco. I can vouch firsthand that the media really played down how serious and widespread the problem was. What I basically learned was that there is a lot more risk out there then people realize and when things go wrong you will get virtually no help from the agencies that are supposed to be looking out for you. For the rest of my life my cash will be in FDIC/NCUA accounts (never going over deposit limits per bank) and in US Treasuries.*[7]

As of 2011 investors have received most of their funds after years of litigation.[8] However, other fund company investors weren't so lucky. Other types of cash funds handed investors large losses in 2008. For example, the Schwab YieldPlus fund lost 42 percent in 2008 during the financial crisis. This fund had been marketed to investors as a conservative cash allocation that would provide "good returns with low principal risk" and "a smart alternative for your cash."[9] Figure 8.1 shows the tragic outcome of this supposedly safe cash fund.

The slight extra yield in these funds was met with a quick evaporation of principal and, in some cases, freezing of redemptions so you couldn't get your money out. The extra percent or so of promised returns a year was not worth it.

It could have been worse; you just weren't being made aware of the problem. From an article on the 2008 credit crisis:

*The level of panic in the money market industry in the fall of 2008 was much greater than previously disclosed, with many Boston firms tapping into billions of dollars the US central bank made available to avoid further financial chaos, data released this week show. Nationwide, nearly 200 money market funds tapped into the Federal Reserve Bank's program, with much of the $217 billion gushing out over five brisk days in late September that year. Bank of America Corps Boston-based Columbia money market funds tapped $13 billion, the Evergreen Funds used $9 billion, and Fidelity Investments sought $5.5 billion, among many others, according to the Fed data released this week.*[10]

---

[7] Crawlingroad.com blog poster discussing his losses during the 2008 market crash, http://crawlingroad.com/blog/2010/12/04/chasing-yield-with-your-cash/.

[8] The Primary Fund In Liquidation Website: http://www.primary-yieldplus-inliquidation.com/pdf/FundUpdate-July2011.pdf

[9] www.cbsnews.com/8301-505123_162-37640409/lessons-from-schwabs-yieldplus-debacle/?tag=mwuser.

[10] "'08 Data Show Hub Firms in Grip of Panic," *Boston Globe*, December 3, 2008, www.boston.com/business/articles/2010/12/03/08_data_show_boston_firms_in_grip_of_panic/?page=full.

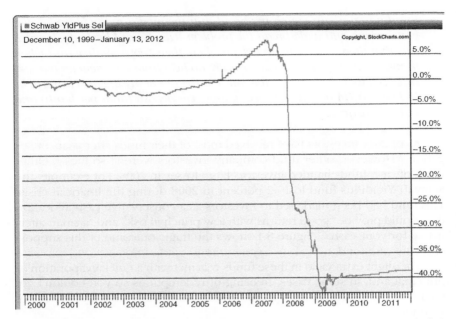

FIGURE 8.1  Schwab YieldPlus from 2000 to 2012. The 2008 financial crises imploded the assets.

Chart courtesy of stockcharts.com.

Can't an investor react on the onset of a crisis and move their money out someplace safer? No, they can't. Things happen so quickly in the markets you'll have no time to react. You'll just be one of many people running for the exits but they'll all be chained shut.

If you own a Treasury Money Market or T-Bill ladder you don't need to worry what risks the fund managers are taking with your money behind the scenes.

Even with the enticement of apparently higher yields, in many cases a riskier non-Treasury money market fund may not outperform the safer T-Bill fund at all. Take a look at a comparison of the Fidelity Select Money Market fund (a popular money market fund) versus the U.S. T-Bill average versus the Industry Money Market benchmark from Morningstar. The longest period they cover is from 1985 to 2012 for this fund. Table 8.9 shows that over this 27-year period the difference between the higher-risk Fidelity Select fund versus the safer and lower-risk T-Bill earned an investor a paltry $108. Or about an extra $4 a year! Seems not worth taking the extra risk for an extra $4 a year on every $10,000 invested in that fund.

TABLE 8.9  Fidelity Select versus T-Bills versus Industry Benchmark
Money Market Fund

| Asset | Growth of $10K from 1985 to 2012 |
|---|---|
| Fidelity Select | $29,539 |
| T-Bills | $29,431 |
| Industry Benchmark Money Market | $27,475 |

An investor taking more risk in an average money market fund only received lower performance out of the arrangement and *no extra profits*.

But it's even worse for the industry average money market funds. Because most funds charge higher expense ratios than a typical T-Bill fund, the returns are actually lower. The T-Bills beat out the standard money market fund by $1,956 over this time period for an advantage of $72 a year for the lower risk and very safe T-Bills. An investor taking more risk in an average money market fund only received lower performance out of the arrangement and *no extra profits*.

For cash, safety should be the first priority. As great as the safety of T-Bills are, it's even better that they still can be competitive to, or often beat, industry standard money markets over time.

## Bank Certificates of Deposit

The U.S. banking system is based on a model under which the bank takes the money you deposit into a Certificate of Deposit (CD) today and makes it available to your neighbor in the form of a loan. The difference between the interest that the bank pays you on your CD and the interest your neighbor pays on his loan is one of the ways the bank makes its profits. This business model means that at any given time the bank will only have a small amount of its depositors' money available for withdrawal (the rest is loaned out to the bank's customers and is tied up in their car, home, business, etc.). But what happens when too many people try to withdraw their money from the bank at the same time? This situation causes the familiar bank runs. The government has attempted to ease the fear of this sort of event through the Federal Deposit Insurance Corporation (FDIC), which was created in the 1930s and insures all deposits up to a certain amount.

Although FDIC deposit insurance has worked to date, the reality is that the FDIC actually has very few assets in relation to its liabilities. That means a wide-scale bank failure could quickly wipe out all of the FDIC's reserves. During the 2008 to 2009 banking crisis, the FDIC did actually run low on reserves and had to go to Congress and the Treasury to obtain a line of credit to deal with the failures—to the tune of around $500 billion. So this threat is not theoretical.[11] The FDIC stated in a February 2009 disclosure[12]:

> *Even though the FDIC has significant authority to borrow from the Treasury to cover losses, a fund balance and reserve ratio that are near zero or negative could create public confusion about the FDIC's ability to move quickly to resolve problem institutions and protect insured depositors. The FDIC views the Treasury line of credit as available to cover unforeseen losses, not as a source of financing projected losses.*
>
> *The FDIC projects that the reserve ratio will fall to close to zero or become negative in 2009 unless the FDIC receives more revenue than regular quarterly assessments will produce, given the rates adopted in the final rule on assessments.*

Although it is likely that the U.S. government would provide the FDIC with financial support in a very bad emergency, there is a chance that it could come with some strings attached. For instance, depositors could experience delays in retrieving their funds for some period of time, or there could be daily withdrawal limits until the crisis passed. Such measures would likely only occur as part of an extreme situation, but extreme situations happen more often than people like to think.

Because the full faith and credit of the United States back T-Bills, they do not need to be insured by FDIC or any other government agency. FDIC is not needed because if the Treasury can't pay you on the T-Bills then FDIC (and the rest of the U.S. government) is kaput anyway.

A nice feature of T-Bills, then, is that there is no insurance limit to worry about. Whether you hold $2,500 worth of T-Bills or $250,000,000, they will be paid in all but the direst of circumstances. And in a financial crisis, holders of T-Bills will be paid before emergency FDIC funding would even be discussed.

> In a financial crisis, holders of T-Bills will be paid before emergency FDIC funding would even be discussed.

---

[11] "FDIC Insurance Fund Near Empty," http://problembanklist.com/fdic-requests-500-billion-to-cover-unforeseen-losses-on-failed-banks/.
[12] www.fdic.gov/news/board/27Feb09_Interim_Rule.pdf.

Ultimately, whether to use a CD or other bank account for the cash in a Permanent Portfolio is a decision that each investor must make for himself. In practice, many people use a hybrid approach where the bulk of their cash is in a solid and safe T-Bills and a portion is in a bank to handle immediate living expenses and emergencies.

If you use a bank account for some or all of your Permanent Portfolio cash, stay informed about the bank's financial health, and consider using accounts at more than one bank. Finally, make sure to remain under FDIC limits at each institution in case the worst does happen. In the 2008 financial panic, many people were shocked at how quickly financial institutions that were thought to be safe could completely collapse. Unfortunately, banks do fail and sometimes very large banks fail in very large ways.

## Municipal Bonds

As discussed above, municipal bonds have credit and call risk. Although it is tempting to think that the tax savings offers a benefit, the reality is that trade-offs with municipal bonds can compromise the safety of the whole portfolio so the savings from the tax-free dividends are often just an illusion.

Since T-Bill interest is not taxed at the state and local level, the only tax advantage offered by municipal bonds would be with respect to federal income taxes.

Table 8.10 compares three popular money market funds. The first is Vanguard's Treasury Money Market Fund. The second is Vanguard's generic Tax-Free Municipal Money Market (a short-term municipal bond fund). The last is Vanguard's Prime Money Market, which holds a variety of debt from government, banks, and corporations.

The data in the table represent the most recent 15 years of fund data from Morningstar, and provides before-tax and after-tax returns. Notice that the Vanguard Treasury Money Market made 2.91 percent a year on a before-tax basis. This return is just slightly less than the Prime Money Market fund's 3.07 percent return over the same period. The tax-free Municipal Money

TABLE 8.10 Vanguard's Treasury Money Market After-Tax Returns versus Vanguard's Tax-Free Municipal Bond Fund versus Vanguard's Commercial Paper Money Market Fund Over the Past 15 Years

| Fund Name | Vanguard Admiral Treasury Money Market Fund | Vanguard Tax-Free Municipal Money Market | Vanguard Prime Money Market |
|---|---|---|---|
| Before taxes | 2.91% | 2.15% | 3.07% |
| After taxes | 1.80% | 1.51% | 1.90% |

Market fund's 2.15 percent before-tax return was significantly lower than the other two funds. This is the difference the markets arbitrage away versus taxable assets.

When you get to the after-tax returns, you find that the taxable Treasury Money Market Fund had a 1.80 percent after tax return versus the Prime Money Market's 1.90 percent. Surprisingly, the tax-free Municipal Money Market fund's returns on an after-tax basis are still lower than the two other funds' after-tax returns. In other words, the perceived additional benefits from the tax-free treatment of municipal bond dividends did not actually translate into higher after-tax returns in the comparison above. This could be for a variety of reasons that affect taxpayers differently.

Why then would an investor want to own a tax-free fund that has higher risks in terms of credit, default, and calls when they could just buy the safer Treasury Money Market for no performance difference? Why get lower after-tax returns *and* more risk?

Even in terms of the Prime Money Market fund, the Treasury fund was lagging by only a scant 0.10 percent after taxes. Another insignificant return advantage for the higher risk that this kind of fund brings to a portfolio versus owning T-Bills.

## Corporate Debt

There are many money market funds that own corporate debt or a mix of corporate and government debt. Often these funds hold debt from banks, industrial concerns like the auto industry, mortgages, and so on. The appeal of these funds is normally a slightly higher yield compared to safer T-Bills. Often, however, this advantage is quite small. As an example, Table 8.10 illustrated how the advantage between the Vanguard Treasury Money Market Fund and the Vanguard Prime Money Market Fund is slim.

Some investors may have objections to loaning their money to the U.S. government. If this is something that bothers you, then you can use commercial debt, but be aware of the risks.

If you elect to allocate cash to something other than T-Bills, use the cheapest money market fund you can buy that holds a wide diversification of debt from many sectors. The fund also should only own AAA-rated debt. These funds are options:

- Vanguard Prime Money Market (Ticker: VMMXX) is a good fund, but does hold some Treasuries from time to time.
- Fidelity Select Money Market (Ticker: FSLXX) is another option, but the current expense ratio significantly reduces the fund's return, and it also holds Treasuries.

Most other money market funds in this sector will be hit or miss and often hold Treasuries as well at manager discretion (as well as being too expensive). Overall, it's strongly encouraged to just use T-Bills for your cash.

## International Funds

The currency and political risk in international currency funds make them unsuitable for use in the Permanent Portfolio. As discussed in the political and currency risk sections already, even the strong Swiss franc has been subject to these problems. If this could happen to the supposedly safe and stable Swiss franc, it could happen anywhere. Then there are the extra tax costs dealing with another country.

For the Permanent Portfolio's cash allocation, investors should only own the currency of the country where they live.

## Shaky Banks

You may sometimes be tempted to buy CDs at shaky banks hoping to rake in some extra interest and get paid off if the FDIC comes to bail things out (chasing yield, but in a dumber way). But you may get burned eventually. Putting money in a shaky bank is like getting into a car with a drunk driver because you think the air bags are going to save you if it wrecks. The better strategy is not to go for the ride.

> Putting money in a shaky bank is like getting into a car with a drunk driver because you think the air bags are going to save you if it wrecks. The better strategy is not to go for the ride.

Don't fall into this trap. Keep your cash in a Treasury Money Market and you eliminate a whole list of potential problems. The rest of the Permanent Portfolio can drive the returns so there is no need to try chasing yield with your cash.

But what if the good bank where you are runs into financial trouble and becomes shaky itself? Simple. Close your account and move your money elsewhere. Don't wait for a disaster to happen and don't let anyone make you feel guilty that you are doing this.

You do not owe the bank any favors. You did *them* the favor by depositing your money in good faith. There is no need to keep your hard earned wealth in a bank that has proven it cannot handle your money responsibly. Protect yourself first and let banks that make bad decisions deal with the consequences of losing customers.

**TABLE 8.11  Cash Risk Matrix—T-Bills Score Best**

|  | *T-Bills* | Bank CD | Municipal | Mortgages | Corporate | International |
|---|---|---|---|---|---|---|
| Default Risk | No | Yes | Yes | Maybe | Yes | Yes |
| Credit Risk | No | Yes | Yes | Maybe | Yes | Yes |
| Call Risk | No | No | Yes | Yes | Yes | Yes |
| Political Risk | No | No | No | No | No | Yes |
| Currency Risk | No | No | No | No | No | Yes |
| Counterparty Risk | Maybe | Yes | Yes | Yes | Yes | Yes |
| International Taxes | No | No | No | No | No* | Yes |
| State/Local Taxes | No | Yes | No | Yes | Yes | Yes |
| Federal Taxes | Yes | Yes | No | Yes | Yes | Yes |

*Only if they are domestic corporations.

## Cash Risk Matrix

Table 8.11 is similar to the one shown in Chapter 7. This is because the same risks that affect other types of bonds also affect different types of cash (which are just a shorter maturity version of these investments). The only difference here is the addition of bank CDs, which although FDIC insured, do have a risk that during a very large bank crisis the FDIC could have problems paying back depositors. Note also that using a T-Bill fund does have counterparty risk if the managers do their job incorrectly. For most investors however, the ability to setup your own T-Bill ladder is not a convenient option so a fund is your best choice even with this small risk.

## Cash and Retirement Plans

Many investors find that they have significant savings in a tax-deferred arrangement, such as an IRA or 401(k) plan. For maximum tax savings investors should try to keep some of their cash in these kinds of plans. Investors should, however, also keep some of their cash outside of retirement plans so they can access it in an emergency without being subject to any taxes or penalties upon withdrawal.

Additionally, many of these plans often have poor choices in terms of the funds they offer. Most probably will not offer any kind of T-Bill fund, for instance. For investors who are choosing to keep some of their cash in these plans the following tips are offered:

- Ask your 401(k) plan administrator to include a T-Bill fund for holding cash. Be sure that any such fund actually is a 100 percent U.S. T-Bill fund (fund names can be deceptive).

■ Ask your 401(k) plan administrator if the plan offers a brokerage window. A brokerage window may allow you to either buy T-Bills directly from the secondary market or buy a suitable T-Bill fund outside of the plan, such as those listed in this chapter.

■ Use the funds that you have to the best of your ability.

If you are forced into the last option, then try to look for the following in your funds that you do have:

■ Lowest expense ratio possible.

■ Uses U.S. T-Bills only, or at least mostly U.S. T-Bills.

■ If it doesn't use T-Bills, then it should be an index fund that owns a large number of commercial securities to diversify its risks broadly. The securities it holds should be of the highest credit rating possible (AAA rated).

■ Avoid all actively managed funds. You want the fund to be 100 percent in short maturity (one year or less) securities to keep the cash as non-volatile as possible. An active fund manager, just like elsewhere, adds no value whatsoever.

## Recap

The Permanent Portfolio holds cash to stabilize the overall returns of the portfolio, make sure emergency funds are always available, and to provide dry powder when the portfolio is rebalanced. Investors should seek as much safety as possible with their cash holdings so it does not become volatile and exposed to risk of loss.

Follow these guidelines for your cash:

■ Debt issued by the United States Treasury should be the first choice for the Permanent Portfolio's cash holdings.

■ You can build your own T-Bill ladder with the help of Treasury Direct or the bond desk at your brokerage if you desire. Alternately, consider using the funds iShares Short Treasury ETF (Ticker: SHV), Fidelity Treasury Money Market (Ticker: FDLXX), SPDR Treasury Bill ETF (Ticker: BIL), Gabelli U.S. Treasury Money Market (Ticker: GABXX), or Vanguard Treasury Money Market [least recommended] (Ticker: VUSXX) for your cash allocation.

■ United States savings bonds can also be used effectively as a part of the Permanent Portfolio's cash allocation.

■ Credit risk, default risk, call risk, currency risk, and political risk should be avoided with the cash in your Permanent Portfolio.

- If you are forced to use a non-Treasury fund for your cash, be sure it is not actively managed and does not modify its strategy trying to chase after performance. Ensure it invests only in the highest-rated securities.
- Bank CDs and money market accounts are not ideal for Permanent Portfolio cash because of the counterparty risk involved in such accounts and exposure to FDIC insurance. However if you use bank CDs for your cash, consider splitting it among several banks.
- If the bank you are using is reporting financial trouble, withdraw your money and move it elsewhere.
- If you object to holding U.S. T-Bills, then use a very high quality, diversified corporate money market fund. However you should recognize the vulnerabilities that using this approach creates.
- Don't chase yield with your cash. Keep it invested in the safest way possible.

# CHAPTER 9

# Gold

## *Gold for Portfolio Insurance*

G old provides an investor with protection during a number of different market environments, including high inflation, political uncertainty, currency crisis, and periods of negative real interest rates. To provide suitable protection, the Permanent Portfolio holds 25 percent of its assets in gold. Although gold offers investors what many think of as an asset of last resort, gold is also a useful asset during times of non-catastrophe as well.

The Permanent Portfolio holds gold because there are periods in which no other asset provides the protection that gold provides. Although gold can be a volatile asset in isolation, when combined in proper proportion with stocks, bonds, and cash, the volatility of gold actually helps to *reduce* the volatility of the overall portfolio. This is an important point to keep in mind concerning all of the Permanent Portfolio's assets (and has been mentioned repeatedly), but especially with respect to gold. Many investors in recent years have probably bought gold without a well-defined strategy for how to make gold ownership both safe and profitable. The Permanent Portfolio provides a framework to benefit from gold's volatility, but also protect an investor against the eventual slumps in this asset.

> Gold is a tool, not a religion.

There are two kinds of investors in this world: those who love gold and those who hate it. There often is not a middle ground. The Permanent Portfolio allocation is agnostic about the issue. Yes, it holds gold. But it also holds long-term bonds, which are the anti-gold.

Gold is a tool, not a religion. Gold does have properties separate from stocks and bonds that can hurt it in some environments, but those same properties prove to be *very powerful* protection when those other assets are in trouble. As a tool, gold can be thought of as a form of portfolio fire insurance. People don't buy fire insurance because they hope their homes will burn down; rather, they buy fire insurance because they know that homes burn down all the time and it is a risk that is worth protecting themselves against.

## Benefits of Gold

Gold does best under high-inflation scenarios. Gold is a form of money, and is probably the oldest form of money in the world that has been in constant use. Since gold is viewed as a form of money, it competes with other paper money. When inflation threatens a currency (especially the U.S. dollar), the value of gold will rise.

> Gold to a politician is like holy water to a vampire.

Gold doesn't change over time and a government can't print more gold when it starts to run low on funds. Gold does not rack up massive debts and unfunded government liabilities. Gold does not care about political speeches or promises about the strength of any particular currency. Gold to a politician is like holy water to a vampire. In terms of purchasing power protection, gold has a long track record of preserving wealth that is unmatched.

The final, and very unique, benefit of gold is that it is a compact and universally recognized form of wealth. Gold can be owned directly by an investor and is not a paper promise as other investments are.

In the 1970s and 2000s gold helped power the Permanent Portfolio to consistent inflation-adjusted returns. When you compare how the four Permanent Portfolio assets performed, it is clear that a portfolio that lacked gold would have struggled to provide positive real returns. Tables 9.1 and 9.2 show the performance of stocks, bonds, cash, and gold over the decades of the 1970s and 2000s.

TABLE 9.1  Asset Class Returns—Gold and Bad Inflation from 1972 to 1979

| Asset | Annualized Return | Real Return | Growth of $10K in Real Dollars |
|---|---|---|---|
| **Stocks** | 5.1% | −2.8% | $8,000 |
| **Bonds** | 3.8% | −4.0% | $7,200 |
| **Cash** | 6.5% | −1.5% | $8,900 |
| **Gold** | 34.1% | 24.1% | $56,000 |

Market data used for equal comparison begins in 1972 after the gold standard ends.

TABLE 9.2  Asset Class Returns—Gold in 2000 to 2009

| Asset | Annualized Return | Real Return | Growth of $10K in Real Dollars |
|-------|-------------------|-------------|--------------------------------|
| **Stocks** | −1.0% | −3.4% | $7,100 |
| **Bonds** | 7.7% | 5.0% | $16,400 |
| **Cash** | 2.8% | 0.2% | $10,200 |
| **Gold** | 14.9% | 12.1% | $31,200 |

During times of high inflation, or expectations of future inflation, gold will experience large price increases. In the 1970s, as both actual inflation and future inflationary expectations gripped the economy, gold saw big price increases some years. There was even a single-year gain in 1979 of over 118 percent as investors fled the U.S. dollar into gold (inflation was raging over 13 percent that year). These explosive price movements are important during a crisis.

During the 2000s the U.S. dollar has been saddled with two wars plus a massive expansion in domestic spending programs (all of which are inflationary). Combined with two bubbles and crashes (tech and real estate), plus unprecedented market intervention by the Federal Reserve central bank, gold was seen as an asset worth owning with all the uncertainty in the markets and it performed very well.

Gold also provides an investor with continuous protection against political, financial, and economic crises even when things look calm. This is important because such events can happen at any time with little or no warning.

> Prudent savers need to invest for the world they have, not the world they want. The world we have is full of uncertainty and that means holding some gold in a portfolio at all times is a good idea.

Prudent savers need to invest for the world they have, not the world they want. The world we have is full of uncertainty and that means holding some gold in a portfolio at all times is a good idea.

## Risks of Gold

Investors should be aware of the risks associated with the assets they own, and that includes the risks of owning gold. Gold has had some long periods of poor performance just like other assets and these should be acknowledged.

When framed in terms of various economic environments, gold does poorly during periods of prosperity, deflation, and recession.

Prosperity will push the price of gold down. When the markets are doing well and inflation is low and stable gold will not be seen as a necessary form of wealth versus the dollar. Since gold does not produce interest or dividends, many investors may shun it in search of higher anticipated returns in the stock and bond markets and this will affect the price.

In recent history, gold has fallen in value by as much as −31 percent in a single year (1981). Gold has also had other losing years where it lost −20 percent or more in value. There have also been strings of years where gold experienced annual single digit losses for an extended period, such as in the 1990s as the stock bubble grew. There was even a 20+ year stretch from 1980 to 2000 where gold was basically flat or declining in value the entire time.

Table 9.3 shows the performance of the four Permanent Portfolio assets during the period of 1980 to 1999 (again, the biggest stock bull market in U.S. history). During this period, gold posted losses of −6.1 percent in real returns if you were unfortunate enough to buy it at the highest price and did nothing else for 20 years (which is unlikely).

The next risk to gold is deflation. Deflation is the opposite of inflation. Whereas during a period of inflation there is too much money in circulation and it falls in value, during periods of deflation there is too little money in circulation and dollars tend to *rise* in value.

Since a dollar that is rising in value can purchase more of everything, it makes sense that a stronger dollar may also purchase more gold. Under deflation it simply takes fewer dollars to buy the same amount of gold so the price falls.

There is an important caveat to this observation about deflation and gold, however, and it is this: in modern times central bankers have shown a willingness to take extraordinary steps to prevent true deflation from developing. The primary tools that central bankers have in their efforts to prevent deflation are increasing the money supply and lowering interest rates. Both of these polices are inflationary if conditions are right.

TABLE 9.3  Gold Can Have Long Periods of Bad Returns: 1980 to 1999

| Asset | Annualized Return | Real Return | Growth of $10K in Real Dollars* |
|---|---|---|---|
| **Stocks** | 17.9% | 13.3% | $122,400 |
| **Bonds** | 10.7% | 6.4% | $34,700 |
| **Cash** | 6.9% | 2.8% | $17,300 |
| **Gold** | −2.3% | −6.1% | $2,800 |

*Rounded to nearest hundred in this and other tables.

Under this view of deflation, it can actually be good for gold because investors may take it as a signal that the central bank is going to take all necessary steps to prevent deflation from actually happening (which may include policies that create the risk of serious future inflation). If this perception exists in the market, gold prices will remain high in anticipation of the coming inflation.

Additionally, even if inflation is low the actions of the central bank can create negative real interest rates in the economy, which mimics higher inflation. For instance, in 2011 U.S. inflation was 2.96 percent, but bank savings rates were hovering around 0.50 percent or less, meaning that after inflation a cash investor's real rate of return was −2.46 percent, or a net *loss*. Gold then can respond as if it were higher levels of inflation because negative real interest rate conditions are similar to a high inflation environment. With that said, if the economy does continue to tip over to true deflation, it will be bad for gold.

The final risk to gold is recession. This is the tight money kind of recession previously discussed. It refers to an economic contraction caused by the central bank raising interest rates when the economy is already very weak. A tight money recession is created by the central bank during a period of bad inflation in an attempt to stop it.

An example of a tight money recession was the period from 1981 to 1982 when the Federal Reserve raised interest rates repeatedly to stop the bad inflation from the 1970s. While the Fed's policy was successful in ending a decade of high inflation in the United States, it also triggered a large decline in the value of gold as inflation came back down.

## Volatility

Just like stocks and bonds, gold is volatile. But it is volatile for different reasons than stocks and bonds.

During the boom years for gold it can go up dramatically in price and offset the losses in your stocks and bonds. During the bad years for gold the stocks and bonds can offset the losses. The volatility assists the portfolio in providing full protection.

As discussed, in the 1970s and early 1980s inflation was bad. The prime rate was around 21 percent by 1981. The dollar was falling fast and there was a panic to move into gold. Gold went from under $100 an ounce in the early 1970s (after breaking the gold standard) to over $800 an ounce by 1981 (that's more than $2,200 an ounce in 2012 dollars).

During this boom time a Permanent Portfolio investor would have been selling down the gold to the 25 percent allocation bands and buying stocks and bonds. These were assets that less people wanted to own because inflation was seen as inevitable (they would soon be proven wrong). Yet, by 1982 gold had fallen in price and the next 17 years were going to be the biggest stock bull market in U.S. history (and *horrible* for gold!).

By selling down your gold when everyone wanted it (in the late 1970s and early 1980s), and buying stocks and bonds when fewer wanted them (in the late 1970s and early 1980s), you intelligently used your money and made good profits. But it was gold's volatility in the 1970s that made this smart move possible. Those big price moves upward allowed an opportunity to take profits and re-direct them to lower-priced assets.

Now the mid- to late 1990s roll around. Stocks are booming. One hot new .com IPO after another was sweeping the nation. The book *Dow 36,000* was being published for the "New Economy." In this New Economy, profits didn't matter as much as how many people saw your sock puppet commercial during the Super Bowl.

Well, during this time you would have been selling down your booming (and volatile) stocks to 25 percent and using that money to buy gold. Gold was an asset that few in his or her right mind wanted at the time. The price sunk to around $250 an ounce and just had almost 20 years of poor returns. *Only a sucker would buy gold, right?*

Then the 2000 to 2002 market crash happened and those big stock gains vanished. The NASDAQ was off −80 percent from its high and the S&P was down around −40 percent. The stock market recovered somewhat, then the big crash in 2008 came wiping out almost all gains over the previous decade. By March 2009 the Dow Index, instead of being 36,000, was at 6,600 and facing one of the biggest crisis situations since the Great Depression.

Yet, gold went from $250 an ounce to $1,600 an ounce over this time. The intelligent move to sell down your stocks and buy gold in the stock boom of the 1990s was built into the portfolio for you. This strategy meant you managed to miss all those terrible stock market losses and turn in a nice profit over the next 10 years when stocks were languishing.

Gold cannot be ignored in its contributions to this performance and it cannot be ignored in a portfolio just because it is perceived as volatile. Any asset can be volatile if given the right economic conditions. It's *how* the asset is combined to offset the volatility that matters most.

## Causes of Inflation

The causes of inflation across an economy are very simple: one way or another, the government allows too much money to get into circulation and spent. Each new dollar that comes into circulation in excess of what the economy requires means each dollar is worth less.

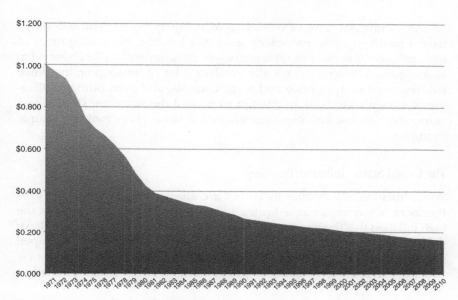

**FIGURE 9.1** Value of U.S. dollar: 1971 to 2010.
**Values based on Consumer Price Index.**

Figure 9.1 shows the reduction in value of the U.S. dollar due to inflation since 1971. The starting date of 1971 has been selected because it was in 1971 that the U.S. broke the last of the dollar's connection to the gold standard and inflation really took off.

The important point to understand about inflation as that it is normally a deliberate policy decision by central banks and politicians. In other words, inflation is not some inevitable phenomenon. Rather, inflation is a *choice* made by policymakers who believe that a steady rate of inflation is required. Inflation allows a government to spend more freshly printed money than it takes in, thereby allowing politicians to avoid the sticky situation of raising taxes to pay for spending. Instead they just print off what they need and let the holders of existing dollars foot the bill in terms of lost purchasing power.

## Gold Protects During Extreme Events

Aside from inflation, gold is also a hedge against uncertainty and extreme events. Any time there is a destabilizing world event the price of gold may move higher as investors buy it to protect against possible declines in the value of other assets, such as dollars.

As a universal form of money, gold is highly liquid. You will never have a problem anywhere selling gold. Not just this, but during times of high inflation it is the natural tendency of governments to lie about what is going on. The scenario usually involves a lot of finger pointing, knee jerk reactions such as price and wage controls, and even outright pillaging of citizen's assets in an attempt to control the situation. Gold is less vulnerable to these activities than stocks and bonds. Let's look at a couple examples.

## The United States' Inflation Two-Step

When inflation and politics meet, lies are always the result. In the 1970s President Nixon implemented price and wage controls to try to rein in the high inflation that the government had caused (and which he may also have deliberately used to help his election campaign according to his own taped conversations).[1] These methods failed miserably and made things worse with product shortages and higher prices when the controls finally ended.

> When inflation and politics meet, lies are always the result.

President Ford followed up with the infamous Whip Inflation Now (WIN) campaign. WIN encouraged people to fill out an enlistment form where they would commit to help beat inflation (and wear a handy button on their shirt). Exactly how a citizen who isn't printing the money can stop inflation is a bit of a mystery, but in times of crisis a little political misdirection can go a long way. President Ford gave a speech on October 8, 1974, in which he proclaimed:

> *There will be no big Federal bureaucracy set up for this [Inflation Control] crash program. Through the courtesy of such volunteers from the communication and media fields, a very simple enlistment form will appear in many of tomorrow's newspapers along with the symbol of this new mobilization, which I am wearing on my lapel. It bears the single word WIN. I think that tells it all. I will call upon every American to join in this massive mobilization and stick with it until we do win as a nation and as a people.*

---

[1] Burton A. Abrams, "How Richard Nixon Pressured Arthur Burns: Evidence from the Nixon Tapes," *Journal of Economic Perspectives* 20, no.4 (Fall 2006): 177–188, http://cba.unomaha.edu/faculty/mwohar/web/links/Donestic_Money_papers/Abrams_jep-v20n42006.pdf.

Alan Greenspan, former Chairman of the Federal Reserve, was an economic advisor in 1974 to the government and stated about the WIN program: "This is unbelievable stupidity," in his book *The Age of Turbulence.*

Later in the decade President Carter tried some other attempts to rein in inflation that also failed. There were speeches, commissions, and economists giving various opinions. But few advocated the obvious solution, which was simply to stop printing and spending money. Inflation started to rage into the double digits. It wasn't until a new Fed Chief named Paul Volcker came in that things were brought under control by deliberate contraction of the money supply (the tight money recession he created in the early 1980s).

What is the lesson from all of this? It's that when high inflation came to the United States the people in charge allowed holders of dollars to roast for nearly a decade before serious action was taken to stop it. No politician wants to take responsibility for inflation. When bad inflation happens, don't be surprised if this kind of history repeats.

## Iceland's Krona Collapse

Currency crises can happen suddenly. In 2008 for instance, Iceland's currency collapsed, affecting the entire population of that country very dramatically. This is a first-world country where this happened, not a banana republic. The aftermath of the problem was very dramatic and disrupted Iceland's economy to the point where even McDonald's decided to get out:

> *Iceland's McDonald's Corp. restaurants will be closed at the end of the month after the collapse of the [Icelandic] Krona eroded profits at the fast-food chain, McDonald's franchise holder Lystehf said. . . . The island's currency collapsed last year following the failure of Iceland's biggest banks. Offshore, the Krona slumped as much as 80 percent against the euro, while capital restrictions this year have failed to prevent an 8.1 percent decline, making the Krona the second-worst performer of the 26 emerging-market currencies tracked by Bloomberg.*[2]

In Iceland, an analysis of the event showed that a Permanent Portfolio being run in that country would have offered significant protection over a conventional stock and bond only portfolio. Gold in Icelandic krona was up

---

[2] Omar R. Valdimarsson, "McDonald's Closes in Iceland After Krona Collapse," *Bloomberg*, October 26, 2009, www.bloomberg.com/apps/news?pid=newsarchive &sid=amu4.WTVaqjI.

+259 percent in value while their stock market sank −88 percent in value.[3] But even more impressive is that as the Icelandic stock market bubble grew, a Permanent Portfolio investor there would have been moving profits out of stocks and into assets like gold *before* the bust. When the bust happened, they were automatically in a position to be protected without having to do any market timing. A good portion of their life savings would have been spared during the disaster.

### Gold Is Not Just for Zombie Attacks

It is common to hear criticisms of gold as some kind of apocalypse asset. Yet, gold has performed well in a diversified portfolio in the past and the world did not end, the dollar did not go into hyperinflation, and zombies did not roam the streets. As shown, in the 1970s gold was able to provide real returns to a stock and bond portfolio that did poorly due to inflation over the entire decade.

> Gold was able to provide diversification to a stock and bond portfolio while the AK-47s and canned beans remained safely buried.

During the 2000s, gold again was the only investment turning in any decent gains. Gold was able to provide diversification to a stock and bond portfolio while the AK-47s and canned beans remained safely buried.

## No Interest, No Dividends, No Problem

One common complaint about gold is that it generates no interest or dividends like stocks and bonds. Fair enough. While not having the same attributes of interest and dividends as stocks and bonds have, gold also doesn't have the same *risks* of stocks and bonds either.

In basic terms, stocks and bonds have an internal rate of return with interest and dividends that allows them to grow on their own that gold does not (e.g., one gold coin will not turn into two no matter how long it sits in a safe deposit box). But it is also true that sometimes investments that have interest and dividends actually are losing to inflation, as shown already, when gold will not.

So even though gold doesn't generate interest or dividends, it can produce *capital appreciation* (price goes up), and those profits can be harvested and used in a balanced and diversified portfolio to produce real returns.

---

[3] "Permanent Portfolio Rescues Icelanders from Total Collapse," http://europeanper manentportfolio.blogspot.com/2009/08/permanent-portfolio-in-iceland.html.

Nobody cares how your portfolio grew in value. It can be interest, dividends, or capital appreciation of gold. The growth is still counted the same no matter what. Don't get wrapped up over chasing interest and dividends alone. Consider the capital appreciation that you get with gold as another weapon in your portfolio protection arsenal.

## Why Do Central Banks Hold So Much Gold?

Another common criticism about gold is that it is just some worthless yellow metal and has no real value. Human history however provides many examples that show owning some gold in a portfolio is an *excellent* idea. This, despite what a government, economist, or investment guru may want to say on the subject.

For instance, major central bank and government vaults are loaded with *tons* of the stuff. You'd think if gold was so worthless and paper currencies were so robust these large banks would sell every last ounce of gold and be done with it, right? Yet, they haven't and probably won't. In fact, growing central banks like China's have been big buyers over the years to *diversify* their holdings.[4] What do these central banks and governments know that you don't?

A safe investment portfolio is diversified across many assets because the future is not predictable. One of those assets that should always be owned for safety is gold. Again, it's important to not make it a religious issue either for gold *or* against. Realize gold's strengths and weaknesses and use it in a portfolio accordingly.

## Owning Gold

The first choice for the Permanent Portfolio's gold allocation should be *physical gold bullion* stored in a safe location and insured against loss. There is no substitute for gold bullion to which you have ready access.

> The first choice for the Permanent Portfolio's gold allocation should be *physical gold bullion* stored in a safe location and insured against loss.

---

[4] Jack Farchy, "China Central Bank in Gold-Buying Push," *Financial Times*, February 16, 2012.

"Gold? That's just a worthless yellow metal. I
can't think of anyone that would want to own it."

Gold can be an asset of last resort. Which means that gold is an asset that you need to be able to access when there may be significant disruptions occurring within the economic or political system. In order to have ready access to the gold in your Permanent Portfolio, you should aim to have as few pieces of paper and people between you and your gold possible.

Realistically, for most investors, the gold allocation will be split among different forms of gold storage options. The most popular ways of owning gold are described below.

# Buying Gold

There are a three basic ways to buy gold for domestic allocations:

1. From a gold dealer.
2. From a bank.
3. From a gold fund.

### Buying Gold from a Dealer

Buying gold from a local coin shop is just a matter of walking in and purchasing bullion from the stock the store has on hand. Using cash for these transactions is often a good idea for additional privacy.

There are gold dealers on the Internet who have been in business for many years and have a good reputation as well. Such dealers will often sell gold for a lower commission than a retail location and ship it directly to your door via insured registered mail. The following dealers have reasonable prices and are reliable and professional:

- AJPM Precious Metals—www.ajpm.com
- American Precious Metal Exchange—www.apmex.com
- Colorado Gold—www.coloradogold.com
- California Numismatic Investments—www.golddealer.com
- Kitco Metals, Inc.—www.kitco.com

When it comes to selecting an Internet-based gold dealer, you obviously must do your own due diligence. In general, the companies that advertise heavily (especially on radio and TV) tend not to have good prices or service. Be careful dealing with such companies, as they often pay for their extensive advertising through higher premiums on their coins.

Before you buy a coin, look up the spot gold price per ounce at a site like www.goldprice.org or by simply searching for "Gold Spot Price" on the Internet.

Take the gold price per ounce and add about 5 percent to it for a markup commission on the coin (this is how dealers pay themselves). That would be a fair price. For example, if gold's spot price is $1,000 an ounce then a fair price on a gold bullion one ounce coin is about $1,050 or thereabouts. Like any other item, when demand for gold is high, premiums may be higher and when demand is low better deals may be available. It makes sense to shop around.

The best gold to hold directly are one-Troy-ounce bullion coins. Bullion coins are either 100 percent gold, or a gold/copper alloy that contain the same amount of gold mixed with copper to make it more durable (pure gold is soft and easily scratched).

In the United States the most common bullion coins are American Eagles, Canadian Maple Leafs, and South African Krugerrands. These coins are minted by their respective governments and in some cases are actually legal tender (although the stamped value on such coins is much less than the actual gold content value). Other coin options include Austrian Philharmonics, Chinese Pandas, Australian Kangaroos, and British Sovereigns. These coins are less popular in the United States.

However, if you live in other countries, there could be tax advantages to buying the issued coins from your government or coins of a specific purity. In Canada, for instance, an investor should purchase Canadian Maples because no tax is charged on them, whereas this may not apply to other types of bullion coins (the coins need to exceed 99.5 percent gold purity to qualify, which the Maple Leafs do).

For a U.S. investor, it is recommended that you buy American Eagles, Krugerrands, or Canadian Maple Leafs. While Krugerrands and Maple Leafs often sell for a lower markup than American Eagles, the American Eagle coin will normally provide a higher premium when you go to sell it (all three coins have the same one-ounce gold content). Any coin dealer will buy these coins so there is no need to worry that you'll get stuck with a coin you can't sell.

> If possible, gold bullion coins should only be purchased in the one-ounce size. Gold coins that are less than one ounce tend to have a high premium relative to their gold content so you get less gold for your money.

If possible, gold bullion coins should only be purchased in the one-ounce size. Gold coins that are less than one ounce tend to have a high premium relative to their gold content so you get less gold for your money.

**DON'T BUY GOLD COINS ON E-BAY**   Don't buy gold coins on E-Bay or other similar auction sites. Although there are some legitimate sellers on these sites, there is a higher risk of fraud associated with this option.

**BE CAREFUL ABOUT CRAIGSLIST**   Sometimes you may come across sellers on places like Craigslist. Unfortunately there have been instances of robberies selling high-value goods this way (jewelry, phones, computers, etc.). Just remember that someone posting gold bullion for sale and offering to meet you knows you'll have a pocket full of cash on hand and this can invite problems. Also, if you are selling on Craigslist, you likewise are a target (especially if you have them come to your home). Using a local coin dealer is a safer option.

**DON'T STORE GOLD AT A DEALER**   Some gold dealers will offer to store gold for you. Never do this. Over the years, there have been cases of gold dealers going out of business and their customer's gold along with them (which they misappropriated). If you buy gold bullion you should *always* take physical delivery of it from the dealer. If you want a bank to store your gold there are options available (discussed below and in Chapter 15, on Geographic Diversification) or do it yourself.

**STORING GOLD IN A BANK SAFE DEPOSIT BOX**   Bank safe deposit boxes are a tried and true method of storing valuables. If you use a safe deposit box to store your gold, bear in mind that the bank will not be aware of what you have in your box and you will need to carry your own insurance on the contents. Keeping the gold outside of your home also protects you against burglary and other common risks.

**STORING GOLD IN HIDDEN LOCATIONS**  In the 1930s President Roosevelt signed an executive order confiscating the gold of American citizens (Executive Order 6102), forcing them to take paper money in exchange. Based upon this historical experience, some people may not trust bank safe deposit boxes and will look for another place to securely store their gold.

If you decide to keep gold outside of a bank just be aware of the risks of fire, burglary, theft (including from friends, relatives, housekeepers, caregivers, etc.). Be careful if you are especially good at hiding things—in the event of your untimely passing or incapacitation your next of kin may have a hard time finding what you have hidden.

> While there are risks associated with storing gold at a bank, being burglarized or having someone you know steal from you is a more likely occurrence than a gold seizure.

The risks of storing gold outside of a bank vault are mentioned as a counterpoint to the arguments you may hear against storing gold in a safe deposit box. While there are risks associated with storing gold at a bank, being burglarized or having someone you know steal from you is a more likely occurrence than a gold seizure. Weigh your options carefully.

## Buying and Storing Gold at a Bank

### Inside the United States

It is possible to buy and store gold at a bank inside the borders of the United States. The biggest drawback for this option for U.S. citizens is that it does not have geographic diversification so it is not ideal for the Permanent Portfolio. Yet some investors (especially those overseas or those that do not want a foreign account) may find the option useful.

Most banks in the United States no longer offer gold custody accounts. A custody account means the assets are not on the bank's balance sheet, but they are holding your property for you. However, Everbank (www .everbank.com) offers a metals account (Metals Select) that can store gold (or silver which is not recommended) in a custody account.

There are two versions of this account:

1. Allocated
2. Unallocated

The allocated account holds gold in your name of a specific lot of coins or bars. The unallocated account stores an amount of gold for many customers in which you have a claim (i.e., you have ownership in the gold, but no specific coins or bars).

The advantage of the allocated account is the gold is held separately in your name directly. If you buy 10 coins, then those 10 coins are put aside for you specifically. The disadvantage of this account is it has a higher annual fee.

The advantage of the unallocated account is that it is cheaper to own. The disadvantage of the unallocated account is that you are not really an owner of a specific lot of gold but rather one of many people with a claim on a pool of gold assets.

> Allocated gold storage should be the first choice for the gold within your Permanent Portfolio.

Allocated gold storage should be the first choice for the gold within your Permanent Portfolio even though the fees are slightly higher than for unallocated storage. Everbank also allows for physical delivery of your gold in the allocated versions of their account providing additional assurance. The more direct you can keep control of the gold the better, and allocated storage does that.

Everbank offers these accounts to foreign customers as well for those looking to hold gold inside the United States from other countries. The Everbank option will be covered in detail in Chapter 15.

### Outside the United States

For international investors with access to a bank that deals directly in gold metal accounts (such banks are common in some parts of Europe for instance), an allocated gold storage account is a good approach to gold ownership.

The topic of bank gold storage has grown very complex or unavailable to many people (either outright or with too high minimums). These options will be more fully covered in Chapter 15 as well.

## Gold Funds

In recent years there has been a huge increase in the assets held in Exchange Traded Funds (ETFs) and so-called "closed-end funds" that own gold. The idea is simple: rather than owning gold yourself and storing it, a fund company buys the gold and you buy a share of the gold fund.

There are risks associated with this approach to gold ownership compared to more direct ownership as already outlined. For one, you have a lot of people and paper between you and the asset and this can be a big problem in an emergency. Additionally, just like other fund types, the managers could be doing things behind the scenes that jeopardize the safety of the asset. There are other unknowns as well.

What these funds do provide, however, is the convenience of being able to trade your gold position as easily as if it were shares of a stock. As with many things in life, with convenience comes less safety.

It's not recommended that you use a gold fund for 100 percent of your gold holdings if you don't have to. Investors who want to use a gold ETF are usually better off using a hybrid approach, with some physical gold in their possession and some held in a gold fund for easy rebalancing of the whole portfolio.

The following exchange-traded funds and closed-end funds are popular options for this type of gold ownership.

1. iShares Gold ETF (Ticker: IAU)
2. StreetTracks Gold ETF (Ticker: GLD)
3. Physical Swiss Gold ETF (Ticker: SGOL)
4. Sprott Physical Gold Trust (Ticker: PHYS)
5. Central Fund of Canada (Ticker: CEF)
6. Central Gold Trust of Canada (Ticker: GTU)
7. Canton Bank of Zürich ETF (Ticker: ZGLD)

These funds all have low expense ratios and should work similarly. However, there are some important differences among the various gold funds.

## iShares and StreetTracks Gold ETFs

The biggest funds in the gold ETF market are the products from iShares (Ticker: IAU) and StreetTracks (Ticker: GLD). These ETFs each hold billions of dollars' worth of gold. They provide the benefit of being highly liquid and well established. The downside to these funds is that these ETFs are probably the most removed an investor can be from actual gold ownership. There are many layers of paper between you and the actual asset.

## Swiss Physical Gold ETF

The Swiss Gold ETF (Ticker: SGOL) is new as of 2009 and has a unique selling point in that it stores its gold in Switzerland. It's unclear whether this feature makes the fund any safer than another gold fund. But for an investor who is seeking geographic diversification against potential risks to gold stored within the United States (such as natural disasters that affect commodity warehouses in the country), this fund may be appealing.

---

## Gold ETF Marketing versus Reality

Some gold ETFs claim additional protection by having their gold in places like Canada or Switzerland. Yet as an investor, the broker often holds the shares of your investments in these ETFs in *their* street name,[5] not yours. The broker then keeps a record themselves of who owns the shares. The ETF will see the shares owned by Fidelity, Vanguard, Merrill Lynch, and so on, not the individual investors. Nor does the individual (normally) have the actual stock certificates proving ownership.

This means it is unclear that you'd really be able to just walk into these ETF offices in the Canadian Rockies or Swiss Alps to pick up your gold and hit the slopes. They would actually have no idea that you were a shareholder unless you had physical stock certificate possession or otherwise could prove direct ownership. Further, since these funds are traded on U.S. exchanges, it's also unlikely you could refuse an order to repatriate assets by the government if so given.

So although these funds may offer protection against natural disasters that affect U.S. gold storage facilities, it is unlikely they are offering any serious diversification against other problems or national emergencies. If you want to pursue stronger protection please see Chapter 15 for options.

---

### Canton Bank of Zürich ETF

Non-U.S. investors may want to consider a gold fund offered by the Canton Bank of Zürich (Zürcher Kantonalbank [ZKB]—www.zkb.ch), Switzerland (Ticker: ZGLD).

---

[5] Street Name as defined by the SEC: "When you buy securities through a brokerage firm, most firms will automatically put your securities into 'street name.' This means your brokerage firm will hold your securities in its name or another nominee and not in your name, but your firm will keep records showing you as the real or 'beneficial owner.' You will not get a certificate, but will receive an account statement from your broker on at least a quarterly and annual basis showing your holdings." Source: www.sec.gov/answers/street.htm.

Zürcher Kantonalbank is a strong bank owned by the canton of Zürich in Switzerland. They are insured by the canton of Zürich as well (the richest canton in Switzerland) and have been around for over 140 years. The bank is required by Swiss law to have 100 percent gold on hand for each share issued. This ETF is only available to non-US investors. One share of this fund is equal to one ounce of gold.

One feature of this ETF is that ZKB will honor pro-rata physical gold withdrawals for shareholders who show up to the bank in Zürich directly, though it seems unlikely an investor could actually do this in reality. However, the bank is very solid and unlikely to be doing things behind the scenes to jeopardize the assets.

While the fees charged by this fund are slightly higher than other ETFs, the fund appears to offer better protections for its gold holdings compared to competitors. For non-U.S. investors this is a highly recommended gold ETF.

> Zürcher Kantonalbank is a strong bank owned by the canton of Zürich in Switzerland. They are insured by the canton of Zürich as well (richest canton in Switzerland). . . . For non-U.S. investors this is a highly recommended gold ETF.

## Sprott Physical Gold Trust Closed-End Fund

The Sprott Physical Gold Trust (Ticker: PHYS) (www.sprottphysicalgold trust.com) is a closed-end fund based in Canada and the gold custodian is the Royal Canadian Mint. This fund is unique in that it lists actual serial numbers on its inventory of gold bars. The fund also allows for conversion of fund shares into physical gold on demand. But again, this is probably more for marketing purposes than actual application. However, they appear to handle the asset behind the scenes more conservatively compared to the larger market players, which is always welcome.

## Central Gold Trust and Central Fund of Canada Closed-End Funds

Like the Sprott Fund discussed previously, the Central Gold Trust (www .gold-trust.com) and Central Fund of Canada (www.centralfund.com) are also closed-end gold funds based in Canada. The Central Gold Trust (Ticker: GTU) holds only gold bullion. The Central Fund of Canada (Ticker: CEF) holds a mixture of gold and silver bullion. For purposes of the Permanent Portfolio, the Central Gold Trust is the better option because it holds only gold and that's what's recommended to use. These funds also hold their gold bullion in Canadian vaults, not in the United States. These funds have been around for decades and offer conservative management of the physical asset as well, compared to the larger gold ETFs.

**TAX ADVANTAGES OF CLOSED-END FUNDS**  One benefit of closed-end gold funds like Sprott, Central Gold Trust, and Central Fund of Canada is that U.S. investors *may* be eligible to elect to have gains from these funds taxed at long-term capital gains rates rather than the higher collectibles rate from the sale of gold as a Passive Foreign Investment Company. For more information regarding this option, check the fund prospectus and consult with your tax advisor to see how it may apply to your situation.

**CLOSED-END FUND PREMIUMS**  Unlike a gold ETF (which tends to track the price of gold very closely), a closed-end gold fund may see the value of its shares trade at 3, 4, or even 10 percent above the price of gold. The values of these funds' shares typically do not ever trade at less than net asset value.

The premiums are listed on each fund's website under the area labeled Net Asset Value and Premium/Discount. Trading above 5 percent would be an indicator to wait a little bit before buying these funds. Normally this premium will only be an issue in very volatile gold markets.

**RISK OF GOLD FUNDS**  U.S.-based ETFs store their gold at one of several approved warehouses/vaults. If there were a national gold confiscation again (unlikely, but not impossible) the first place the authorities will go are to these commodity warehouses.

There could also be a problem at the warehouse relating to a manmade or natural disaster. A mild earthquake hit the East Coast of the United States in 2011 and was felt as far north as New York City. Thankfully there was no damage, but it was a reminder that something bigger could cause significant problems to the financial sector and where they store their assets.

The attacks of September 11, 2001, impacted gold storage facilities in the basement of the World Trade Center used by commodity exchanges. Luckily nobody in the facility was killed and the markets were able to cope. Yet, no one had ever considered what storing gold in a high-risk target could mean if something very awful were to happen (the buildings had already been attacked in 1993 with a bomb). Force Majeure clauses are buried in many contracts, which absolve the insurer from any responsibility during acts of God, war or terrorism. The attacks of September 11, 2001 buried tons of gold under the rubble that was being stored for commodity traders:

*A fortune in gold trapped for seven weeks in the ruins of the World Trade Center officially returned to the global bullion trade Friday, but dealers had already closed the book on the tale of tragedy and buried treasure. . . . The $230 million in precious metals has been moved from* *the basement vaults of ScotiaMocatta Depository at 4 WTC, where it was stored on behalf of the New York Mercantile Exchange when the September 11 attacks brought down the twin towers. All warehouse staff got out safely.*[6]

With this said, if you decide to use an ETF it makes sense for you to split the allocation among a couple of them listed here to help diversify these risks. It also may make sense to ensure the gold is not stored at a major financial center in your country as well.

**OVERSEAS GOLD STORAGE** An important aspect of the Permanent Portfolio's diversification strategy is to keep some money outside of the country where you live (Rule #13 of the 16 Golden Rules of Financial Safety). There are a number of legitimate reasons for seeking geographic diversification of your investments:

1. To diversify against natural disasters.
2. To diversify against manmade disasters.
3. To diversify against individual threats to your account.
4. To diversify against government attempts to seize assets.

Effective geographic diversification for a U.S. investor has become a complex matter. Expanded reporting requirements have made overseas gold storage much more difficult, and many non-U.S. financial institutions have simply chosen to stop doing business with U.S. citizens.

Still, it's recommended that you keep some gold within close access locally for emergencies and some overseas if you are able. This topic is covered in more detail in Chapter 15 on Geographic Diversification.

## Assets to Avoid

### Storing Gold in an IRA

The IRS says that American Eagle gold coins can be put into an IRA. This is probably not a good idea for two reasons:

1. Gold has no interest or dividends to shelter so you're consuming valuable tax-deferred space that is better used for bonds, cash, and stocks.
2. You can't get to your gold quickly if you should find you need it. The IRA custodian will store it with all the inherent risks in doing so.

---

[6] Reuters News Service, "Buried WTC Gold Returns to Futures Trade," November 17, 2001, www.rediff.com/money/2001/nov/17wtc.htm.

Gold is the last asset an investor should put into a retirement account. Fill these accounts first with stocks, bonds, and some cash. Even if there were space still available, an investor would be wise to not keep all their gold in the IRA space just in case.

## Swiss Francs

The Swiss franc was once viewed as an excellent currency to hold for diversification against inflation in the United States and other countries. Since 2000, however, Switzerland severed the last link between the value of the franc and gold. This made the franc just another world currency subject to the whims of politicians and a central bank.

In 2011 the Swiss National Bank responded to world currency markets bidding up the value of the franc by announcing they were going to intervene to keep it at a certain value of the euro. An investor who had been holding Swiss francs to protect against declines in the value of the U.S. dollar or euro saw an immediate loss. The Swiss National Bank's announcement shocked the markets:

> *The Swiss franc, which has been a popular sort of safe haven for currency traders, depreciated 7.8 percent against the euro. The Swiss National Bank said it is aiming to preserve the Swiss currency to at least above 1.20 against the euro, and that it is "prepared to buy foreign currency in unlimited quantities," according to a statement released by the central bank Tuesday.*[7]

There is no paper money today that can be relied upon to protect an investor from declines in the value of the U.S. dollar (or any other currency). Since no central authority controls the price of gold, it can react as markets deem appropriate in terms of price and is less subject to artificial manipulations.

## Commodities

Some investors believe that a basket of commodities will work just as well (or better) than holding gold. They won't.

Commodities are not as directly tied to the U.S. dollar and inflation threats and will not react like gold to certain economic conditions. In 2008, for instance, some commodity funds lost more than 45 percent of

---

[7] Heather Struck, "Swiss Take Firm Currency Action, Franc Tumbles," *Forbes*, September 6, 2011, www.forbes.com/sites/heatherstruck/2011/09/06/swiss-bank-takes-firm-currency-action-u-s-markets-poised-for-losses-at-open/.

their value compared to the 5 to 10 percent *gain* that gold had for the year. When the financial system was teetering on collapse, people wanted gold, not oil futures.

> When you want the ultimate in inflation protection you should have exactly what the major central banks *themselves* own. That's gold. Central banks hold tons and tons of gold. The people in charge of the money don't own a basket of commodities, so why should you?

When you want the ultimate in inflation protection you should have exactly what the major central banks *themselves* own. That's gold. Central banks hold tons and tons of gold. The people in charge of the money don't own a basket of commodities, so why should you?

Figure 9.2 illustrates the difference between the gold ETF (Ticker: GLD) and PowerShares commodity index fund (Ticker: DBC) during the market crash in 2008. Obviously the markets view commodities much differently than gold bullion when a crisis comes around. Gold is a commodity, but it's also money and that makes all the difference.

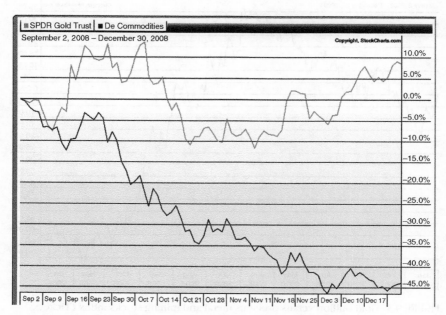

FIGURE 9.2 Gold bullion versus commodity futures index in 2008.
Chart courtesy of stockcharts.com.

Unlike commodities, which can only be owned through futures contracts, gold can be owned directly and stored securely. This is something that can't be said for barrels of oil and wheat. In terms of emergency reserves, gold simply provides better protection.

## Gold Mining Companies

Owning mining company stocks is not the same as owning physical gold bullion. Mining company stocks are subject to the same market pressures that affect all other publicly traded stocks, even when the price of gold is rising.

Figure 9.3 compares the physical gold market and the Standard and Poor's precious metals and mining index (which tracks mining stocks) during the 2008 financial crisis. The price of gold showed a gain for the year, while the precious metals and mining index posted a loss of 60 percent and almost 75 percent at the worst of the crisis!

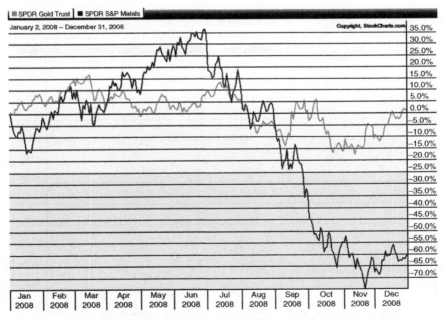

**FIGURE 9.3** Gold bullion versus precious metal and mining stocks index (Ticker: XME) in 2008's crash.

Chart courtesy of stockcharts.com.

## Collectible Coins

Avoid any type of numismatic (collectible), rare, or antique coins. Also avoid all coins that are not from a recognized source, such as commemorative coins.

Since numismatic coins derive much of their value not from the metal content, but from their collectible rarity, they are not as reliable store of wealth as gold bullion.

Many commemorative coins sold on TV are often gold-plated metal and have no value in terms of gold content. Yes, that even includes the limited edition Elvis collection. Stick to recognized bullion coins.

## One-Ounce Bullion Bars

Investors should avoid small gold bullion bars (usually sold in one-ounce sizes from issuers like PAMP Suisse). Small bullion bars are not as recognizable as the popular gold bullion coins, and often come in tamper-proof packaging that can make verifying their authenticity difficult.

## Pre-1933 Coins

Some gold dealers tell people that if you own pre-1933 coins they will be exempted from government gold confiscation if it should happen again. This is a bogus argument. For one, the possibility of another gold confiscation in the United States is remote as we are no longer on a gold standard. Second, there is no telling what the politicians may do if they feel like they want to make a play to seize assets of U.S. citizens again.

> The government could decide to pass a law to seize all Teddy Bears and the courts would rule it valid.

The government could decide to pass a law to seize all Teddy Bears and the courts would rule it valid. So don't think that just because some gold dealer claims that a particular coin can't be seized that it actually means anything.

What you should know is that pre-1933 coins fall into that numismatic category and have higher markups due to their rarity over and above their gold content. What you are really doing is lining the gold dealer's pocket by paying more for these coins.

## Silver in Most Cases

Silver is more of an industrial metal than a monetary metal and it is not as reliable as gold for protection against a range of political and economic problems. The price of silver may or may not track the price of gold.

With that said, keeping some junk silver coins around for emergencies may not be a bad idea (U.S. coins minted before 1965 were 90 percent silver). However, silver shouldn't be your primary hard asset in the Permanent Portfolio over gold.

## Fake Gold

With respect to counterfeit coins, if you buy from a reputable dealer this is unlikely to happen. However if you are buying privately you should be careful about counterfeits. There are two devices, which are a very simple way to tell if a coin is a fake.

1. Gold Coin Balance—www.goldcoinbalance.com
2. Fisch Coin Balance—www.fisch.co.za

These devices take three measurements in seconds:

1. Checks the thickness of the coin.
2. Checks for the correct diameter.
3. Checks for the correct weight.

Gold has a very specific density that makes it hard to copy and match all three of these measures with common metals.

If you are going to do a lot of gold buying from private individuals these devices may be worth purchasing. The Fisch detectors are expensive, but the Gold Coin Balance (see Fig. 9.4) is very cheap and works just as well. These devices work on most major bullion coin types including Eagles, Maple Leafs, and Krugerrands.

If you see a deal that is too good to be true, it probably is. Someone trying to sell you gold bullion far below market price is probably a crook. If you limit yourself to buying from reputable dealers it is unlikely you're going to run across a fake gold coin.

**FIGURE 9.4** Gold Coin Balance.
Source: Gold Coin Balance

## Treasury Inflation-Protected Bonds

A common temptation among investors is to use Treasury Inflation-Protected Securities (TIPS) instead of gold in the Permanent Portfolio. TIPS are not a suitable replacement for gold in the Permanent Portfolio for a number of reasons.

**TIPS HAVE A CONFLICT OF INTEREST**  TIPS purport to provide an investor with a return that is adjusted to the effects of inflation. The basic problem with this idea is that the entity offering the inflation protection is the *same entity* that is causing the inflation.

The role of gold in the Permanent Portfolio is, in part, to provide diversification against political and economic decisions that results in high inflation. The idea that TIPS could serve the same role as gold in an investment portfolio is unrealistic; it would be like buying fire insurance from an arsonist.

> The idea that TIPS could serve the same role as gold in an investment portfolio is unrealistic; it would be like buying fire insurance from an arsonist.

Among the risks involved with TIPS is the integrity of the reporting process for inflation, also known as the Consumer Price Index (CPI). Even if one believes that the CPI provides an accurate picture of inflation in the broader economy right now, the question is whether the government would be tempted to manipulate the CPI during some future period of severe inflation. In fact, the U.S. CPI has been changed a number of times through the years for various reasons. There is nothing to say it can't be changed again in the future.

Argentina is the poster child for currency destruction and an example of what kind of behavior to expect from government when dealing with high inflation (a review of the United States in the 1970s is also instructive, as already discussed). As recently as 2011 they were up to their old tricks again in understating inflation. Their response however is typical: manipulate the Consumer Price Index and discredit anyone that objects. This is a warning of what to expect in terms of how holders of inflation-indexed bonds will likely be treated regardless of where you live:

> *And when inflation remained stuck at about 10 percent in 2006, Kirchner [Argentina's Prime Minister] replaced the officials in charge of the CPI report. Since then, Lavagna says, the government has*

*underreported the consumer price index. The bureau says prices rose just 10.9 percent last year, while research firm Ecolatina, which Lavagna founded 30 years ago, says the gain was 26.6 percent.*[8]

Financial history suggests that it's a good idea to not entrust 100 percent of your wealth to paper currencies. This isn't a prediction of imminent financial doom. It's just a nod to history that when currency problems happen, they often do so very quickly and with very unpredictable outcomes.

**TIPS DO NOT HAVE ENOUGH UPSIDE PRICE MOVEMENT**   Even if TIPS weren't unsuitable for the Permanent Portfolio for the reasons outlined above, the increases in the value of TIPS during periods of high inflation will never be great enough to offset the losses in the rest of the portfolio. TIPS are simply not as volatile as gold. As already discussed, in a crisis gold can have explosive price movements in excess of 100 percent annually. The chances of TIPS ever doing this are basically zero due to how they are priced by the markets.

During certain economic environments the Permanent Portfolio *needs* gold's volatility to carry the whole portfolio. That means gold's upward price movements must be able to completely offset losses in cash, stocks, and long-term Treasuries. The price movements in TIPS will not be powerful enough to do this, but gold's price movements will.

**TIPS HAVE NEVER BEEN PUT UNDER STRESS**   TIPS have only been available in the United States since 1997 and have not been through a period of high inflation. Therefore, anyone stating how TIPS would do during a period of high U.S. inflation is just guessing regardless of what credentials they hold. If the United States were to encounter a period of high inflation, TIPS owners could easily begin to feel more like crash test dummies than investors.

The final word on TIPS is this: *Don't buy inflation insurance from the people causing the inflation.* Stay away from TIPS and only buy gold for the Permanent Portfolio to guard against inflation.

Don't buy inflation insurance from the people causing the inflation.

---

[8] Eliana Raszewski. "No One Cries for Argentina Embracing 25% Inflation of Fernandez." *Bloomberg*, March 28, 2011, www.bloomberg.com/news/2011-03-29/no-one-cries-for-argentina-embracing-25-inflation-as-fernandez-leads-boom.html.

# Limit Gold Bullion Sales Taxes

Sale of gold bullion is subject to special collectibles capital gains rates for U.S. citizens. This topic is discussed in Chapter 13, Taxes and Investing, in more detail. However there are other taxes you can avoid upfront with some planning.

## State Sales Taxes

Some states charge sales tax on bullion coin purchases. Gold minted by the U.S. Treasury is legal currency, however. Why should a gold bullion buyer pay a sales tax on legal money? Should they pay a sales tax when they take dollars out of an ATM?

What an investor should do in this case is drive over the state line and buy where they don't charge sales tax on such purchases (many states do not impose sales tax on gold bullion and often border ones that do).

Since this may be illegal to then bring the coins back into your state without paying a tax, you can open a safe deposit box in a bank in the state where purchased to store your coins there. This gives you mild geographic diversification as well and you are no longer bringing the coins back into the state so sales tax obligations shouldn't apply. You will, however, have to declare any sales you make to appropriate authorities on your tax returns. But at least you will avoid unfair taxation on the purchase.

## National Sales Tax

Some countries charge sales taxes on gold bullion. Others may do so if it is not a particular purity (as in Canada and other places). In the case of purity restrictions (where the gold must usually be 99 percent or more pure to qualify for tax exemption), then just buy the tax-free coins allowed in your country. In Canada this would be Maple Leafs, which are in excess of 99 percent pure gold (24K) for instance.

# Other Considerations

## Safe Deposit Box Risks

You should make sure your insurance carrier covers gold bullion. Many plans do not cover this asset by default and you'll need to purchase an additional rider. Uninsured gold at home is a potentially serious problem if you are burglarized or there is a fire. Safe deposit boxes also are not covered by the bank's insurance policy (they don't know what's in them to know how to insure) so you should make sure your own insurance policy covers the contents.

There is also a chance the bank could turn your safe deposit box over to the state for auction if state regulations think it is abandoned (this varies by state but it could be as little as a few years). This is a backdoor way for a state government to collect funds in hopes the actual owners never come forward.[9] You can still claim this money, but if you have sentimental valuables in your safe deposit box it may not mean much to get cash back instead. To prevent this, it's advised you visit your safe deposit box at least once a year. Just having an account in good standing at the bank is not enough. Physically visit the box so they have a record of it.

## Risks in Metal Accounts

For metal account holders, if the institution should go bankrupt you could have a hard time recovering assets that the bank was holding for you. Check with the bank to ensure assets are not promised to creditors in any way (i.e., make sure it is a *custody account* agreement and not carried as an asset of the bank).

Even then, agreements alone cannot prevent outright fraud. In 2011 MF Global, a very large trading house, went bankrupt due to fraudulent activities. The management of the firm went into customer accounts and used assets in ways they were not authorized to do. They also did this on physical gold and silver bars they held on behalf of customers. Here is how *Barron's* described the depth of the problem:

> *It's one thing for $1.2 billion to vanish into thin air through a series of complex trades, the well-publicized phenomenon at bankrupt MF Global. It's something else for a bar of silver stashed in a vault to instantly shrink in size by more than 25 percent.*
>
> *That, in essence, is what's happening to investors whose bars of silver and gold were held through accounts with MF Global.*
>
> *The trustee overseeing the liquidation of the failed brokerage has proposed dumping all remaining customer assets—gold, silver, cash, options, futures and commodities—into a single pool that would pay customers only 72 percent of the value of their holdings. In other words, while traders already may have paid the full price for delivery of specific bars of gold or silver—and hold "warehouse receipts" to prove it—they'll have to forfeit 28 percent of the value.*

---

[9] "Anguished Tales of Property Taken by State," www.sfgate.com/cgi-bin/article.cgi?f=/c/a/2007/07/02/LOSTPROPERTY.TMP&ao=all.

*That has investors fuming. "Warehouse receipts, like gold bars, are our property, 100 percent," contends John Roe, a partner in BTR Trading, a Chicago futures-trading firm. He personally lost several hundred thousand dollars in investments via MF Global; his clients lost even more. "We are a unique class, and instead, the trustee is doing a radical redistribution of property," he says.*[10]

As of this writing, the question on who actually owns the assets is tied up in court and is unlikely to get resolved equitably. This kind of risk is rare, yet it does happen.

## Keep the Dogma on a Leash

For the Permanent Portfolio the ideal is to have some physical gold in your possession stored securely and the rest stored overseas for geographic diversification. That's ideal.

*But we sometimes don't have the ideal available.* At this point it's a question of degrees and not letting the dogma get in the way. A smaller portfolio may want to purchase the gold directly and store it securely locally. Larger portfolios simply can't do this for logistical reasons. Many may find they need a combination of physical gold they store in small amounts and some type of bank or other gold investment product to handle the remaining bulk.

Owning gold exposure that is not ideal (such as ETFs) is a *far better idea* than owning none at all. Don't let dogma get in the way of useful action. If ETFs make the best sense for your situation, then do it. Don't fail to implement any part of the portfolio strategy just because you don't have an ideal way to do it. You can work up to the other options as you are able.

# Recap

The Permanent Portfolio holds gold to protect against threats of high inflation and other political and economic crises. Here is why and how you need to hold gold in your Permanent Portfolio:

- Gold is a powerful asset that reacts strongly to high inflation and can offset losses in the other assets in a diversified portfolio to provide real returns.

---

[10] Erin Arvedlund, "The Silver Rush at MF Global," *Barrons*, December 17, 2011, http://online.barrons.com/article/SB50001424052748703856804577098740322633760.html.

- Gold does not produce interest or dividends like stocks and bonds. However it does have capital appreciation that can produce profits when stocks and bonds cannot.
- Never substitute Treasury Inflation Protected Securities (TIPS) for gold bullion in the Permanent Portfolio.
- Gold mining companies and commodity indices are not a substitute for gold in the portfolio.
- Gold should be held in a way that has as few pieces of paper between you and the asset as possible.
- Store some gold in a way that it can be easily accessed in an emergency if needed.
- Buy gold bullion coins like American Eagles, Canadian Maple Leafs, and South African Krugerrands for your gold allocation.
- Gold bullion funds are for convenience, not safety.
- Don't buy collectible or antique gold coins for the portfolio.
- If you buy gold from a gold dealer, don't pay too high a commission and always take delivery of the metal.
- You are better off holding gold of some type, even if it is not ideal, then holding none at all. When it comes to gold ownership, don't let the perfect be the enemy of the good.
- Geographic diversification of your gold holdings is a good idea regardless of where you live.

Gold is a powerful asset that has unique properties to protect a portfolio in times of inflation or serious crisis. Like all the assets of the Permanent Portfolio, it works together to provide safety and stability for the entire allocation.

# CHAPTER 10

# Implementing the Permanent Portfolio

## *Multiple Ways to Achieve Safety*

N ow that the economic theory behind the Permanent Portfolio has been laid out, and the individual assets have been covered in depth, it's time to talk about implementation.

There are several ways to implement the portfolio that range from very easy to more involved. You must determine which approach is appropriate for your situation.

When implementing your Permanent Portfolio, it is much more important to follow the basic strategy than to achieve a perfect implementation. Every investor has different constraints based upon factors such as where he lives, his tax situation, the size of his portfolio, and so on. In practice many investors must assemble their Permanent Portfolios based upon what is most practical. In other words, when implementing your Permanent Portfolio keep in mind the adage: "The perfect is the enemy of the good."

Don't let the search for the perfect portfolio keep you from implementing a portfolio that is good enough. You can always implement further enhancements later as your situation changes.

## Key Concepts

### Buy All of the Assets

Remember that the diversification provided by the Permanent Portfolio comes from having exposure to all four of its asset classes. Those asset classes are: Stocks, Bonds, Cash, and Gold.

It is imperative that all four of these assets be held in the portfolio *at all times* without making any attempts at market timing. Trying to correctly guess when to be in or out of any asset leaves your portfolio exposed to serious risks, and these risks can show up suddenly and without notice.

It's also important to stay within the guidelines outlined in the previous chapters for each asset class. Straying outside of those parameters can easily cause an investor to move from investing to speculating, often without even realizing it.

## Eliminate Risks Where You Can

An investment strategy that is simple and easy to follow will often out-perform an approach that is more complicated. A Permanent Portfolio can be put together using very basic investment funds and instruments, and it is helpful to own each asset in the *simplest* possible way.

For instance, a basic stock index fund is going to be better than one that uses active trading. It is better to own gold directly or in allocated storage than to have it in a gold fund. Owning Treasuries through a fund is fine, but if you can own them directly at your brokerage with little trouble then why not do it? Always remember that complicated investments can hide many risks behind the scenes. Try to own assets as directly as you can within reason (e.g., owning bonds directly is fine, but don't go out and try to build your own stock index fund!).

These are the kinds of considerations you should keep in mind with respect to individual assets classes when deciding how to implement your Permanent Portfolio:

- What is the *simplest* way to get exposure to this asset?
- Is there a way to reduce the number of parties standing between you and the asset you are seeking to own?

## Consider Using Different Financial Institutions

You will need a brokerage account to implement the Permanent Portfolio, since you will be buying ETFs or mutual funds for a portion of the portfolio's assets. A suggested approach is to open accounts at *two* different brokerages to protect you against the risk of a problem arising at any one financial services company. While this approach may seem to add more complexity to the portfolio, it only takes a little extra effort to set up accounts at two companies. After the initial setup there is little ongoing maintenance other than checking on the whole portfolio occasionally to see if a rebalancing event has occurred.

The reason for using more than one brokerage for your assets is covered in Chapter 14 on Institutional Diversification.

## Consider Using Different Fund Providers

Another simple way of reducing potential risks in your Permanent Portfolio is to use different fund providers for the major portfolio assets.

For instance, instead of keeping all your stock exposure in the Vanguard Total Stock Market fund, you can split it 50/50 between the Vanguard fund and Fidelity's Total Stock Market index, just in case a problem were to arise in one of the funds. This goes for the other assets as well. There is no need to store all your cash in a Fidelity Treasury Money Market when you can break it between Fidelity and iShares for example.

It is important to remember that you may be protecting yourself against remote risks with these steps, but if the protection requires nothing more than typing in another ticker symbol when doing your purchase, the reduced risk is coming at virtually no cost.

However many may find it too much trouble to split up each asset class into multiple funds. So another approach is to consider using different fund companies for different asset classes. For example, you might choose to use a Vanguard fund for the stock exposure, an iShares ETF for the cash holdings, hold the bonds directly, and put the gold in allocated storage. This way you could still use one broker for the stocks, bonds and cash but still know that a single fund having a problem is unlikely to impact the entire portfolio.

## Four Levels of Protection

Below is a description of four different levels of protection in various Permanent Portfolio implementation methods. Each level represents a higher level of overall protection of your assets.

The four levels are:

**Level 1—Basic—All ETFs and/or mutual funds for stocks, bonds, cash, and gold**

Level 1 will provide you with strong diversification and safety. It will allow you to implement the Permanent Portfolio strategy in a quick and easy way. This approach may, however, involve some fund manager risk in the bond and gold funds and in extreme circumstances such as natural or man-made disasters that affect the financial sector.

This approach is a basic implementation strategy for the portfolio and may be a good choice for smaller amounts, or for those who are looking for simplicity above all else.

**Level 2—Good—ETFs and/or mutual funds for stocks, cash and most gold. Bonds and some gold owned directly**

The Level 2 approach will provide more protection to the portfolio by owning bonds directly (and thereby eliminating bond fund manager risk). Some gold is owned in physical form and stored locally so it can be quickly accessed in an emergency. There is, however, limited geographic diversification for the bulk of the gold allocation and there is also manager risk associated with gold ownership through a fund.

### Level 3—Better—ETFs and mutual funds for stocks and cash. Bonds owned directly. Gold stored in country securely

Level 3 further diversifies your assets by ensuring you not only have more direct control over your bonds, but your gold will be stored in physical form at a bank or other secure location of your choice. This approach enables you to have more diversification against serious problems in the financial sector, including natural or man-made disasters that could disrupt markets.

### Level 4—Best—ETFs and mutual funds for stocks and cash. Bonds owned directly. Gold split between in country and overseas storage for geographic diversification

The Level 4 approach offers the highest level of safety and diversification for the overall portfolio. Stocks are owned in a simple equity index fund. Cash can be a T-Bill ladder or high quality Treasury Money Market fund. Owning long-term Treasuries directly eliminates bond manager risk. Your gold allocation is geographically diversified, and can provide a meaningful asset of last resort during a serious crisis. This approach can provide a high degree of confidence that your life savings won't be entirely wiped out even under extraordinary circumstances.

While it is easy to achieve Level 1, Level 2, or Level 3 portfolio implementations with minimal effort, the highest level of protection is also well within reach using the banking and investment tools available today.

The implementation levels described above are not set in stone; they are laid out in this way so they can be built upon. For instance, starting at Level 1 and then purchasing some physical gold bullion and long-term Treasuries directly rather than using a fund moves the portfolio to Level 2.

From Level 2 you can modify your gold ownership and get to Level 3. Using this approach, your gold is more directly controlled, lowering the risk that it won't be there if you need it.

From Level 3 it is a matter of finding an overseas storage option for gold to achieve Level 4 protection.

With a little bit of planning it is possible to jump right to Level 4 when setting up your portfolio initially. You are probably already halfway there with the accounts you are currently using.

# Level 1—Basic—All Funds

Level 1 offers the most basic level of diversification. Buying these funds in equal amounts will diversify your portfolio against most market risks. This is an all ETF and/or mutual fund Permanent Portfolio. Select one fund from each category (the funds listed are illustrative, but not exhaustive).

### 25 Percent Stocks

> iShares Russell 3000 (IWV)
> Vanguard Total Stock Market (VTSMX or VTI)
> Fidelity Spartan Total Stock Market Index (FSTMX)
> Schwab Total Stock Market (SWTSX)

### 25 Percent Bonds

> iShares Treasury Long-Term ETF (TLT)
> Fidelity Spartan Treasury Long-Term Mutual Fund (FLBIX)
> Vanguard Treasury Long-Term Mutual Fund (VUSTX)

### 25 Percent Cash

> iShares Short Treasury Bond Fund (SHV)
> State Street SPDR Treasury Bill ETF (BIL)
> Fidelity U.S. Treasury Money Market (FDLXX)
> Gabelli U.S. Treasury Money Market (GABXX)
> Vanguard Treasury Money Market (VUSXX)

### 25 Percent Gold

> iShares Gold ETF (IAU)
> State Street Gold ETF (GLD)
> Physical Swiss Gold ETF (SGOL)
> Zürich Canton Bank Gold ETF (ZGLD) (non-U.S. preferred choice)
> Sprott Physical Gold Trust (PHYS)
> Central Gold Trust of Canada (GTU)

## Sample Level 1 Portfolio—Same Fund Company

Here is how one simple portfolio would look using the commonly available funds listed above.

### iShares Portfolio

> A sample Level 1 portfolio using iShares funds:
>> 25 percent stocks—iShares Russell 3000 ETF (IWV)

25 percent bonds—iShares Treasury Long-Term ETF (TLT)
25 percent cash—iShares Very Short-Term Treasury ETF (SHV)
25 percent gold—iShares Gold ETF (IAU)

This portfolio can be implemented through any broker using just one ETF provider (Barclay's iShares). If you can obtain free trades on the ETFs (which many brokers are now providing up to a certain number a year) then this portfolio can be setup at virtually no cost.

### Vanguard Portfolio

If you have an account at Vanguard, consider this option:

25 percent stocks—Vanguard Total Stock Market (VTSMX)
25 percent bonds—Vanguard Long-Term Treasury (VUSTX)
25 percent cash—Vanguard Treasury Money Market (VUSXX)[1]
25 percent gold—iShares Gold ETF (IAU)

This portfolio uses Vanguard funds for 75 percent of the portfolio. The 25 percent gold allocation requires a fund like the iShares ETF because Vanguard does not offer an acceptable gold bullion fund (their Precious Metals and Mining fund is *not* a substitute for gold bullion). However, the iShares fund is easily purchased through Vanguard's brokerage service, making this a convenient way of implementing the portfolio.

### Fidelity Portfolio

Fidelity also offers simple options to implement the portfolio:

25 percent stocks—Fidelity Spartan Total Stock Market (FSTMX)
25 percent bonds—Fidelity Spartan Treasury Long-Term (FLBIX)
25 percent cash—Fidelity Treasury Money Market (FDLXX)
25 percent gold—iShares Gold ETF (IAU)

As with Vanguard, Fidelity does not offer a suitable gold bullion fund, but the iShares gold ETF is easily included in the portfolio by using Fidelity's brokerage service.

Using the approaches above is convenient, though there is some risk involved in keeping all of your money at one fund company or brokerage.

## Sample Level 1 Portfolio—Different Fund Companies

Using multiple fund providers can diversify against something unthinkable happening at any one of them. This type of portfolio might be implemented as follows:

---

[1] Currently closed to new investors as of 2012. Consider using the Vanguard Short-Term Treasury (VFISX) fund instead.

**Level 1–Funds Only**

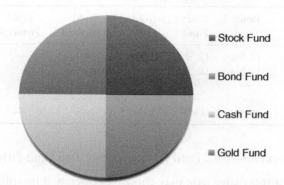

- ■ Stock Fund
- ■ Bond Fund
- ■ Cash Fund
- ■ Gold Fund

Funds at one or two brokerages. Different fund provider for each asset (e.g., Vanguard, Fidelity, iShares, and State Street ETFs).

**FIGURE 10.1** Basic level 1 Permanent Portfolio.

1. 25 percent stocks—Vanguard Total Stock Market ETF (VTI).
2. 25 percent bonds—iShares Treasury Long-Term ETF (TLT).
3. 25 percent cash—State Street Treasury Bill ETF (BIL).
4. 25 percent gold—Swiss Gold ETF (SGOL).

This portfolio is also just as easily setup at any brokerage but it diversifies your money across *four* different fund providers (Vanguard, iShares, State Street, and ETF Securities). Figure 10.1 and Table 10.1 illustrates.

> Under this approach, a problem at any one fund company will not lock you out of all your assets. Yes, this is a small possibility, but it's something to consider and protecting yourself from this risk is easy to do.

Under this approach, a problem at any one fund company will not lock you out of all your assets. Yes, this is a small possibility, but it's something to consider and protecting yourself from this risk is easy to do.

**TABLE 10.1** Level 1 Portfolio with One Brokerage

| Asset Location | Stock Fund | Bond Fund | Cash Fund | Gold Fund | Gold Allocated | Gold Physical | Total |
|---|---|---|---|---|---|---|---|
| Broker | 25% | 25% | 25% | 25% | — | — | 100% |
| Bank | — | — | — | — | — | — | — |
| Local | — | — | — | — | — | — | — |
| **Total** | **25%** | **25%** | **25%** | **25%** | — | — | **100%** |

TABLE 10.2 Level 1 Portfolio with Two Brokerages

| Asset Location | Stock Fund | Bond Fund | Cash Fund | Gold Fund | Gold Allocated | Gold Physical | Total |
|---|---|---|---|---|---|---|---|
| Broker 1 | 12.5% | 12.5% | 12.5% | 12.5% | — | — | 50% |
| Broker 2 | 12.5% | 12.5% | 12.5% | 12.5% | — | — | 50% |
| Bank | — | — | — | — | — | — | — |
| Local | — | — | — | — | — | — | — |
| **Total** | **25%** | **25%** | **25%** | **25%** | **—** | **—** | **100%** |

## Sample Level 1 Portfolio—Two Fund Companies and Two Fund Providers

To make your portfolio safer, you may choose to operate it by splitting your funds between accounts at two different brokerages. By using this approach you get some diversification at the broker level *and* the fund level.

A problem at one broker or fund won't lock you out of all your money while you get it resolved. If you are choosing to implement a Permanent Portfolio using *only* funds, this is the recommended approach. Table 10.2 has a sample breakdown.

Table 10.3 shows how a portfolio would look with an account at Vanguard and Fidelity, and split half in each (any broker would work). Since each fund will largely mirror the growth of the fund at the other provider, when it comes time to rebalance you can do the transactions equally at each provider very easily.

TABLE 10.3 50/50 Split Between Vanguard and Fidelity Accounts

|  | Vanguard | Fidelity |
|---|---|---|
| Stocks | Vanguard Total Stock Market | Fidelity Total Stock Market |
| Bonds | Vanguard Treasury Long-Term Fund | Fidelity Treasury Long-Term Fund |
| Cash | Vanguard Treasury Money Market | Fidelity Treasury Money Market |
| Gold | iShares Gold ETF | Swiss Gold ETF |

# Level 2—Good—Funds, Bonds, and Gold

Level 2 seeks to eliminate bond manager risk through direct ownership of the portfolio's bonds. Under the Level 2 approach, a portion of the gold allocation is also held in the form of physical bullion for emergencies. ETFs or other funds are used for the allocations to stocks, cash, and the remainder of the gold allocation not held in the form of bullion.

To implement a Level 2 Permanent Portfolio, choose a fund from the Level 1 lineup for the allocations to stocks, cash, and gold. For the bond allocation, contact your broker's bond desk or use the broker's online tools and purchase U.S. Treasury bonds with 25 to 30 years to maturity either at auction or on the secondary market. You could also open a Treasury Direct account and purchase Treasury bonds directly at auction if you wish.

For the gold purchases, you will need to visit your local coin dealer or an online vendor and purchase some gold bullion coins that you can store safely.

## Sample Level 2 Portfolio

1. 25 percent stocks—Vanguard Total Stock Market ETF (VTI).
2. 25 percent cash—iShares Short Treasury Bond ETF (SHV).
3. 25 percent gold—Swiss Gold ETF (SGOL) and some physical bullion.
4. 25 percent bonds—Bought on secondary market and held by your broker or purchased at Treasury Direct.

This portfolio maintains the fund provider diversification of the Level 1 portfolio (with three different fund providers), but you have now taken control of the bond allocation through direct bond ownership. You no longer need to worry about the missteps of a bond manager because there will no longer be a bond manager. Also, you've eliminated the annual expense associated with bond fund management. In other words, you will now have lower risk *and* lower costs. That's hard to beat.

> The basic idea is to have some gold that you can get your hands on quickly if you need to.

The Level 2 approach calls for some direct ownership of gold, which should be stored under your control in case of emergencies. The remainder of the gold allocation will be held in a gold ETF or other fund. The 5 percent figure shown in Table 10.4 was chosen as an example. You will need to pick

TABLE 10.4 Level 2 portfolio with One Brokerage and Physical Gold

| Asset Location | Stock Fund | Bonds | Cash Fund | Gold Fund | Gold Allocated | Gold Physical | Total |
|---|---|---|---|---|---|---|---|
| Broker | 25% | 25% | 25% | 20% | — | — | 95% |
| Bank | — | — | — | — | — | — | — |
| Local | — | — | — | — | — | 5% | 5% |
| **Total** | **25%** | **25%** | **25%** | **20%** | **—** | **5%** | **100%** |

**Level 2–Bonds and Gold**

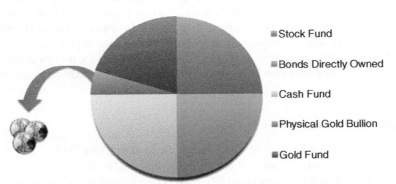

- Stock Fund
- Bonds Directly Owned
- Cash Fund
- Physical Gold Bullion
- Gold Fund

Funds at one or two brokerages. Different fund provider for each asset.
Bonds bought directly and not with a fund. Some physical gold bullion
held securely for quick access.

**FIGURE 10.2** Level 2 with some gold bullion under your direct control and directly
owned bonds.

out a percentage that is appropriate for your situation. Investors with smaller
portfolios may want to store 100 percent of their gold locally. Investors with
larger portfolios won't be able to do this for logistical and security reasons.
The basic idea is to have some gold that you can get your hands on quickly if
you need to. Figure 10.2 illustrates taking some control of your gold in the
Level 2 implementation.

Table 10.4 shows how to implement a Level 2 portfolio with one brokerage. Table 10.5 shows how to implement the portfolio with two brokerages.

Table 10.6 again shows how it would look with an account at Vanguard
and Fidelity, and split half in each.

**TABLE 10.5** Level 2 Portfolio with Two Brokerages and Physical Gold

| Asset Location | Stock Fund | Bonds | Cash Fund | Gold Fund | Gold Allocated | Gold Physical | Total |
|---|---|---|---|---|---|---|---|
| Broker 1 | 12.5% | 12.5% | 12.5% | 10% | — | — | 47.5% |
| Broker 2 | 12.5% | 12.5% | 12.5% | 10% | — | — | 47.5% |
| Bank | — | — | — | — | — | — | — |
| Local | — | — | — | — | — | 5% | 5% |
| **Total** | **25%** | **25%** | **25%** | **20%** | — | **5%** | **100%** |

TABLE 10.6  50/50 Split Between Vanguard and Fidelity Accounts

|         | Vanguard                            | Fidelity                            |
|---------|-------------------------------------|-------------------------------------|
| Stocks  | Vanguard Total Stock Market         | Fidelity Total Stock Market         |
| Bonds   | Direct from Bond Desk               | Direct from Bond Desk               |
| Cash    | Vanguard Treasury Money Market      | Fidelity Treasury Money Market      |
| Gold    | iShares Gold ETF plus some gold coins | Swiss Gold ETF plus some gold coins |

# Level 3—Better—Funds, Bonds, and Gold

Under the Level 3 approach you are exercising even more direct control over your money. In this configuration you are using ETFs or mutual funds for the stocks and cash, but the bonds you now own directly. Further, all of your gold is owned in the form of physical bullion locally and in allocated storage rather than shares of a gold fund.

## Sample Level 3 Portfolio

1. 25 percent stocks—Vanguard Total Stock Market ETF (VTI).
2. 25 percent cash—iShares Short Treasury Bond ETF (SHV).

**Level 3–Bonds, Domestic Allocated and Physical Gold**

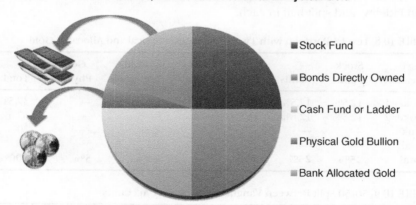

- Stock Fund
- Bonds Directly Owned
- Cash Fund or Ladder
- Physical Gold Bullion
- Bank Allocated Gold

Funds at one or two brokerages. Different fund providers for stocks and cash. Optionally use your own T-Bill ladder. Bonds bought directly and not with a fund. Gold stored in allocated storage in a domestic bank. Some physical gold bullion held securely for quick access.

FIGURE 10.3  Level 3 with gold in allocated bank storage, some gold owned close by and bonds owned directly.

TABLE 10.7  Level 3 Portfolio with One Brokerage, Physical and Allocated Gold

| Asset Location | Stock Fund | Bonds | Cash Fund | Gold Fund | Gold Allocated | Gold Physical | Total |
|---|---|---|---|---|---|---|---|
| Broker | 25% | 25% | 25% | — | — | — | 75% |
| Bank | — | — | — | — | 20% | — | 20% |
| Local | — | — | — | — | — | 5% | 5% |
| **Total** | **25%** | **25%** | **25%** | **—** | **20%** | **5%** | **100%** |

3. 25 percent bonds—Bought on secondary market and held by your broker or purchased at Treasury Direct.
4. 25 percent gold—Securely stored physical bullion.

Some of the Level 3 gold allocation can be stored locally, while the remainder can be stored with an institution that deals with metal accounts (discussed in the Gold chapter). The gold storage should be the allocated variety for extra safety.

A Level 3 portfolio's assets are now spread across both paper *and* physical assets. This kind of diversification makes it unlikely that any single financial, political, or economic event will ever be able to completely wipe out your life savings.

Tables 10.7 and 10.8 show how to implement a Level 3 portfolio with either one or two brokerages plus a bank that offers allocated gold storage.

Table 10.9 again shows how it would look with an account at Vanguard and Fidelity, and split half in each.

TABLE 10.8  Level 3 Portfolio with Two Brokerages, Physical and Allocated Gold

| Asset Location | Stock Fund | Bonds | Cash Fund | Gold Fund | Gold Allocated | Gold Physical | Total |
|---|---|---|---|---|---|---|---|
| Broker 1 | 12.5% | 12.5% | 12.5% | — | — | — | 37.5% |
| Broker 2 | 12.5% | 12.5% | 12.5% | — | — | — | 37.5% |
| Bank | — | — | — | — | 20% | — | 20% |
| Local | — | — | — | — | — | 5% | 5% |
| **Total** | **25%** | **25%** | **25%** | **—** | **20%** | **5%** | **100%** |

TABLE 10.9  50/50 Split Between Vanguard and Fidelity Accounts

|  | Vanguard | Fidelity |
|---|---|---|
| Stocks | Vanguard Total Stock Market | Fidelity Total Stock Market |
| Bonds | Direct from Bond Desk | Direct from Bond Desk |
| Cash | Vanguard Treasury Money Market | Fidelity Treasury Money Market |
| Gold | None—Stored at a bank in allocated storage and some locally | None—Stored at a bank in allocated storage and some locally |

## Level 4—Best—Funds, Bonds, Gold, and Geographic Diversification

Level 4 seeks to provide the highest possible level of safety and protection for your portfolio.

To implement a Level 4 portfolio, an investor will take a Level 3 portfolio and add geographic diversification in the form of allocated gold storage with an overseas institution. This approach provides *extremely* robust diversification and is not difficult to setup with a little planning.

### Sample Level 4 Portfolio

1. 25 percent stocks—Total Stock Market Index Fund.
2. 25 percent cash—T-Bill Ladder or Treasury Money Market Fund.
3. 25 percent bonds—Bought and held at your broker or purchased at Treasury Direct.
4. 25 percent gold—Securely stored physical bullion, a portion of which is held in an allocated storage account at an overseas institution.

This portfolio provides maximum safety:

- Your stocks are indexed and enjoy exposure to the entire stock market without relying upon timing and at very low cost.
- Your cash is in a safe T-Bill ladder or suitable Treasury money market fund.
- Your Treasury bonds are owned directly without any manager risk.
- Your gold is held in physical form with geographic diversification against natural and man-made disasters as well as other emergencies.

At this point you have very strong protection for your life savings. Plus, you have good options to deal with a wide range of extraordinary events if they should occur. Figure 10.4 illustrates.

Table 10.10 lists out a sample split using the strategy described above.

Table 10.11 shows how it would look with an account at Vanguard and Fidelity, and split half in each.

If this approach seems like too much trouble, then consider Table 10.12 using one brokerage. You likely already have the bank and brokerage accounts, so all you would need would be an overseas allocated gold storage account.

This allocation would provide very strong diversification and would be easy to maintain once it was set up.

Table 10.13 shows how it would look with an account at Vanguard.

**Level 4—Bonds, Overseas Allocated and Physical Gold**

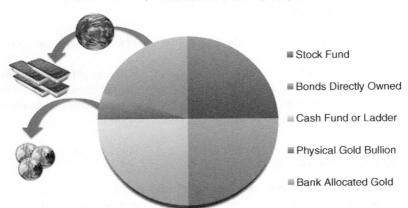

■ Stock Fund

■ Bonds Directly Owned

■ Cash Fund or Ladder

■ Physical Gold Bullion

■ Bank Allocated Gold

Funds at two brokerages. Different fund providers for stocks
and cash. Optionally use your own T-Bill ladder. Bonds bought directly
and not with a fund. Gold stored in allocated storage outside your home
country. Some physical gold bullion held securely for quick access.

FIGURE 10.4  Level 4 has gold stored overseas, stocks are indexed, cash is in a solid
T-Bill fund or ladder, and bonds are owned directly.

TABLE 10.10  Asset Split Between Two Brokerages, Locally and Overseas

| Asset Location | Stock Fund | Bonds | Cash | Gold Fund | Gold Allocated | Gold Physical | Total |
|---|---|---|---|---|---|---|---|
| Broker 1 | 12.5% | 12.5% | 12.5% | — | — | — | 37.5% |
| Broker 2 | 12.5% | 12.5% | 12.5% | — | — | — | 37.5% |
| Overseas | — | — | — | — | 20% | — | 20% |
| Local | — | — | — | — | — | 5% | 5% |
| **Total** | **25%** | **25%** | **25%** | — | — | **5%** | **100%** |

TABLE 10.11  50/50 Split Between Vanguard and Fidelity Accounts

| | Vanguard | Fidelity |
|---|---|---|
| Stocks | Vanguard Total Stock Market | Fidelity Total Stock Market |
| Bonds | Direct from Bond Desk | Direct from Bond Desk |
| Cash | Vanguard Treasury Money Market | Fidelity Treasury Money Market |
| Gold | None—Stored overseas in allocated storage and some locally | None—Stored overseas in allocated storage and some locally |

TABLE 10.12  Asset Split Between One Brokerage, Locally and Overseas

| Asset Location | Stock Fund | Bonds | Cash | Gold Fund | Gold Allocated | Gold Physical | Total |
|---|---|---|---|---|---|---|---|
| Broker | 25% | 25% | 25% | — | — | — | 75% |
| Overseas | — | — | — | — | 20% | — | 20% |
| Local | — | — | — | — | — | 5% | 5% |
| **Total** | **25%** | **25%** | **25%** | — | **20%** | **5%** | **100%** |

TABLE 10.13  50/50 Split Between Vanguard and Overseas Account

|  | Vanguard | Overseas |
|---|---|---|
| Stocks | Vanguard Total Stock Market | |
| Bonds | Direct from Bond Desk | |
| Cash | Vanguard Treasury Money Market | |
| Gold | None | Allocated storage and some locally |

## Maximum Protection Is Easy to Achieve

Once it is set up, this portfolio requires little maintenance and monitoring and is powerfully diversified against a wide range of risks to your life savings. Everything from normal market risks to a crisis that affects where you live is included in this protection.

Here are the steps you need to take to get started with a Level 4 portfolio:

1. Open an account at one or two brokerages.
2. Split your cash, stock, and bond money between the two brokerages or, if you opt for a single brokerage, deposit all of your cash, stock, and bond funds into the single account.
3. Buy a total stock market index at the brokerage(s) with the stock allocation funds.
4. Buy T-Bills or a Treasury money market fund with the cash allocation funds. Keep some cash at your local bank for emergencies.
5. Buy Treasury bonds with the bond allocation funds.
6. Buy some gold locally and keep it stored securely nearby for emergencies.
7. Open accounts at one of the locations listed in Chapter 15 on Geographic Diversification and use the remaining gold funds to purchase allocated gold bullion.

# All In, or Wait?

A common question about the Permanent Portfolio is whether it is better to buy all of the assets at once or wait and move in slowly over time. Go all in. Waiting is a euphemism for market timing.

Waiting is a euphemism for market timing.

Purchasing all of the portfolio assets at the same time will provide the following benefits:

- It will immediately diversify your portfolio in a way that will likely make it safer than it is currently.
- You will be able to begin enjoying steady and stable investment returns without the gut-wrenching swings in value that test your nerves.
- You will begin to feel less anxiety about your money and you will find it much easier to ignore world events.
- You will have your assets diversified in a way that provides options to deal with even extreme emergencies.
- You can get on with your life without the distraction of constantly having to worry about protecting your wealth.

## Dollar Cost Averaging May Not Help You

In the investment industry, "dollar cost averaging" refers to the practice of buying into an asset over time in hopes of reducing the chances that the asset is being purchased at too high of a price.

This idea sounds fine in theory, but in practice there are several problems with this approach, especially when it is applied to the Permanent Portfolio:

- There is no assurance that the asset you are buying is going to go lower in price. It may just keep going up and you'll miss out on the gains while waiting for a lower price.
- Most investors are not disciplined enough to follow through on purchasing the required amounts on schedule.
- Each time an investor needs to buy into an asset it gives him another chance to second guess his decision and be influenced by the financial media, friends, investment gurus, and so on.
- By not buying all the assets in the portfolio, the level of protection is compromised.

Once you have decided that the Permanent Portfolio is right for you, it is normally best to just buy into the entire portfolio rather than trying to time the individual asset purchases. When you take this all-in approach, you get the full protection of the portfolio *immediately* and you can start enjoying the peace of mind offered by the portfolio that much sooner.

Craig relates his experience about why timing asset purchases is a bad idea: "Let's look at some real world examples that I've experienced about timing assets in the portfolio. In Spring 2008 inflation was threatening and oil prices just hit historic highs, pushing gasoline to over $5 a gallon in some places. Everyone was certain that inflation was coming, which is very bad for bonds as rates go up. Yet I felt that falling real estate prices could be very deflationary and that long-term bond rates *could* go lower and that would make the bond prices go way up. This was around April of 2008. By Fall 2008 the markets were crashing along with housing prices and long-term bond yields fell, pushing bond prices up very quickly. Inflation was out and deflation was in. Bonds gained over 30 percent by the end of the year, while the stock market sank by much more. People that waited to buy bonds because they thought they were going to fall in price ended up missing out on a lot of gains and had no protection from the falling stock market.

"Then in late 2008 and early 2009 I was running my investment blog and people would write me and say they didn't want to buy stocks because of the market crash. They thought stocks would fall to even lower levels. I told them that if anything, it was the best time to buy stocks because they were on sale with prices not seen in a decade. I also wrote on my blog that investors should rebalance as the Permanent Portfolio strategy recommends because a sharp rebound in stock prices was quite possible. Some still decided to wait. Well, in 2009 the stock market posted massive gains approaching 30 percent and bonds fell in value by around 20 percent. So someone not buying stocks in 2009 missed out on those stock market gains.

"Now 2010 is rolling around. Someone would write and say 'In 2009 long-term bonds fell a lot in price and I think they'll keep doing that so I'm not buying them yet.' Of course, I would advise them not to time the markets and just buy everything at once to get the full protection. Sure enough, in 2010 long-term bonds posted a 9 percent gain for the year! Then in 2011 long-term bonds looked like an even *worse deal*. People were again saying that they weren't going to buy bonds because they were certain interest rates 'had nowhere to go but up' (which is bad for bonds). Well, guess what? Rates fell dramatically in 2011 and long-term bonds posted gains in excess of 33 percent for the year, while the stock market had only about a one percent return!

"And when it comes to gold, things are much the same. In 2007 gold was around $600 an ounce and plenty of people thought it couldn't go any higher and waited to buy. But by early 2012 it was trading at $1,600 an ounce!

"If the investors in the situations above had just bought all four parts of the portfolio at once and held on to them they would have made over 8 percent compounded annual returns in the very volatile 2008 to 2011 period. This even included the very bad year of 2008, where the portfolio was basically flat when the markets were down almost 40 percent during the worst parts of the crisis. It also included 2009 when bonds fell by over 20 percent and it also covered 2010 and 2011 that were extremely volatile as well. The assets worked together to nullify the losses in the portfolio's individual asset classes and handed investors solid real returns with very little volatility.

"The markets are just not predictable. That's why I tell people to buy all the assets at once and be done with it. Without all the assets you don't have all the protection."

## Other Portfolio Ideas

### Using a Portfolio-Building Service

If you are intimidated by the idea of managing a portfolio at a brokerage or simply want a simpler way to set up your Permanent Portfolio, you may want to consider a portfolio-building service. A portfolio-building service bundles together a group of funds or ETFs into a single portfolio into which you can deposit money. The service will take care of buying the shares and can even handle rebalancing for you.

The drawback is that these services will charge a fee if you do not perform enough trades each quarter (and a Permanent Portfolio involves very little trading once it is set up). However, the fees may be reasonable enough to you that it would be worth paying for the convenience.

**FOLIO INVESTING** Folio Investing (www.folioinvesting.com) will allow you to very easily set up a Permanent Portfolio using all ETFs as outlined in this chapter. Once set up, you can deposit money and deploy it or rebalance as needed. It charges $15 a quarter if you do fewer than three trades (which is quite possible). It also charges $4 per trade. So expect to pay around $60 a year for this service plus per-trade commissions.

**SHAREBUILDER** ShareBuilder (www.sharebuilder.com) is similar to Folio Investing. It is operated by ING Direct and has some features that make it easy to automatically save.

ShareBuilder allows periodic automatic investing (e.g., every month) that will buy your specified ETF shares for $4 per transaction. The money is taken directly from your bank account. Just like Folio Investing, you can space out the buy-ins so that they only occur when you have accumulated a significant contribution in order to keep transaction costs under control.

**PORTFOLIO SERVICE PLUS PHYSICAL GOLD**   You can use the ETFs and other funds recommended in this chapter for the stocks, bonds, and cash and set an equal amount to each for the portfolio service. That way each month you will buy equally into all of them. Then use the remaining amount of your monthly savings to purchase physical gold.

This is a good plan for investors with smaller portfolios. By using this approach, eventually the gold allocation will become large enough to make the overseas storage option appealing for a portion of it, and you can grow into that part of the portfolio implementation.

# Final Considerations

## Turn off Automatic Reinvestments

You should turn off automatic reinvestments of fund interest and dividends. This feature automatically reinvests dividends and interest paid by your stock and bond funds back into the same fund. Automatic reinvestment of interest and dividends can make it difficult to track fund purchases for tax purposes, and can distort the rebalancing bands that are used to determine when to buy and sell each asset in the portfolio.

Instead of having payments reinvested, consider having all of the funds deposited into your cash allocation (sometimes called a "Sweep Account"). By using this approach, your recordkeeping will be easier because you will no longer need to track small buy transactions into your stocks and bonds. Plus you can pool your money into your cash and use it to rebalance into your lagging asset once a year or when you hit a rebalancing band, which can help reduce transaction fees.

## Dogma versus Reality

This idea was touched on in Chapter 9 on Gold, but it bears repeating here because the options can get overwhelming when it comes to designing the ideal portfolio.

*Often you don't have the ideal available.* Your particular situation is going to vary from everyone else's and that is normal. As an investor you should do what you can with the options that you have to protect yourself. If all you have available to you is an all-fund Permanent Portfolio, then that is much better than keeping your money in risky and/or speculative investments. If it means you use some funds and keep a few gold coins in your safe deposit box because that's all you can do right now, that's fine as well. It's better to get started with a good plan than to wait for the perfect plan to come along.

## Recap

By using the following Permanent Portfolio implementation strategies, you can create increasing levels of safety for your portfolio:

> Level 1—All funds.
> Level 2—Funds with direct bond ownership and some gold bullion.
> Level 3—Funds with direct bond and gold ownership.
> Level 4—Funds with direct bond and gold ownership plus overseas gold geographic diversification.

Holding the portfolio's assets at more than one brokerage can further enhance portfolio diversification. When building a portfolio, consider implementing the highest level you can initially. You can build on it later.

Don't dollar cost average or try to time the markets when purchasing the four assets. Just buy them all at once and get the full protection of the portfolio immediately. Finally, don't let the search for the *perfect* plan keep you from implementing a *good* plan.

# Portfolio Rebalancing
# and Maintenance

The Permanent Portfolio starts off with an even allocation among four simple asset classes. However, over time the value of each of the assets will diverge from the initial percentage and the portfolio will become unbalanced. Eventually it becomes necessary to rebalance the whole portfolio in order to maintain its safety and stability.

For example, Figure 11.1 shows the initial Permanent Portfolio configuration with assets split equally into 25 percent portions. Over time, one asset will begin to outpace the others, depending on what is going on in the underlying economy. As time passes, the portfolio may start to look like Figure 11.2 instead. If an investor waits too long, the portfolio can become very lopsided as one asset (shown as stocks in this example) comes to dominate the whole allocation, as shown in Figure 11.3.

> One asset is going to be doing great and another will be in the doghouse much of the time.

Over time, all diversified portfolios will experience this kind of unbalanced growth. One asset is going to be doing great and another will be in the doghouse much of the time. The problem is if you wait too long before restoring the assets to a balanced state, there is an increased risk of taking a loss if the leading asset suddenly reverses course.

Although you want to capture as much gain as possible in assets that are performing well, in the example above an investor who simply

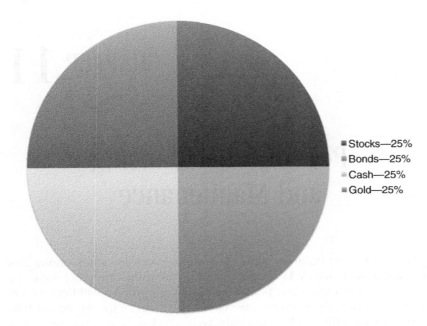

Stocks—25%
Bonds—25%
Cash—25%
Gold—25%

**FIGURE 11.1  Initial Permanent Portfolio 25 percent split.**

"lets it ride" and does nothing creates a huge exposure to movements in the stock market. If the stock market happens to hit a bad stretch (and sooner or later it will), then stocks could create trouble for the whole portfolio. In Figure 11.3 a portfolio that has grown to 50 percent stocks means if there is a 50 percent drop in the stock market the whole portfolio could see a potential 25 percent loss (i.e., 1/2 of 50 percent of the portfolio).

There is, of course, a good chance that if one asset falls in value one of the other assets will rise to offset the loss somewhat. However, by letting the other assets fall to lower levels an investor is taking a risk that there won't be sufficient holdings to offset the losses. For example, Figure 11.3 shows gold dropping to 10 percent of the allocation, yet if the economic environment that caused stocks to lose value were inflation, an investor would only have a small slice of gold to help offset the decline.

The example above illustrates why it is important to have a method for capturing gains in the assets that have appreciated in value without allowing the overall portfolio to become too unbalanced. The profits need a way to be sent to the laggards so they can pull their weight when required. This process is called "rebalancing."

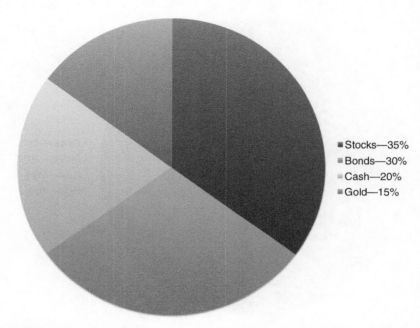

**FIGURE 11.2** Over the years, one or more assets will start to grow more than others.

## Two Primary Purposes of Rebalancing

Rebalancing serves two primary purposes for the Permanent Portfolio:

1. Control risk.
2. Capture additional returns.

In terms of controlling risk, rebalancing ensures that you are never too exposed to any one asset in the portfolio. By taking some money off the table from the hot-performing asset you are forcing yourself to adopt a "sell high, buy low" mentality. This lowers your risk of the hot performer suddenly turning cold and dealing out losses.

A second by-product of rebalancing is that it allows you to capture additional returns over time by selling a portion of your winning assets and buying more of the losers. This is a good long-term investing strategy.

Table 11.1 shows the differences from 1972 to 2011 between a Permanent Portfolio that has been rebalanced annually compared to one that has not. The rebalanced portfolio returned significantly more over time. The returns of the rebalanced portfolio were not only higher, but the rebalanced portfolio also had one-half the market volatility as

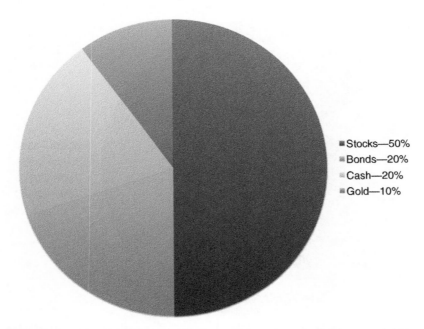

**FIGURE 11.3** Eventually one asset may grow much too large and an investor is in serious risk of experiencing a large loss if it should drop in value.

well (not shown in the chart, but for those interested, the standard deviation of the unbalanced portfolio was 14.3 percent and the rebalanced one was only 7.7 percent).

The worst year for the rebalanced portfolio was around −5 percent in 1981 (−12.7 percent in real terms). However, in that same year the unrebalanced portfolio turned in larger losses of −21.6 percent (−28 percent in real terms). In reviewing years in which the unrebalanced portfolio saw losses, the rebalanced portfolio always had smaller losses and in most cases had no losses at all, as shown in Table 11.2. Rebalancing controls risk *and* improves performance.

**TABLE 11.1** Rebalanced versus Unrebalanced Portfolios 1972 to 2011

| Portfolio | Compound Growth | Real Returns | Growth of $10K | Growth of $10K Real Dollars |
|---|---|---|---|---|
| Rebalanced | 9.5% | 4.9% | $379,800 | $69,200 |
| Unrebalanced | 8.8% | 4.3% | $300,400 | $54,700 |

TABLE 11.2  Losses of a Rebalanced Portfolio versus Unrebalanced Version

| Year | Rebalanced Loss | Unrebalanced Loss |
| --- | --- | --- |
| 1975 | None | −7.9% |
| 1981 | −4.9% | −21.6% |
| 1983 | None | −3.3% |
| 1984 | None | −5.4% |
| 1988 | None | −0.9% |
| 1990 | None | −1.5% |
| 1994 | −0.9% | −1.0% |
| 2000 | None | −2.1% |
| 2001 | −0.7% | −5.7% |
| 2002 | None | −5.8% |
| 2008 | −2% | −12.2% |

# Rebalancing Maintains Firewalls

A firewall is a feature designed to contain damage in the event of a fire. The idea is if a fire breaks out the damage will not spread and cause worse problems. In a townhouse, for example, there are firewalls between residences so that in the event that a neighboring home goes up in flames it will be less likely to burn down the entire block. Similarly, automobiles have a firewall separating the passenger compartment from the engine to increase safety in the event of a vehicle fire. Conceptually, a firewall is a good design strategy to limit the damage from unexpected events.

Part of the overall safety provided by the Permanent Portfolio is the fact that it has firewalls built in and this is why rebalancing is so important. By limiting each asset class to an initial 25 percent allocation (stocks, bonds, cash, and gold) any one of them can take a large loss and the damage to the portfolio can be minimized.

## Thought Experiment on Large Losses

Try the following thought experiment involving the containment of large losses. How would a hypothetical loss to any one asset in the portfolio impact the *entire* value? It's a valuable exercise to consider worst-case scenarios.

How about a 50 percent loss to an asset? What if gold (or stocks or bonds) crashed by 50 percent tomorrow morning? It could happen. A 50 percent loss of a 25 percent allocation to gold is a 12.5 percent loss to the entire portfolio value, as shown in Table 11.3.

Now a 12.5 percent loss is not great, but it's not a *disaster*. This example also assumes that as one asset is crashing none of the other

TABLE 11.3  A Large Loss to a Single Asset is Contained

| Asset | Initial Value | Loss | Final Value |
|-------|---------------|------|-------------|
| Stocks | $10,000 | 0% | $10,000 |
| Bonds | $10,000 | 0% | $10,000 |
| Cash | $10,000 | 0% | $10,000 |
| Gold | $10,000 | −50% | $5,000 |
| **Total** | **$40,000** | **−12.5%** | **$35,000** |

assets is rising in value to help offset the impact of the falling asset (which is what typically happens). If gold crashes, stocks or bonds are probably going to be rising, which will help offset potential losses to the whole portfolio.

Let's take it one step further. Let's say that tomorrow morning you wake up to find that gold has become *worthless.* Maybe someone finally perfects alchemy and gold becomes so cheap that you can make it in your backyard and pave the patio with it.

Now your 25 percent gold allocation goes to *zero.* In terms of the total portfolio value this would be a 25 percent loss. Table 11.4 shows the results. A 25 percent loss is again not great, but is not an unrecoverable catastrophe. Again, this assumes no other asset goes up in price to offset those losses either.

In contrast to the examples above, consider the kind of losses stock investors expose themselves to on a regular basis without this firewall-type protection in place. In 2008, for example, some stock-heavy allocations took losses of 40 percent or more at the worst of the crash. In the Great Depression, the stock market lost almost 90 percent over a three-year period! Anyone with large stock concentrations can easily take losses well in excess of 25 percent that may never be recovered. The firewalls in the portfolio help contain this kind of catastrophic damage.

TABLE 11.4  A Catastrophic 100 Percent Loss to a Single Asset is Contained

| Asset | Initial Value | Loss | Final Value |
|-------|---------------|------|-------------|
| Stocks | $10,000 | 0% | $10,000 |
| Bonds | $10,000 | 0% | $10,000 |
| Cash | $10,000 | 0% | $10,000 |
| Gold | $10,000 | −100% | $0 |
| **Total** | **$40,000** | **−25%** | **$30,000** |

## A Firewall for Your Life Savings

Periodic rebalancing prevents your portfolio from seeing any single asset become too overweight. By using this approach you are building a portfolio for your life savings with built-in firewalls. This ensures that a crash in any single asset can never destroy a large part of your wealth.

As the table in Chapter 3 on performance illustrates, taking a 40 percent loss means that you need to earn a 66 percent return just to get back to where you started! How about a hypothetical 90 percent decline as happened in the Great Depression? That means you need to earn a 900 percent return on that asset to get back to where you started.

Contrast the losses above with a loss of 12.5 percent in the example where a single Permanent Portfolio asset loses 50 percent in value. That would mean that you would need to earn only 14.3 percent to get back to where you started. That's a much easier hurdle to clear. That kind of return can occur in a single year (and has), but a 66 percent return in a single year to make up a prior large loss? That's not very likely. A loss like that typically takes many years to recover from.

> A disciplined rebalancing strategy keeps the possibility of large losses to a minimum. Don't let the greed of watching one asset go up in value distract you from the serious risk being taken if that asset is allowed to become too large a part of the overall portfolio.

A disciplined rebalancing strategy keeps the possibility of large losses to a minimum. Don't let the greed of watching one asset go up in value distract you from the serious risk being taken if that asset is allowed to become too large a part of the overall portfolio.

# How to Rebalance: Rebalancing Bands

The entire portfolio should be rebalanced when any single asset reaches either a high of 35 percent of the total allocation or falls to a low of 15 percent of the total allocation (referred to as 35/15 percent). These trigger points are called "rebalancing bands," and they are designed to force an investor to mechanically buy and sell assets based upon the percentages within the portfolio (and nothing else).

Normally, it is only necessary to look at the portfolio once a year or so to check up on these percentages. It is rare to need to rebalance more often than once a year. Rebalancing bands have historically been triggered every

TABLE 11.5  Portfolio Out of Balance After 18 Months

| Asset | Original Value | Current Value | Percentage of Portfolio |
| --- | --- | --- | --- |
| Stocks | $25,000 | $21,500 | 18.17% |
| Bonds | $25,000 | $29,350 | 24.80% |
| Cash | $25,000 | $25,650 | 21.68% |
| Gold | $25,000 | $41,800 | 35.33% |
| **Total** | **$100,000** | **$118,300** | **100%** |

few years (assuming no new money is being added to the portfolio). The 35/15 percent rebalancing bands have been used in a variety of markets through the years and they strike a good balance between performance and risk.

With the above said, sometimes if you hear about a really big event going on in the markets (e.g., a big run-up in gold prices or a large stock market crash) then it makes sense to check in on things and such events may occasionally require a rebalancing sooner than your one year point if a band is hit.

Rebalancing the portfolio when a band has been reached involves selling a portion of any assets that have risen above 35 percent of the total value of the portfolio and using the proceeds to buy the assets that have fallen below 25 percent of the total value of the portfolio. After rebalancing, the overall portfolio should have 25 percent in each asset class, as it did when it was initially set up.

For example, assume a Permanent Portfolio was initially set up with a total of $100,000, with $25,000 placed in each asset class. The investor looks in on the portfolio 18 months later and finds that the four assets are now worth the values shown in Table 11.5.

Since one of the assets in the example above has reached a rebalancing band of 35 percent (gold), the investor would need to do the following.

1. Take the total value of the portfolio ($118,300) and divide it by 4 to get $29,575. This is the value of each of the four assets in the portfolio following the portfolio rebalancing.
2. Sell the gold holdings down to $29,575.
3. Take the profits from the gold sale and buy enough of each of the other assets so that each asset has $29,575 allocated to it after the portfolio rebalancing.

Table 11.6 shows the results of the above actions.

Note that even though only one of the assets held in the portfolio reached a rebalancing threshold, the entire portfolio is rebalanced.

TABLE 11.6 Rebalancing Assets

| Asset | Old Value | New Value | Percentage of Portfolio | Action |
|-------|-----------|-----------|-------------------------|--------|
| Stocks | $21,500 | $29,575 | 25% | Buy $8,075 |
| Bonds | $29,350 | $29,575 | 25% | Buy $225 |
| Cash | $25,650 | $29,575 | 25% | Buy $3,925 |
| Gold | $41,800 | $29,575 | 25% | Sell $12,225 |
| **Total** | **$118,300** | **$118,300** | **100%** | |

This basic approach to rebalancing provides a near-optimal method of capturing gains while minimizing risk to the overall portfolio. There are a few rebalancing-related topics that arise in practice, however, that are useful to cover in more detail.

## Withdrawals and Rebalancing

In theory, rebalancing bands can be triggered because an asset either rises or falls in value. In practice, however, all four of the assets held in the Permanent Portfolio tend to rise in value over time. Therefore, it is more common for one of the assets to exceed 35 percent of the total portfolio value than it is for one of the assets to fall below 15 percent of the total portfolio value.

An exception to this tendency is when an investor is in the process of drawing down the value of the portfolio, such as during retirement. For an investor who is in the process of drawing down his Permanent Portfolio, the withdrawals should come from the *cash* component.

The process of drawing down the portfolio will eventually cause the cash component to near the 15 percent rebalancing band. When this threshold is reached, the entire portfolio should be rebalanced to the initial 25 percent × 4 allocations to bring the cash back up.

Because the stocks, gold, and bonds will likely grow more over time than the cash, an investor in the withdrawal phase is better off leaving those assets alone as long as possible. In this case, taking the cash down to 15 percent before touching the other components will give them the best chance to grow.

## Timing Can Influence Rebalancing

Another factor that influences when rebalancing bands are hit is when you set up your portfolio. If you happen to set up your portfolio when one of the Permanent Portfolio assets is at an all-time high or when one of the assets just saw a dramatic decline in value, you might encounter a rebalancing band sooner than the portfolio typically sees. Just rebalance as normal anyway.

> Over longer periods of time, most Permanent Portfolio investors can expect to encounter rebalancing events every few of years or so.

Over longer periods of time, most Permanent Portfolio investors can expect to encounter rebalancing events every few of years or so. Infrequent rebalancing means that transaction fees and taxable gains can be kept to a minimum, which helps to keep the cost of maintaining the portfolio very low. The portfolio also requires little monitoring so you can do more important things with your time.

## Adding New Money to the Portfolio

Another factor influencing when rebalancing bands are hit is the amount of new money that is being contributed to the portfolio through savings. Harry Browne suggested that new money be contributed to the cash portion of the portfolio and then rebalanced into the other Permanent Portfolio assets when cash reached 35 percent of the entire portfolio.

However, an alternative approach that might lead to slightly better long-term returns would be to add new money to the cash allocation until it reaches 25 percent (if it isn't already at or above 25 percent) and next add new money to the *worst performing* of the portfolio's other three assets until it reaches 25 percent.

Generally, it's a good idea to buy the worst performing asset because it will be on sale at the lowest price. Who doesn't like a good sale? When you buy an asset on sale you'll get more of it (stocks, bonds, cash, or gold) for each dollar. This is the exact opposite behavior of many investors that love piling into hot assets only to see them drop later.

## Allocating Dividends

Another factor that influences when rebalancing bands are hit involves the allocation of dividends generated by the portfolio.

Investors who use ETFs or mutual funds for the portfolio's stock market and treasury exposure have the option of automatically reinvesting the dividends generated by the funds (called "Dividend Reinvestment Plans" or DRIPs). This means that dividends paid by a fund will immediately be used to buy shares of the *same* fund. In effect, the fund creates profits and those profits buy more of the fund itself.

As discussed in Chapter 10, Implementing the Permanent Portfolio, instead of reinvesting dividends, you should choose to have all the interest and dividend payments go right into your cash allocation. For tax-free accounts it does not make much difference, but for taxable investors this approach can reduce the burden involved in keeping up with many small portfolio transactions and tax management.

By pooling your dividend payments into cash, you also have the option to use the cash to buy the lagging assets and not be forced into reinvesting into assets that have gone up a lot in price. Again, over time, this is usually the best approach.

## Different Approaches to Rebalancing

While Harry Browne recommended a rebalancing approach based upon 15 and 35 percent bands, tighter 20 percent and 30 percent rebalancing bands were also considered acceptable (under this approach you would rebalance the entire portfolio if any asset reached 30 percent or 20 percent of the overall portfolio). This approach has historically provided slightly lower returns compared to the 35/15 percent approach.

The appeal of the 30/20 percent approach is that it can help calm market jitters you may have from watching one asset reach 35 percent of the whole portfolio (particularly if it is an asset that you don't personally like). Just be aware that using the tighter bands will result in higher transaction and tax costs and these can eat into your profits versus just leaving things alone until you hit the 35/15 percent bands.

> Because annual rebalancing can *significantly* increase tax costs, this approach is only recommended for investors who have their money primarily in tax-deferred accounts.

Another approach to rebalancing that is often used is to simply rebalance the entire portfolio back to 25 percent in each asset class once a year regardless of the percentage in each asset class. This approach will virtually always cause the portfolio to be rebalanced prior to reaching the 35/15 percent bands (and has provided slightly lower long term returns when compared to the 35/15 percent rebalancing methodology). But it has the benefit of providing the investor with the ability to honestly say that he spends no more than 15 minutes or so a year monitoring and managing his investments. Because annual rebalancing can *significantly* increase tax costs, this approach is only recommended for investors who have their money primarily in tax-deferred accounts.

The bottom line is that rebalancing is an important part of the Permanent Portfolio strategy. However, there is some flexibility in how a particular investor chooses to approach the topic of rebalancing.

## Emotional Aspects of Rebalancing

Over time the Permanent Portfolio requires an investor to watch as his portfolio becomes increasingly unbalanced as one or more of the portfolio's assets begin to make up a larger and larger proportion of the overall portfolio's value. An investor can run into trouble if the asset that happens to be outperforming is an asset that the investor *personally* dislikes. Investors can also get into trouble when it comes time to rebalance and they are buying a lagging asset that they (and the market at the time) don't like.

For example, consider the Permanent Portfolio's gold allocation. Many investors just dislike gold despite the reliable way it has performed historically in relation to the other assets in the portfolio. What can happen in practice is that an investor who was nervous holding 25 percent of his investments in gold can become *very* nervous when he finds himself holding 34.9 percent of his investments in gold following an upward move in the price. It is these periods of waiting for a disfavored asset to make the climb from 31 percent or 32 percent to the 35 percent rebalancing threshold that can be the source of stress. In such cases, using a 30/20 percent rebalancing approach can allow an investor to sleep better at night (even if it does result in slightly lower overall returns).

> The asset an investor hates today may be the one that saves him in the future. It has happened many times in the past and likely will in the future.

Or consider an ardent gold lover being told that he needs to sell down his 35 percent in gold and use it to buy bonds, an asset that he may personally dislike. Emotionally he may not like the idea, but historically buying the lagging asset with profits from a winner has been a very good idea. This investor should hold his nose and just get it over with and recognize that the future is not predictable. The asset an investor hates today may be the one that saves him in the future. It has happened many times in the past and likely will in the future.

Rebalancing is an important part of what makes the Permanent Portfolio so safe and stable. In order to fully enjoy this safety and stability, though, it's important to follow a *disciplined* rebalancing strategy. In other words, don't try to time your rebalancing moves based upon your hunches, market opinions, or the words of your favorite market commentator. Keep your emotions out of the decision and stick to the rebalancing bands.

## Rebalancing and Taxable Accounts

Rebalancing can be expensive in terms of taxes. However, there is a balance between paying too much in taxes and allowing your portfolio to get lopsided. A lopsided portfolio with no rebalancing means you may risk a large loss that dwarfs what you would hand over to the government in taxes by rebalancing. Therefore, you have to rebalance sometimes and just accept the tax consequences to ensure your future performance is not compromised. Luckily, the Permanent Portfolio requires very little in terms of rebalancing and this means a lower tax bill all around.

If your portfolio consists of mostly taxable accounts, please consider the following guidelines to help improve the tax efficiency of the overall portfolio:

1. Use the 35/15 percent rebalancing bands. This approach will minimize portfolio transactions, which will help to reduce the taxable capital gains generated by the portfolio.
2. During the rebalancing process, if more than one asset is above 25 percent, but not yet at the 35 percent upper band, you can simply leave it alone to save on taxes and transaction costs. In this case, use the proceeds from the asset that has hit 35 percent to buy the other lagging assets that are below 25 percent, but leave any assets above 25 percent alone.
3. When you have to do a sale, pick transaction lots you've owned the longest to get favorable long-term capital gains treatment.
4. Gains from the sale of gold in the United States are currently taxed either at an investor's marginal tax rate or the collectibles tax rate (currently 28 percent), whichever is lower. You may want to rebalance gold holdings across more than one tax year depending on your marginal tax rate, or have some of it in your tax-deferred accounts to rebalance that portion tax-free.
5. If you use a CPA to prepare your taxes, make sure he understands the taxation of precious metals like gold, gold ETFs and closed end gold funds.

6. Have your dividend and interest payments sent to your cash allocation and not automatically re-invested. This will help eliminate a lot of book-keeping hassles and will not kick off a "wash sale" if you are doing tax-loss harvesting.
7. Don't use rebalancing as an excuse to tinker with your portfolio. It is expensive in tax costs to trade frequently and it is unlikely that you'll get better returns than just leaving things alone.

## Recap

Rebalancing a portfolio controls risk and can help capture additional overall returns. By rebalancing the assets when needed, you limit the chances of taking a catastrophic loss. Think of rebalancing as a firewall for your life savings.

Rebalancing bands are a simple way of keeping a portfolio aligned. The default rebalancing bands for the Permanent Portfolio involve selling an asset down to 25 percent when it gets to 35 percent or more of total portfolio value and buying an asset back up to 25 percent if it falls to 15 percent or less of the total portfolio.

There are many ways to rebalance the portfolio, but the simplest approach is when an asset hits 35 or 15 percent you simply restore the whole portfolio back to 25 percent in each asset. If you are nervous about your portfolio it may be helpful to have the rebalancing bands set at 30 percent on the high side and 20 percent on the low side. Just be aware of the potentially higher transaction and tax costs of using this approach.

If you want to simplify the portfolio so that it requires virtually no monitoring, you can simply rebalance all of the assets back to 25 percent once a year and be done with it (though tax issues should be considered before adopting this approach).

Taxable investors should try to limit transactions in the portfolio as much as possible. Stick to the 35/15 percent rebalancing bands and you will probably only have to rebalance once every two or three years. Do not ever allow an asset to exceed 35 percent of portfolio value or fall to less than 15 percent. Doing so seriously compromises the safety of the strategy.

Lastly, don't let your emotions drive your rebalancing decisions. Sometimes assets you dislike will prove you wrong and perform the best. Sometimes assets that perform the best should be sold down and profits used to buy something that is out of favor. Be happy that you're able to buy those assets on sale with your profits.

# CHAPTER 12

# Implementing the Permanent Portfolio Internationally

There are people all over the world who implement the Permanent Portfolio today and many more who would like to. The most common question is: "Does it work where I live?" The answer is yes it does.

The caveat is that the portfolio is designed to work *inside* of your own country's economy. So if you live outside the United States, you do not want to concentrate your assets in U.S. stocks, U.S. bonds, and U.S. cash assets. You want to hold these assets, as best as you can, inside your own country's economy and currency. This prevents having your returns erode through currency fluctuations or being overly impacted by what is going on in a foreign economy. There are some exceptions to this rule that will be discussed (mainly for developing countries), but in general you're better off concentrating the Permanent Portfolio assets where you live and work.

## The World Is Not Flat

It's important to understand that the economic cycles of prosperity, inflation, recession, and deflation that the Permanent Portfolio uses are going to be *country dependent.* This means that the economy in Canada could be very prosperous, yet at the same time the economy in the United Kingdom could be inflationary. Likewise, a period of deflation in Japan may have no effect at all on someone living in Australia.

Table 12.1 illustrates this idea. We are going to take a limited look at the economic climates of several countries by central bank interest rate, inflation rate, unemployment rate, and GDP growth.

> The world economy is very diverse despite the recent hoopla around globalization and "the world is flat" mantras.

The world economy is very diverse despite the recent hoopla around globalization and "the world is flat" mantras. Sure, there is a greater dependence on trade than before, but economies in various regions still tend to move independent of each other much of the time.

The important thing about Table 12.1 is not the year it covers (the table is for 2011). What matters is that the countries themselves are all going to be in *different economic states* at all times. One country may have low inflation (Germany), another may have higher inflation (UK), yet another could be in deflation (Japan), and another may be in prosperity (Australia). It all varies each year and is not predictable. Most importantly, it is unique to each country.

## Kangaroos versus Eagles

In 2011, the United States was still recovering from the problems caused by the real estate crash that started several years earlier. The result was that the central bank in the United States decided to adopt a very low interest rate policy (sometimes called "ZIRP"—Zero Interest Rate Policy) and had interest rates set very low at 0.25 percent. The official rate of inflation, however, was reported to be 2.96 percent. In real return terms, putting cash in your local bank account in 2011 would have earned perhaps 0.50 percent a year in

TABLE 12.1  Every Country Has its Own Economic Conditions. The World is Definitely not flat

| Country | Central Bank Interest Rates* | Inflation Rate | Unemployment Rate | 2011 GDP Growth |
|---|---|---|---|---|
| United States | 0.25% | 2.96% | 8.5% | 1.6% |
| Canada | 1.0% | 2.29% | 7.5% | 2.4% |
| United Kingdom | 0.50% | 4.19% | 8.4% | 0.8% |
| Germany | 1.0%*** | 2.09% | 6.6% | 2.5% |
| Japan | 0.1% | −0.20% | 4.5% | −0.7% |
| Australia | 4.25% | 3.1% | 5.2% | 2.1% |
| Israel | 2.5% | 2.17% | 5.4% | 4.7% |

*From www.global-rates.com as of February 2012, Australian rates from Reserve Bank of Australia, EU rates from European Central Bank.
**As of Q4 2011 or Q3 2011 if Q4 data unavailable from www.tradingeconomics.com.
***European Central Bank Interest Rate.

interest, but with inflation at 2.96 percent a year, you would have seen a negative return after inflation. In other words, the United States is currently in *a negative real interest rate environment*. This is not very prosperous at all and the unemployment and growth rates reflect that.

Now look at Australia's numbers for 2011. Australia did not have a large real estate bubble and crash like the United States in recent years (at least not yet). They have a central bank interest rate of 4.25 percent and inflation rate of 3.1 percent. Yet Australian banks offer savings accounts paying around 6 percent a year instead of the near zero percent in the United States. An Australian saver therefore would have a positive real return versus the negative real return someone in the United States might see.

Additionally, the Australian stock market over the past decade dramatically outperformed the U.S. market, as shown in Figure 12.1. An Australian citizen who decided to invest all of his money in the U.S. stock market and ignore where he lived not only was pulled into the stock market turbulence experienced in the United States, but also was being subjected to policies in the United States that made the dollar weaker around the world.

The discussion above isn't meant to suggest you should put all of your money into the Australian markets. Next year the situation could

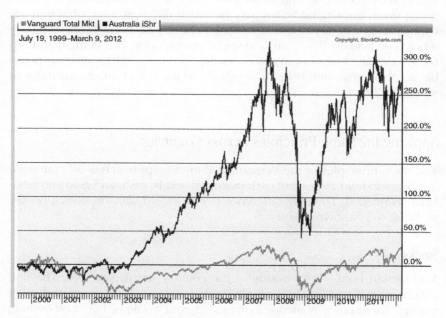

**FIGURE 12.1** Australian Stock Index (ASX) versus U.S. Total Stock Market 1999 to 2012—longest period of data for the index comparison from Ishares ASX Index and Vanguard Total Stock Market.

easily reverse. The point is that each country is going to have its *own economic situation* going on independent of other countries. This is going to be true despite what economists and business books would have you believe about the world economies being more or less all tied together as a result of globalization.

The world economies are not flat nor are they a monolith. Each country still has its own interests it will protect and own problems unique to that region that will affect their own economy. Leaders in each country are going to implement policies for their own purposes and those policies will be to benefit themselves first. Yes, lip service is paid to fair trade, cooperation, strong currencies, and so on but at the core this is just a fantasy. Each country will look out for their own interests through their own economic policies and actions and these will affect each region separately. U.S. policies are to benefit the U.S. economy just as those of China, Japan, Europe, Australia, and so on are there to benefit those economies.

### Invest Where You Live

We have already discussed why, for example, if you live in another country you don't want to concentrate all your funds in the United States. What is going on in the United States may be much different than what you are experiencing where you live. You want to have your funds invested mostly where you actually live, earn, and spend your money. The Permanent Portfolio is designed to work in any economy. The economic conditions possible do not change simply because you live in the U.K., Canada, Australia, or wherever.

## Applying the Same Principles Across Countries

The same principles of the Permanent Portfolio apply across all countries. You want to hold 25 percent each in stocks, bonds, cash, and gold and rebalance as needed. The only difference is you should bias the stocks, bonds, and cash to your own country.

### Stocks

You should hold stocks mostly in the country where you live. The one exception is if you live in a country with a very small economy and stock market. For instance, someone living in Belgium would be better off owning the entire European Union (EU) stock index. This is because the economy of the entire EU is going to affect them. Someone in Singapore might want to own a Pacific Rim stock index for similar reasons.

## Bonds

An international permanent portfolio investor should seek the longest term government bonds that are available that are considered to be more or less risk-free. Such bonds would ideally be issued by an investor's home country, but in the example above the Belgian investor might use 30 year German bonds for his Permanent Portfolio. Someone in Canada, for instance, should own Canadian government bonds, not U.S. Treasury bonds. A German investor would want to own German bonds and not those of the U.K.

The reason for this is that each currency is going to be strong or weak relative to each other as economies transition between states of prosperity, inflation, deflation, and recession. This movement is going to push bond interest rates all over the map. As shown earlier, Australia's economic condition is much different than Japan's right now. Looking at bond interest rates between the two, we have Table 12.2 using 15-year government bonds because that is the longest the Australian government offers.

In Table 12.2 we see that Japanese bond yields are significantly below Australia's (1.43 percent versus 4.35 percent). This is because Japan has been fighting deflation for years and its interest rates have fallen and remained low as a result (remember interest rates fall in response to deflation). However, Australia does not a problem with deflation, but it does have higher inflation than Japan and bond rates reflect that by paying higher rates. In this example, if you are non-Japanese and buying Japanese bonds you not only have to worry about the interest rate fluctuations inside the Japanese markets, but you also have to worry about exchange rates between the yen and your own currency. The situation gets extremely complicated and risky which is always something investors want to avoid.

Not all governments offer long-term bonds as recommended for the Permanent Portfolio (20 to 30 years). For instance, you may only have access to 15-year long-term bonds as the Australian example showed (or 10-year or less in other countries). This can be a problem because the bonds will not move as powerfully in response to deflation if it should happen where you live.

In this case, use the longest bonds you have available. You will get the same benefits as U.S. investors have with U.S. Treasury bonds in terms of

**TABLE 12.2** Long-Term Bond Yields Japan versus Australia 2012

| Country | 15-Year Bond Yields[1] | Inflation[2] |
|---------|------------------------|--------------|
| Japan | 1.43% | −0.2% |
| Australia | 4.35% | 3.1% |

[1]The longest term Australian bond is 15 years—Bloomberg Government Bond Yields, March 2012.
[2]Australian rates from Reserve Bank of Australia from www.global-rates.com as of February 2012.

low credit or default risk from your own government (assuming you live in a relatively stable industrialized economy). An investor in this situation could buy the 10 or 15 years bonds for the long-term bond portion of the portfolio and just hold less cash to emulate the longer maturity that U.S. bond investors may have. For example, hold 15 percent in cash instead of 25 percent. Take the other 10 percent and use it to buy more bonds, making the final allocation 35 percent bonds and 15 percent cash with shorter maturity bonds.

In simpler terms, the 25 percent long-term bonds (20 to 30 years) and 25 percent cash of the U.S.-based Permanent Portfolio mixes together to form an average maturity approximating 10 to 15 years. So if you can only get 15-year bonds where you live, you would want to own more of those to get closer to the 10- to 15-year *average* maturity across the entire cash and bond holdings portion of the portfolio. At the same time, however, you still need to hold some cash for emergencies and living expenses, so if at all possible you don't want to go to 100 percent bonds at the expense of your cash holdings.

## Cash

Cash holdings in an international Permanent Portfolio follow similar principles to those used by U.S. investors: own the shortest-term bonds issued by your own government. This is the safest way to hold cash in most economies. Most governments will have very short-term debt you can hold even if they don't offer very long-term bonds. The important point is you want your cash in the currency where you live, work and spend money. You do not want to purchase currency from foreign countries, which may not work out in your favor if exchange rates are moving around. Currency markets are just as volatile and unpredictable as any other market (maybe even worse).

## Gold

Permanent Portfolio investors in any country should take the same approach to gold ownership. Own some of it in physical form if you can for local emergencies. Own the rest in one of the options discussed earlier in the book, including the use of geographic diversification if you are able. All investors should hold gold no matter how stable they may believe their local currency situation is.

## Various Country Options

Listed below are various countries and the assets that would make good candidates for use in your local Permanent Portfolio.

Please keep in mind that there are many options in various parts of the world and that just because it's not listed here does not mean it's not viable where you live.

Please keep in mind that there are many options in various parts of the world and that just because it's not listed here does not mean it's not viable where you live. If you follow the basic asset class guidelines in this book you are very likely going to be able to build your own very robust Permanent Portfolio. Use these recommendations then as a blueprint for what to look for where you live and invest.

Each country will have varied taxes on investments. Some foreign locales will tax investments and then your own country may tax them again (double taxation). Then some countries may tax all foreign investment income much more heavily than investment income from domestic firms. It will all be very different across tax jurisdictions and is constantly changing. To be sure you are receiving the best possible tax treatment for where you live, please see a qualified tax expert.

## Canada

Being so close to the United States and a major trading partner, Canada's economy is tightly linked to the United States in many ways. However, it also has some significant differences. The biggest difference is that the Canadian economy is very dependent upon natural resource production, as they are a large exporter of timber, oil, natural gas, and other commodities. Despite being so close to the United States, Canadian users of the Permanent Portfolio have found that the ideas work just as well inside their country with mostly Canadian assets. So a Canadian-focused Permanent Portfolio is a good option to grow and protect wealth.[3]

### Stocks

#### iShares S&P/TSX 60 Index (Ticker: XIU)
This index is comprised of the 60 largest companies on the Toronto Stock Exchange (TSX). This ETF has been around since 1999 and

---

[3] Thanks to Mike Barber for his input on this section for Canadian options.

has a very low 0.17 percent management fee. Because it only holds the top 60 companies, it is focusing more on large-cap stocks and won't hold smaller Canadian companies.

### iShares S&P/TSX Capped Index Fund (Ticker: XIC)

Like the TSX 60 ETF above, this index fund tracks Canadian companies, but with a twist. First, it holds more than the top 60, so it more closely mirrors the total Canadian market (over 250 stocks which represents about 95 percent of the Canadian public companies). Second, the Canadian exchange is much smaller than that in the United States. As a result, in the past companies in Canada have grown to take up a large part of the Canadian stock index during bubbles (e.g., Nortel). This can cause one stock to dominate and if it has problems the entire index is affected disproportionately. The capped index attempts to prevent this by limiting any single stock to no more than 10 percent of the total index.

This iShares fund has a very low 0.25 percent management fee and has been around for over a decade so it has a long track record as well. The higher expense compared to XIU is likely related to the fact that it owns smaller companies as part of its portfolio, which tend to generate higher management expenses.

### Vanguard MSCI Canada Index ETF (Ticker: VCE)

Vanguard has just jumped into the Canadian markets with their own index offering. The MSCI index tracks the larger companies in the Canadian market (about 100) with a very low expense ratio of 0.09 percent. This fund is brand new, but with Vanguard's reputation it should be a good option.

### BMO Dow Jones Canada Titans 60 ETF (Ticker: ZCN)

This ETF tracks the 60 largest Canadian companies on the TSX as well, and does it for a very low 0.15 percent management fee. This fund has been around since 2009.

## Bonds

### Buy Direct

Canadian long-term bonds can be bought directly and this is *always* the best option as you avoid manager risk. Contact your brokerage bond desk for assistance if you need it. You can follow the guidance in Bonds, Chapter 7, on the kind of Canadian government bonds to buy, but try to make sure they are in the 25 to 30 year-to-maturity range.

### BMO Long Federal Bond ETF (Ticker: ZFL)

This ETF holds 100 percent Canadian government long-term bonds with an average maturity of around 21 years. While *not* as good as holding the bonds directly, it would be a convenient choice if you cannot buy bonds directly.

### iShares DEX Long-Term Bond Index ETF (Ticker: XLB)

This ETF holds a mix of national government, provincial, and corporate long-term bonds. The average maturity is around 22 years. This bond fund is not as good as the BMO ETF option because it is not 100 percent government bonds. However, it might be an alternative worth considering if you cannot access the BMO option.

## Cash

### Buy Direct

Brokerages can help you build your own ladder of Canadian government short-term bonds if you wish. This is a good option if it can be done conveniently for you.

### BMO Short Federal Bond ETF (Ticker: ZFS)

This ETF has a mix of Canadian government bonds, but unfortunately contains some mortgage exposure along with it. This is not ideal, but could be okay if it is all you have access to. The maturity is also on the long side for cash, at an average of 2.74 years. Ideally it should be below one year.

### iShares Short-Term Bond Index ETF (Ticker: XSB)

Like the BMO option above, this iShares product is a mix of bonds, but is mostly government debt (with mortgages). The maturity is about the same so it's not an ideal cash component, but would be okay if mixed with other options.

### CDIC Insured Account

Just like the U.S. investor's FDIC, a problem in the Canadian Deposit Insurance Corporation (CDIC) could be a problem if you have all your money at a bank and large failures happen. However, if you keep your accounts below the insured limit and spread it between two banks, this may be a good option for a portion of your cash.

With the options above it's still recommended that you try to utilize Canadian Government securities as much as possible for ultimate safety. They are the safest to hold for a Canadian for the same reasons U.S. Treasuries are best for U.S. citizens.

## Gold

### Physical Bullion

The Canadian Maple Leaf is a beautiful coin and also is not subject to sales taxes in Canada, as it meets the purity guidelines (in excess of

99 percent gold). For a Canadian Permanent Portfolio's physical gold holdings, it makes a great choice. Other pure gold coins like the U.S. Buffalo would also be acceptable.

**Overseas Gold**

As a Canadian, you may have more options for overseas storage of gold than an American. Chapter 15 on Geographic Diversification has options available to you if you wish to take this step. Be warned that some Swiss banks are now not accepting Canadians or Americans for accounts. Other options are all still available.

**Central Gold Trust (Ticker: GTU.UN)**

A good fund for gold in Canada is the one offered by the Central Gold Trust. This is a closed-end fund described in Chapter 9 and has been in existence since the 1960s. It holds physical gold bullion inside of Canada.

## Canadians and the U.S. Dollar

If you are a Canadian spending a lot of time in the United States, it may make sense to hold exposure to U.S. dollar assets mixed with Canadian assets. This means that if you're spending the winters down south, it may make sense to hold some U.S. stocks, U.S. Treasury Bonds, and T-Bills as well because you will be spending a portion of your money in the United States Owning some U.S. Permanent Portfolio assets can help hedge you against fluctuations between the value of the Canadian dollar and U.S. dollar.

## Links

- iShares Canada—ca.ishares.com
- Vanguard Canada—www.vanguardcanada.ca
- BMO Canada—www.etfs.bmo.com
- Central Gold Trust—www.gold-trust.com
- Bank of Canada—www.bankofcanada.ca

# Europe

Unless you live in Germany or France, in Europe it normally makes sense to diversify across the entire Eurozone instead of concentrating your assets inside your own country. The primary reason for this is that each country has its own economic strengths and weaknesses, but are linked together under one currency. While some of the countries such as Germany and France are quite strong, others have had a lot of problems historically (e.g., Spain, Greece, and Italy). An investor is better served by spreading his wealth around if he lives in a country with a very small economy or repeated history of financial upheavals.

## Stocks

### Vanguard MSCI Europe Index

Vanguard offers a stock index fund that is registered in multiple countries and tracks the MSCI European index. This index holds 450 stocks from 16 different countries inside Europe all for a low expense ratio.

### STOXX 600 Index

The STOXX 600 index is comprised of the largest 600 companies in Europe. It would be very similar to the S&P 500 for a U.S. investor and would make another excellent choice for the stock allocation.

### db X-Trackers

Deutsche Bank offers a range of products under the db X-Tracker name. These ETFs are available across a range of countries. It offers the Euro STOXX 50 ETF, which tracks the largest 50 companies in Europe. It also offer a DAX index, which concentrates inside of Germany.

## Bonds

### Buy Directly

If possible, try to buy the bonds of your government if you live in one of the larger economies inside Europe. Various countries will have their own maximum maturity, but try to get between 20 to 30 years if you are able. If you can only get shorter maturity bonds, you will have to own more of them than the 25 percent allocation and less cash to get the same effect in the portfolio.

Many European Permanent Portfolio investors will simply buy German bonds regardless of where they live. German bonds are perceived to be the safest European government bonds to hold.

### db X-Tracker Sovereign Eurozone 25+ (Ticker: X25E [varies])

This index tracks government debt with 25+ years to maturity from a variety of Eurozone countries. The average maturity of this fund would make it an excellent choice for the Permanent Portfolio in Europe.

### iShares Barclays Capital Euro Government Bond 15 to 30 Year (Ticker: IBCL)

This ETF holds a diversified allocation to bonds from a variety of Eurozone countries. The maturity is 22 years and the expense ratio is 0.20 percent. This would be a good fund to consider for a diversified bond portfolio if you don't want to or can't buy bonds directly.

### Vanguard European Bond Index

This fund really has too short of an average maturity for use in the bond allocation (average eight years), but it would be okay if it is all you have access to. If you are using this fund you'll have to hold more of it and less cash to get the same performance as longer-term bonds in the portfolio.

### IBOXX German and Eurozone Bond ETFs

IBOXX indices are available through db X-Trackers that follow the German and Eurozone bonds. These ETFs do not have the maturity needed for the long-term bond portion of the Permanent Portfolio, but again you could choose to hold more of these ETFs and less cash to get similar volatility. The IBOXX Sovereign Eurozone Treasury (variety of countries) and IBOXX Germany Treasury (Germany only) are both options.

## Cash

### Buy Directly

If you can set up your own short-term bond ladder with your country's bonds at your broker that is a good option.

### iShares Barclays Capital Euro Treasury Bond 0–1 Year (Ticker: EUN6)

Like Barclay's bond fund, this fund holds a mix of government securities that will function well as a cash allocation. The short maturities and higher quality bonds ensures a high degree of safety and diversification across multiple countries.

### EasyETFs IBOXX Liquid Sovereigns Extra Short (Ticker: ISS)

This ETF holds a mix of very short-term sovereign debt primarily from France, Germany, and Italy for a diversified cash holding.

### Amundi ETFs (Ticker: C3M)

Amundi offers a government bill ETF that track various countries' sovereign debt that would also work well as a cash holding.

### iShares Barclays Capital Euro Treasury Bond 1–3 Year (Ticker: IBCA)

This ETF would be a good option for investors who have at least a year's living expenses saved and would like to put the remaining cash allocation into a fund with a slightly higher yield, but with slightly higher interest rate risk. Like the other offering, this fund holds a variety of bonds from multiple countries in the Eurozone.

### IBOXX German 1- to 3-Year Treasury ETF

IBOXX indices are available through db X-Trackers that follow German short-term government bonds. This would be a good option for investors who want more yield with slightly more interest rate risk.

## Gold

### Physical Bullion

Gold dealers are available throughout Europe. In some countries banks still sell gold bullion over the counter. Austria produces its own gold coins called the Vienna Philharmonic which could be a good choice along with American Eagles, Krugerrands, or Canadian Maple Leafs. British Sovereigns are also an option. Credit Suisse and PAMP Suisse produce gold bullion bars in various sizes, but coins are still recommended where possible. Investors in countries where obtaining gold bullion coins is difficult should consider holding some junk gold chain jewelry for emergencies.

### Swiss Bank Gold

If you are close enough to travel to Switzerland and can open a gold metal account then by all means take advantage of this option. Recommended banks are listed in Chapter 15. Account minimums may be lower for EU residents than they are for investors from other countries (especially Americans). Banks in Austria and Lichtenstein would also be options to explore for gold storage.

### Overseas Gold

As a resident of Europe you may want to store your gold using one of the options listed in Chapter 15 that involves moving your gold holdings outside the European continent.

### Zürcher Kantonalbank Gold ETF (Ticker: ZGLD)

This ETF is run by the Canton Bank of Zürich and is based in Switzerland. This ETF is highly recommended as a gold ETF if you can buy it and need to use an ETF.

### ETF Securities Physical Gold ETF (Ticker: PHAU or PHAUP)

ETF Securities offers an ETF that holds physical gold in the United States.

## Links

- Vanguard Global—global.vanguard.com
- iShares Global—www.ishares.com/global
- STOXX Indices—www.stoxx.com
- db-X Trackers—www.etf.db.com
- Amundi ETFs—www.amundietf.com
- Easy ETFs—www.allcountry.easyetf.com
- Austrian Mint—www.muenzeoesterreich.at
- Canton Bank of Zürich—www.zkb.ch
- Silber Corner—www.silber-corner.de

# United Kingdom

UK Permanent Portfolio investors should focus on holding assets denominated in pounds. However, an option to consider is to diversify the stock allocation between the UK and the EU because of the deep connection between mainland EU companies and those in the UK.

## Stocks

There are several index fund providers that track the FTSE 100 or 350 index. These would all be good choices. Mixing in some market exposure from mainland Europe is also an option.

### iShares FTSE 100 (Ticker: ISF)
This is a low-cost ETF that tracks the 100 largest companies on the London exchange and is a good option.

### Eurozone Options
See the previous section for mainland EU options that will work well for a UK Permanent Portfolio stock allocation.

## Bonds

### Buy Directly
UK gilts can be purchased directly at auction or on the secondary market. Contact your brokerage bond desk for assistance or you can visit the Debt Management Office website listed below to get more information. Owning gilts directly avoids manager risk present in bond funds.

### iShares FTSE UK All Stocks GILT (Ticker: IGLT)
This ETF tracks long-term UK gilts. However, it has an average maturity of only 13 years, which is on the short side, but you can hold more of this ETF and less cash in your portfolio to make up for the maturity difference.

## Cash

### Buy Directly
If you can setup your own short-term ladder at your broker, that is a good option.

### iShares FTSE Gilts 0–5 (Ticker: IGLS)
This ETF invests in UK gilts with maturities up to five years. Average maturity is about 2.8 years, which can introduce some volatility to

the cash holdings in a UK portfolio. This ETF would be a good option for investors who have at least a year's living expenses saved and would like to put the remaining cash allocation into a slightly higher yielding option, but with slightly higher interest rate risk.

## Gold

### Physical Bullion

Holding some physical bullion in the form of British Sovereigns, Austrian Philharmonics, American Eagles, Krugerrands, or Canadian Maple Leafs are all good options. Credit Suisse and PAMP Suisse produce gold bullion bars in various sizes, but bullion coins are still recommended over the bars if you have the option.

### Swiss Bank Gold

If you are able, open up a Swiss bank gold metal account. Recommended banks are listed in Chapter 15.

### Overseas Gold

A UK investor may consider storing some of his gold in one of the foreign location listed in Chapter 15.

### Zürcher Kantonalbank Gold ETF (Ticker: ZGLD)

This ETF is run by the Canton Bank of Zürich and is based in Switzerland. This ETF is highly recommended as a gold ETF if you can buy it and need to use an ETF.

### ETF Securities Exchange Traded Gold (Ticker: PHGP)

This ETF trades on the London exchange and holds physical gold bullion.

## Links

iShares UK—uk.ishares.com
ETF Securities—www.etfsecurities.com
UK Debt Management Office—www.dmo.gov.uk
Canton Bank of Zürich—www.zkb.ch

# Australia

A very solid Australian Permanent Portfolio can be assembled using the funds below. Followers of the Permanent Portfolio in Australia have had good success thus far with results matching other regions.

## Stocks

### Vanguard Australian Shares Index (Ticker: VAS)

Vanguard offers a fund that tracks the S&P Australian 300 index. The expense ratio starts at a relatively high 0.75 percent, though it tiers downward as certain account balances are reached. Vanguard also offers an ETF version of this fund that has a much lower 0.15 percent expense ratio.

### iShares MSCI Australian 200 Index (Ticker: IOZ)

iShares offers an ETF that tracks the top 200 companies on the ASX for a cost of 0.19 percent a year.

### State Street SPDR S&P/ASX 200 Index (Ticker: STW)

The State Street SPDR index ETF tracks the 200 top companies on the ASX for a cost of 0.286 percent a year.

## Bonds

### Buy Directly

If possible, try to buy the bonds directly. The Reserve Bank of Australia lists purchase methods on its website or you can try working with your brokerage. The longest term bond currently being sold by the government is 15 years, so this is the one you should purchase.

### Vanguard Diversified Bond Index

This fund is a mix that is 40 percent Australian and 60 percent international bonds. The bonds are mostly government bonds with some corporate holdings. Most of the bonds are AAA or AA rated. The biggest problem with this fund is that the average maturity is much too short for the desired long-term bond exposure in the Permanent Portfolio. However, if you are using this fund you can simply reduce your cash allocation and buy more of this fund in its place to try to get more volatility for the bond portion of the portfolio.

## Cash

### Buy Directly

If you can set up your own short-term bond ladder at your broker with your country's bonds that is a good option.

### Vanguard Cash Plus Index

This index fund invests in a broadly diversified set of securities from the states and banks in Australia. It is not as safe as holding government securities only, however, though it would be a more diversified way to hold cash than keeping it in one location. Unfortunately, the annual fee of 0.70 percent a year for smaller accounts is relatively high for a cash fund.

## Gold

### Physical Bullion

Australia is fortunate to have the Perth Mint, which produces gold bullion coins of the highest quality, and coins from the mint would be a good option for physical gold ownership. You can read more about the Perth Mint in Chapter 15.

### Perth Mint Gold ETF (Ticker: PMGOLD)

The Perth Mint also offers a gold ETF that is backed by physical gold held at the Perth Mint. The ETF is related to the Perth Mint's gold certificate program, which is discussed in Chapter 15. The Perth Mint offers discounts on its minimums for residents of Australia and New Zealand and citizens can deal directly with the mint.

### Overseas Gold

Although the Perth Mint has one of the best programs for overseas gold storage, that won't help if you actually live in the same country as the mint. Look at "Geographic Diversification," Chapter 15, for some other ideas you can consider for holding gold in the United States or Switzerland.

## Links

- Vanguard Australia—www.vanguard.com.au
- State Street Australia—www.spdr.com.au
- iShares Ausralia—au.ishares.com
- Perth Mint—www.perthmint.com.au
- Reserve Bank of Australia—www.rba.gov.au

## Asia, Middle East, and the Rest of the World

There are many different exchanges throughout Asia, the Middle East, and the rest of the world so listing all possible options in this book is not feasible. In general, follow the guidelines listed at the beginning of this chapter in terms of stock index, bonds, cash, and gold allocations. If you live in a very small country you may want to consider diversifying into an all-world or even U.S.-focused portfolio simply because your local economy may not provide very good options for building the portfolio. This is especially true if you live in a country with an unstable economy or a government bond market with a history of debt defaults.

In terms of assets like gold, different countries may have restrictions on purchasing or availability. Consider keeping some junk gold chains in lieu of physical bullion for emergencies, at a minimum. Other overseas gold options are listed in Chapter 15 that you may want to consider for additional protection and privacy.

## Developing Country Investing

Unfortunately, many countries around the world are corrupt and this affects the citizens who live there and their economy, especially those with wealth that they would like to protect.

The reality is that the Permanent Portfolio is designed to work in an economy that is not corrupt. Yes, it has features to diversify against really bad risks (like gold stored overseas). Yet, it can't work magic if your local stock market is riddled with corruption and your government has a history of not paying back its debts and periodically confiscating citizens' hard earned wealth.

Many times the best way to protect yourself is to have most of your assets invested elsewhere while you work at home to build your savings. Bring back funds when you need to spend them for living expenses, but otherwise keep them out of reach of the corrupt local government and shaky economy.

If this is your situation, it's recommended you use Chapter 10, Implementing the Permanent Portfolio, for the U.S. portfolio or the international portfolios listed above, and see if you can buy those assets on your local exchange or through a broker elsewhere that is insured and trustworthy. Here are some general recommendations on what to look for in your portfolio construction.

### Stocks

Purchase an all-world index fund. Vanguard has begun offering such an index fund (Ticker: VT) on U.S. exchanges and this is a good option if you can access it. It was discussed in more detail in Chapter 6. This fund attempts to mirror the relative weightings of all countries around the world.

- Vanguard Total World Index Mutual Fund (Ticker: VTWSX)
- Vanguard Total World Index ETF (Ticker: VT)

This fund will provide simple one-step diversification if you are able to buy the fund where you reside with the help of a domestic or U.S.-based broker. Figure 12.2 is a reprint of the breakdown of this fund discussed in Chapter 6.

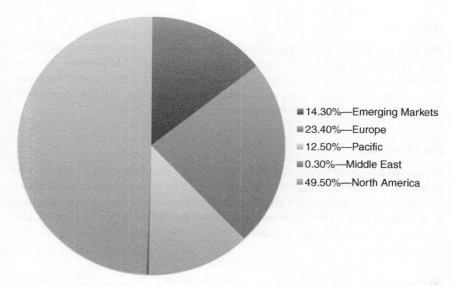

**FIGURE 12.2** Vanguard Total World Index: A good option if you can buy it where you reside.

*Source:* Portfolio breakdown according to Vanguard, early 2012.

## Bonds

All-world government bond exposure is hard to find in a single fund, since most funds focus on individual bond markets or regional bond markets. If you can find a broad-based bond index to buy, use one that has 10+ years average maturity from a variety of developed countries. If you can't do this, then try to see if you can buy U.S. Treasury bonds directly as they are very liquid and trade globally. Since many countries rely on the U.S. dollar extensively, you will still get strong diversification by using this approach.

## Cash

Keep some cash in the local currency for emergencies and spending purposes. But keep the rest in a globally diversified short-term bond fund. Again, pickings here may be slim depending on what exchanges you can access. Otherwise, consider purchasing a U.S. Treasury money market or short-term bond fund as described in Chapter 8 on Cash.

## Gold

Physical gold bullion may be difficult to purchase in some countries or outright prohibited. Instead, consider buying some junk gold jewelry you can use for barter in an emergency, but keep that as private as possible for security reasons. The rest of your gold allocation can be stored overseas securely as additional protection against currency problems at home.

## Fund Companies

Vanguard has great international fund offerings and is starting to offer more funds on foreign exchanges. Vanguard would be a good option to consider checking out first at www.vanguard.com. iShares also offers many good international funds (www.ishares.com). Other European index fund providers may also be open for you to purchase so consider them as well.

# Recap

The world is not flat. Each country will have its own unique economy and economic cycles that are not necessarily going to match up with other countries around the world.

Try to concentrate your bond and cash holdings inside your own government's debt and currency. Purchasing foreign debt exposes you to currency fluctuations that can hurt your performance.

Broad stock market exposure in most industrialized countries can be obtained through inexpensive index fund products. If you live in a very small country with a small stock market, consider diversifying across the region (e.g., Europe, Pacific Rim, or the United States).

There are good foreign gold storage options for non-U.S. investors, even though Americans have seen their foreign gold storage options restricted in recent years. Review Chapter 15 for some ideas about how to safely store gold in a foreign location.

If you live in a developing country with lots of corruption, consider building a diversified portfolio made up of global or U.S. assets. Try to keep some assets outside of your country.

The guidelines for a U.S. investor in terms of stocks, bonds, cash, and gold apply internationally as well. Calling up your broker and asking for specific products that you can use to build the portfolio will often lead to additional options that may not have been covered here.

# CHAPTER 13

# Taxes and Investing

Taxes are an inevitable part of investing. There are taxes on interest income, taxes on dividends, and taxes on capital gains when you sell an asset for a profit. The particular investing tax situation you will face will vary depending on where you live, but all investors recognize the basic point that *taxes erode your total investment returns.* Managing taxes effectively is an important part of successful investing.

Every penny you pay in taxes today is one less penny that can compound over time. As the years pass, the impact of taxes on investment returns can be dramatic. It is not uncommon for investments with unfavorable tax treatment to reduce annual returns anywhere from 10 to 30 percent a year or more. Over an investing lifetime this can result in growth that is much lower than that of an investor who managed to avoid paying any taxes as shown in Table 13.1.

Investors should take tax costs into consideration at every turn. Not doing so means turning over more of your hard-earned money to the government instead of keeping it for you and your family.

## Simplicity Is Often the Best Tax Strategy

The Permanent Portfolio is premised, in part, on the idea that an investment strategy should be simple. The same should be true of an investor's tax management strategies. A simple approach to investing like the Permanent Portfolio is easier to manage with lower costs than many other strategies, but for purposes of minimizing taxes it offers clear advantages:

1. Using simple passive investing avoids managers and strategies that can churn a portfolio and generate unnecessary taxes.
2. The simple allocation requires less management and rebalancing which reduces the chance of experiencing frequent taxable events.

TABLE 13.1 Each Percent of Tax Impact on Annual Returns Drastically Reduces
Overall Returns

| Starting Value | Tax Load | Annual After Tax Return | Years | Ending Value |
|---|---|---|---|---|
| $10,000 | 0% | 10% | 20 | $67,275 |
| $10,000 | 1% | 9% | 20 | $56,044 |
| $10,000 | 2% | 8% | 20 | $46,609 |
| $10,000 | 3% | 7% | 20 | $38,696 |

3. Simple portfolios are less likely to get dragged into complicated tax
   planning schemes, which can be affected by future tax law changes and
   be expensive to adjust if (or *when*) the rules change.

When thinking about tax-planning strategies, bear in mind that paying the
smallest allowable amount of taxes should be the goal of all investors. Fortunately, there are many legitimate opportunities to minimize the tax burden of
your investments and these strategies should be used as much as possible.

There are also, however, tax strategies that are either very aggressive or
arguably outright illegal, and these should be avoided completely. There is no
point in putting together a safe and stable portfolio only to see yourself lose
much of it in penalties and interest (potentially along with your freedom) by
being reckless in your approach to taxes. If a strategy is difficult to understand,
or seems too good to be true, *be careful.* Always talk to a qualified accountant
or tax attorney if you have questions about a particular tax strategy.

# Tax-Free Savings Vehicles

Many governments have created savings mechanisms you can use to shelter all, or part, of your retirement investments from taxes. These vehicles vary by country, but they tend to have one or more of the following features:

- They allow interest and dividends to collect tax-free.
- They allow capital gains to be harvested tax-free.
- They may allow deposits or withdrawals to be tax-free.
- They may allow other types of tax-free savings and investing with specialty bonds, and so on.

Because there are so many different tax-deferred savings vehicles and strategies available to investors (with laws constantly changing), this book cannot cover each one individually (that would require its own book). The discussion in this chapter focuses on tax strategies available to U.S. investors. However, virtually any Permanent Portfolio investor can utilize some or all of these techniques to build a more tax efficient overall portfolio with the tools you may have available where you reside.

# Types of Taxable Events

As an investor, you primarily need to understand what *kinds* of events will trigger taxes in each asset class and position assets within the correct tax shelter or tax-deferred account that applies to your situation. Once you understand the sources of taxes in each investment you'll have a better understanding of how to use your tax shelter options most effectively.

At the core, a Permanent Portfolio investor is going to encounter four main types of tax situations in the course of managing his investments:

1. Interest Taxes
2. Dividend Taxes
3. Capital Gains Taxes
4. Collectibles Gains Taxes

## Interest Taxes

Interest from Treasury bonds and T-Bills is treated as taxable income. For the U.S. Treasury bonds and bills held by the Permanent Portfolio, the interest income is taxable at the U.S. federal level. However, interest from Treasuries is not currently taxed at the state level, which is a nice benefit for investors in states with income taxes.

Since the Permanent Portfolio generates interest income constantly, there is no good way for an investor to avoid paying tax on the payments unless the bonds and bills are held in a tax-deferred account.

## Dividend Taxes

Dividends are the profits paid out by corporations to shareholders, and dividend income is taxable. A stock index fund held by a Permanent Portfolio investor will pay dividends that are taxable at the federal and state levels. Like interest income, dividend income is received regularly and investors cannot avoid paying taxes on it without some type of tax-deferred account.

## Capital Gains Taxes

Capital gains are profits you receive from the sale of assets that have appreciated in value. For example, if you buy an asset for $100 and you later sell it for $150, the $50 profit is a capital gain. For U.S. investors, capital gains on assets held more than one year are considered long-term capital gains and, in recent years, these gains have been taxed at a lower rate than ordinary income. Capital gains on assets held for less than one year are considered short-term capital gains and are taxed at normal income tax rates. States may also have taxes that apply to capital gains.

In the Permanent Portfolio there is no reason to ever pay the higher short-term capital gains rates, since the strategy doesn't require frequent trading. Although taxes on long-term capital gains are inevitable for an investor with taxable accounts, there are strategies available that can help you match up losses with capital gains to help minimize your overall capital gains tax liability.

> Capital gains are beneficial to taxable investing because you can delay when you pay taxes by not selling the asset until you are ready.

The Permanent Portfolio can generate capital gains from bonds, cash, stocks, or gold (gold typically generates a special type of gain discussed below). Capital gains are beneficial to taxable investing because you can delay when you pay taxes by not selling the asset until you are ready. Capital gains are not a problem for funds held within tax-deferred accounts.

## Collectible Gains Taxes

Under the U.S. tax system, gold is treated as a "collectible" and any gains from investments in gold are taxed differently than stocks or bonds. Gains on the sale of collectibles are currently taxed at the lower of 28 percent or your marginal tax rate (i.e., the tax rate you pay on your last dollar of taxable income). Gains from the sale of gold in the Permanent Portfolio are subject to taxation at the collectibles tax rate if held outside a tax-deferred account.

One important point about the collectibles tax is that gains from the sales of certain closed-end gold funds (such as CEF, GTU, and others discussed in Chapter 9) can be treated as long-term capital gains under some circumstances if the investor completes the appropriate IRS forms (Form 8621 for a Passive Foreign Investment Company). If you are interested in more information about this tax planning opportunity, you should discuss the matter with your tax advisor.

Gains on collectibles are only realized when an investor sells an asset, so an investor can delay paying the taxes until a sale actually occurs. Like the other kinds of taxes, only a tax-deferred account can prevent the taxation resulting from the sale of gold (though the options for owning gold in a tax-deferred account are somewhat limited).

## Ordering of Assets and Tax Planning

Once you are familiar with the different types of taxable events that a Permanent Portfolio is going to experience, it is next necessary to determine the portfolio assets that are least and most tax efficient (i.e., the degree to which an asset allows you to manage the taxes from its income and/or appreciation in value). In general, here are the tax efficiency guidelines for each Permanent Portfolio asset, listed from least to most tax efficient:

1. Bonds generate the highest amount of taxes because of the regular payment of interest income and potentially large capital gains when the portfolio is rebalanced.
2. Cash is next because it also generates taxable interest income, and can also generate small capital gains.
3. Stocks come in third because of their regular taxable dividend payments and capital gains that can be triggered when the portfolio is rebalanced.
4. Gold brings up the rear because it generates capital gains at the time of sale. However, it does not generate any dividend or interest income that is taxed.

Given the guidelines above, investors would first want to put bonds into their tax-deferred accounts, then cash, then stocks, and finally gold.

Given the guidelines above, investors would first want to put bonds into their tax-deferred accounts, then cash, then stocks, and finally gold.

Now this approach is only a *theoretical* optimum. Reality may dictate a different approach in different situations. The discussion below covers selected tax matters related to each Permanent Portfolio asset.

## Bonds

Bonds can produce returns in the form of interest payments or capital appreciation under market conditions where interest rates are falling. The constant stream of interest payments provided by bonds can be a challenge for taxable investors. However, potential capital gains can be managed to some extent by deciding when to sell bonds that have appreciated in value.

Although the interest from U.S. Treasury bonds is not taxable at the state and local level, interest payments can generate additional taxes at the federal level that investors should try to minimize as much as possible. Using Morningstar's tax cost analysis in Table 13.2 you can see the result of returns from the Vanguard Treasury Long-Term fund (Ticker: VUSTX) both before and after taxes have been paid over the past 15 years, which is the longest period it covers.

Morningstar's tax analysis tools allow an investor to apply a reasonable expectation regarding what a tax load may look like based on past data. It is best to only rely on data from funds that are at least 10 years old. A period of at least 10 years will ensure that the fund has been through a variety of market conditions so you can see how the managers handled taxes in good and bad times.

Table 13.2 shows how nearly 25 percent of the fund's returns were lost to taxes over the period covered, which is a severe blow to overall returns. Given this kind of tax impact, you would normally want to put all, or nearly all, of your bonds into tax-deferred accounts in order to allow those returns to escape taxation for as long as possible. The ability to prevent the bond interest from spilling over into taxable accounts can be a big advantage over the years.

In addition to the taxable interest discussed above, there can be sizeable capital gains in bonds when interest rates are falling. Sometimes the price

**TABLE 13.2 Before and After Taxes on Vanguard's Long-Term Bond Fund Over the Past 15 Years**

| Fund Name | Pre-Tax | After-Tax | Difference |
|---|---|---|---|
| Vanguard Treasury Long Term | 8.5% | 6.3% | 2.2% |

*Source:* www.morningstar.com tax cost analysis.

appreciation of the bonds can go up so much in value that you will hit a rebalancing band and have to sell them down to the correct level. This situation occurred in many Permanent Portfolios during the 2008 stock market crash when bond prices went up over 30 percent as the stock market fell almost 40 percent. When rebalancing occurs under these circumstances, your bond holdings will generate capital gains in addition to the taxable interest payments received on the bond holdings. This scenario demonstrates why having as much of your bond holdings as possible in a tax-deferred account is a good idea.

## Cash

Like bonds, cash held in the form of T-Bills (or similar instruments) also produces interest income, but unlike bonds, T-Bills provide little potential for capital gains. This is because T-Bills are very stable in price due to their short maturities. The interest income on T-Bills also tends to be lower than the interest paid by the long-term bonds the portfolio holds. Taxes are, however, still a problem for cash. Table 13.3 shows the effects of taxes on the Vanguard Short-Term Treasury fund over the past 15 years and how tax-deferred accounts can help.

**CASH AND EMERGENCIES**  There is a need to keep enough cash outside of tax-deferred accounts to meet living expenses or emergencies, such as when retired or in the event of a job loss, illness, and so on.

If you put all of your cash in a tax-deferred account, and later need to access it because of an emergency, there can be penalties for early withdrawal and delays in getting access to the funds (assuming that the funds can be withdrawn at all). Therefore, you don't want to put *all* of your cash in a tax-deferred savings or retirement account. Instead, a suggested approach is to keep several months' worth of living expenses in cash outside of your retirement accounts just in case you need to get access to these funds. By taking this approach you will avoid delays and/or the payment of penalties if you find you need to get to your cash quickly.

Once you have some living expenses set aside in a taxable account, putting the rest of your cash in a tax-deferred account is a good way to minimize the tax burden on the overall portfolio.

**TABLE 13.3** Vanguard Short-Term Treasury Before and After Taxes

| Fund Name | Pre-Tax | After-Tax | Difference |
|---|---|---|---|
| Vanguard Short-Term Treasury | 4.6% | 3.1% | 1.5% |

*Source:* www.morningstar.com tax cost analysis.

## Stocks

Stock funds pay out dividends and capital gains to investors. The problem with these payments, however, is that they cause the value of the fund to *decrease* by the amount of the dividend and capital gains distributions. Once the dividend and capital gains are distributed to shareholders, the payments are subject to taxation. With these distributions you are essentially just pulling money from one pocket, paying a tax on it, and putting it into another pocket (the same is true of bond funds as well).

Although the stock fund distribution scenario described above can create unwanted taxable income, the use of a broadly based stock index fund (as recommended for the Permanent Portfolio) is actually very efficient in terms of taxes. A broad market index fund has little churning of stocks internally, and as a result generates minimal gains subject to capital gains taxes (assuming an investor doesn't sell any of his shares). Plus, a broad market index fund will also typically generate not more than 2 to 3 percent in dividend income, reducing the tax bill even further.

Table 13.4 shows the comparison of pre-tax and after-tax returns of the Vanguard Total Stock Market Fund (Ticker: VTSMX) and how they stack up against the large, actively managed Magellan fund from Fidelity (Ticket: FMAGX) over the past 15 years.

In terms of tax efficiency, the Vanguard index fund gave up less than 10 percent in total returns to taxes (0.5 percent of 5.7 percent pre-tax). The Fidelity managed fund, however, gave up nearly 30 percent of its returns to taxes (1.0 percent of 3.5 percent pre-tax). In addition to reduced tax efficiency, the Fidelity actively managed fund also significantly underperformed the total stock market index before taxes are considered. This is a double blow to an investor looking for strong after-tax performance.

Because stock index funds do generate taxable dividend and capital gains (even though they are relatively tax efficient), it makes sense to place some of your stock index fund holdings in tax-deferred accounts (assuming you have room in your tax-deferred accounts after the bond and cash allocations).

TABLE 13.4 Vanguard Total Stock Market versus Fidelity Magellan Tax Efficiency Over the Past 15 Years

| Fund Name | Pre-Tax | After-Tax | Difference |
|---|---|---|---|
| Vanguard Total Stock Market | 5.7% | 5.2% | 0.5% |
| Fidelity Magellan Fund | 3.5% | 2.5% | 1.0% |

*Source:* www.morningstar.com tax cost analysis.

**TABLE 13.5** Before and After Taxes on State Street's Gold ETF Over the Past Five Years

| Fund Name | Pre-Tax | After-Tax | Difference |
|---|---|---|---|
| State Street Gold ETF | 20.1% | 20.1% | 0% |

*Source:* www.morningstar.com tax cost analysis.

## Gold

From a tax perspective, gold is an unusual asset because it generates no interest or dividends at all. It does, however, generate taxable gains when sold for a profit. Despite the potential for taxable gains, however, gold is the last asset you should put into tax-deferred accounts.

Table 13.5 uses the popular State Street Gold ETF (Symbol: GLD) as a proxy for gold during the past five years (which is the longest period of data available from Morningstar). Notice that the returns before and after taxes are identical. This is because the fund is not generating taxable events internally (no interest, no dividends, and no capital gains). Investors will pay taxes individually on their gains when they sell shares of the fund, but these taxable events are not reflected in Morningstar's results. The only caveat is that some ETFs require special tax handling in how they pay their expenses. We recommend visiting the ETF website and reading their prospectus on tax issues.

Gains from gold ETFs may be taxed at the collectibles rate. Gains from closed-end gold funds can be taxed as long-term capital gains, as discussed earlier with the filing of the correct IRS forms. If you hold physical gold, you will also not owe any taxes on it until you make a sale that results in a gain. However, the gains from the sale of physical gold bullion are subject to the collectibles tax rates and not the lower rates on long-term capital gains. The Permanent Portfolio's design makes the most of gold's tax efficiency by engaging in infrequent transactions within the portfolio.

The discussion of gold and taxes assumes your gold holdings are not within a tax-deferred account. If you have room in a tax-deferred account after making your allocations to bonds, cash, and stocks, a *portion* (but not all) of your gold holdings can be placed within it. This will have to be in the form of a gold fund or gold bullion if it is an Individual Retirement Account that holds American Eagle gold coins (see the discussion below for more information about gold bullion in tax-deferred accounts). A gold allocation within a tax-deferred account (even if small) can help reduce the tax effects if you sell gold at a profit during a future rebalancing of the portfolio.

**GOLD AND EMERGENCIES**  If you choose to place a portion of your gold holdings in a tax-deferred account, you should still keep some of it in a form that can be easily accessed in an emergency, just like a portion of your cash holdings. You never know when you might need to have quick access to your gold in an emergency. If you did find yourself in such a situation, you wouldn't want to have a lot of people and institutions standing between you and your gold. Of course, we all hope to never find ourselves in such a situation, but history shows that people are frequently caught by surprise at how quickly the world can change. Unfortunately, disasters don't provide notice for you to contact your broker before they occur.

## Retirement Accounts and the Permanent Portfolio

While it is not possible to cover every type of retirement account in which an investor may hold assets, most U.S. investors have some combination of a 401(k) plan account through an employer and one or more Individual Retirement Accounts (IRAs). The discussion below addresses some of the opportunities and challenges involved in using the Permanent Portfolio strategy with these types of accounts.

### 401(k) Plans

Most private sector employers offer 401(k) plans. These plans have exploded in popularity in recent years for a variety of reasons, including employers' desire to shift investment and longevity risk to employees (a traditional defined benefit pension plan puts these risks on the shoulders of the employer). Another factor in the popularity of 401(k) plans is Wall Street's desire to sell the idea that everyone can get rich from investing if they are just given the right tools. The reality is that 401(k) plans present investors with the same challenges that they face in other investment accounts.

In the same way that the Permanent Portfolio can provide an investor with a welcome sense of safety and stability in his taxable accounts, it can also help to make a 401(k) account safer and more secure. One of the problems with many 401(k) plans, however, is that the investment lineups from which participants must choose are normally made up primarily of stock funds with a handful of bond funds included almost as an afterthought. While the typical 401(k) plan usually won't have funds that cover all of the components of the Permanent Portfolio (i.e., stocks, bonds, cash, and gold), a 401(k) account can be combined with other taxable and tax-deferred accounts to create an overall portfolio that meets the Permanent Portfolio's specifications.

**STOCKS IN A 401(K) ACCOUNT**  In the past, many 401(k) plans only offered actively managed stock funds, but in recent years virtually all 401(k) plans have started offering basic low-cost S&P 500 index funds, which work perfectly well for the stock portion of the Permanent Portfolio.

If your plan does not offer a stock index fund, then look for a fund within the plan's investment lineup that invests in the U.S. stock market using a broadly based strategy (avoid sector funds) and stays invested in stocks 100 percent of the time without market timing. In general:

1. Make sure the fund charges the lowest management fee of your available options.
2. Select a fund that is 100 percent invested in stocks at all times and provides the broadest possible exposure to the entire stock market.
3. Check the funds on Morningstar and see what their annual turnover is. High turnover in a fund is a red flag indicating active management that can result in lower performance. Try to avoid these funds if you can. This topic is discussed in more detail in Chapter 6.

**CASH IN A 401(K) ACCOUNT** Since virtually no 401(k) plans offer short-term Treasury funds, a 401(k) investor is usually going to have to compromise a bit with the Permanent Portfolio's cash allocation. Of course, if your 401(k) plan does offer a short-term treasury fund then use it for your cash holdings, though you should read the fund's prospectus to find out how it actually invests its assets (many "Treasury" funds actually own a lot of non-Treasury assets).

Here are some guidelines to use in selecting a fund from your 401(k) plan's lineup for your cash allocation:

1. Avoid funds that are offered in a plan that involve interest-rate risk (i.e., the fund can lose money when interest rates rise), which is inappropriate for the cash piece of the Permanent Portfolio. You need the fund that holds your cash to be very stable. This means that you don't want to buy any fund with an average maturity over three years, since funds with longer average maturities are subject to more interest rate risk. If possible, choose a fund with an average maturity of less than one year.
2. Try to select a fund with a low expense ratio and as little manager discretion as possible regarding the way the fund's assets are invested.
3. Most 401(k) plans offer a so-called "stable value fund", which can be a good choice for your cash allocation. Stable value funds are designed to offer modest returns with little or no risk of loss of principal. However, they do have counterparty risk that is not present with investments in Treasury bills.
4. If you choose to use the stable value fund in your 401(k) plan for the cash portion of your Permanent Portfolio, make sure to read the fund's prospectus and make sure you understand the risks involved with the fund. Be aware that any fund that is not invested in 100 percent (or near 100 percent) Treasury bills carries more risk.

**BONDS IN A 401(K) ACCOUNT** In general, 401(k) plans tend not to offer bond funds with long average maturities. While the Permanent Portfolio's bond allocation calls for treasury bonds with at least 20 years to maturity, most 401(k) plans tend to offer bond funds with average maturities of only 5 to 10 years. Additionally, these funds tend to hold only a small amount of their assets in Treasuries (if any). In other words, virtually no 401(k) plan is going to include a suitable long-term Treasury bond fund for use with the Permanent Portfolio.

In light of the limited availability of long-term Treasury bond options in most 401(k) plans, here are a few suggestions:

1. Ask your employer to add a long-term Treasury bond index fund to the plan's investment lineup (it can't hurt to ask).
2. If your only option is a fund that holds intermediate Treasuries (such as 7 to 10 year maturity) then hold more of that fund and less in your cash allocation. For instance, consider buying 35 percent of the intermediate bond fund and 15 percent in cash. By increasing the allocation to intermediate-term Treasuries and reducing the cash allocation, it can cause the overall portfolio to behave similarly to a portfolio with equal parts cash and long-term Treasury bonds.
3. If you do not have access to a fund that holds long-term Treasuries, try to find one that only holds very high-quality corporate bonds with long maturities.
4. Try to use a fund that keeps a *constant* maturity. This means that if the fund states it is 10-year average maturity you don't want to wake up one day to find the manager has shifted the bonds down to one-year maturity. You want to avoid any fund where a manager can move around the fund's assets trying to outguess the markets.

If none of the options above provides a workable solution for your Permanent Portfolio bond allocation, review the brokerage window discussion that follows. Some brokerage windows offer the option to purchase long-term Treasury funds or to directly purchase Treasury bonds for your 401(k) plan account. If you have access to a brokerage window, find out what assets it allows you to purchase.

**GOLD IN A 401(K) ACCOUNT**   Virtually no 401(k) plans will offer a suitable bullion fund for the Permanent Portfolio's gold allocation. Be aware that precious metals and mining funds are *not* a substitute for a gold bullion fund. However, the lack of gold bullion options within a 401(k) plan is less problematic when you consider that gold is the most suitable of the portfolio's assets for holdings outside of tax-deferred retirement accounts.

If you do have access to an acceptable gold bullion fund in your 401(k) plan (again, *not* a precious metals and mining stocks fund), then you can use it for a portion of your gold allocation.

**401(K) PLAN BROKERAGE WINDOWS—A SOLUTION?** Understanding the 401(k) plan limitations described above, one excellent (and often overlooked) tool offered in some plans is known as a "brokerage window". A brokerage window allows a 401(k) participant to bypass the plan's normal investment lineup and instead access a much wider range of investment options, almost as if the 401(k) plan account was an investment account with a brokerage company.

> Most brokerage windows in 401(k) plans are only utilized by a handful of employees. In many 401(k) plans there is almost no mention of the brokerage window option in any of the plan's documentation.

Most brokerage windows in 401(k) plans are only utilized by a handful of employees. In many 401(k) plans there is almost no mention of the brokerage window option in any of the plan's documentation. Brokerage windows are normally not heavily advertised due to a combination of factors. First, the plan sponsor does not want participants to take excessive risk with their accounts, and brokerage windows are often used by 401(k) plan participants to take greater risk than what is offered in the plan's regular investment lineup. Second (and more likely), the plan's fund provider wants as much of the assets as possible to be invested in the *provider's* investment products. The fees on these products are how the plan provider makes its money.

If your plan's documentation doesn't say anything about a brokerage window, it is still useful to ask your plan administrator about it (many plans that don't appear to have brokerage windows actually *do*).

If a brokerage window is available in your plan, and there are not too many restrictions on its use (some brokerage windows only permit some types of funds to be purchased), an investor can easily set up an all-ETF Permanent Portfolio within his 401(k) plan account, using the same approach discussed in Chapter 10 for putting together a fund-based Permanent Portfolio.

## Individual Retirement Accounts

Individual Retirement Accounts (IRAs) are self-directed retirement savings accounts that provide favorable tax treatment. IRAs typically allow an investor to choose from most ETFs, mutual funds and individual stocks available through a brokerage company, so setting up an all-ETF or mutual fund Permanent Portfolio with an IRA is easy to do.

There are two basic types of IRAs: Traditional and Roth (with some variants, such as SEP-IRAs). The main difference between them is that Traditional IRAs allow you to deposit funds before taxes (and deduct them from your income) and pay taxes on withdrawals once you reach a certain age and begin taking distributions. Roth IRAs, on the other hand, involve the contribution of funds that have already been taxed, but future earnings on these contributions are not subject to any additional taxation and future withdrawals after retirement age are tax-free.

Whether an investor uses a Traditional or Roth IRA, the basic approach to setting up a Permanent Portfolio in an IRA will be the same. The decision on which one to use is highly dependent on your own particular situation, including your taxable income, future expectations of tax rates, and so on. If you are unsure which is best for your situation you should review your options with a tax advisor.

Once you have opened an IRA, you can set up the portfolio as outlined in Chapter 10. These assets will simply reside in your IRA account instead of a taxable account.

## Gold and IRAs

The IRS allows American Eagle gold bullion coins to be deposited into qualified custodian IRA accounts. Given the hassle and potential expense involved with this option, however, it's not clear that there is an advantage rather than just using one of the gold bullion funds that are available.

> Holding gold in an IRA is for convenience, not safety.

Whether you use a gold bullion IRA or a gold fund held in an IRA, in both cases you are isolated from the gold asset by the custodian or fund provider, so similar risks are present in each method. Holding gold in an IRA is for convenience, not safety. As noted above, it's always a good idea to keep some gold outside of your tax-deferred accounts for emergencies.

## Creditor Protection

Individual Retirement Accounts and 401(k) plan accounts provide some protection from the claims of creditors. 401(k) plan accounts are protected from the claims of creditors by a federal law known as ERISA, while IRAs are protected from the claims of creditors based upon laws that vary from state to state. Thus, in addition to providing tax advantages, retirement accounts can also offer lawsuit and creditor protection under certain circumstances.

You should contact an attorney who is familiar with the laws of the state in which you live for more information regarding the scope of creditor protection offered by various types of retirement accounts. However, this is one additional benefit of using tax-deferred accounts for a portion of your savings.

## Pensions, Social Security, and Other Plans

If your employer offers a traditional pension plan, count yourself lucky. These plans are becoming less and less common and those who have benefits under them often don't realize how valuable a lifetime stream of income really is. Similarly, Social Security provides what is essentially a small pension benefit to workers who pay into the system long enough to qualify. However, the future of traditional pension plans and even Social Security is uncertain. The Permanent Portfolio can give peace of mind to an investor who is concerned about these types of programs by providing a nest egg that is completely independent of any other retirement plan or government program.

Any retirement benefits you are entitled to under pension plans or other arrangements (such as an annuity) should be kept separate from your Permanent Portfolio. The reason is that a monthly payment for life is not the type of asset that can be incorporated into a rebalancing strategy. Plus, it's hard to tell how much a monthly benefit is worth when compared to the rest of a Permanent Portfolio. Finally, there are many possible future scenarios under which Social Security benefits could be paid out at lower levels than workers are currently expecting (or maybe not at all). Likewise, pension plans can run into trouble if they aren't managed properly, which can lead to the reduced availability of distribution options.

The best approach is to simply treat your Permanent Portfolio as a separate pool of assets from any pension or Social Security benefits to which you may be entitled. A Permanent Portfolio should be viewed as insurance against something that might go wrong in the future with a pension plan or government-provided retirement benefit such as Social Security.

## Tax-Loss Harvesting

If you have a significant portion of your investments in taxable accounts, you may want to explore the option of using "tax-loss harvesting" to write off losses within your portfolio and boost your portfolio's overall tax efficiency.

Tax-loss harvesting is based on the concept that if you have a loss in an asset, you can sell the asset and recognize the loss for tax purposes. The losses you recognize in one asset can then be used to offset gains you may have in another asset. You can write off a fixed amount of your losses every year until the losses are depleted, or use them all at once to offset gains in any particular year.

For example, assume that in one year you own a stock fund and it drops in value by $10,000. You sell it and lock in the $10,000 loss. Next, you generate gains in bonds of $10,000 due to rebalancing. Normally, you would owe taxes on the $10,000 bond gain. However, since you have a loss of $10,000 from the stocks, you can apply it against your bond fund gain of $10,000 to provide a net gain of $0.

In other words, you would owe *no taxes* as a result of combining the tax effects of the two transactions. If you have no gains to offset (say you didn't rebalance) you can still write off a fixed amount of loss each year until it reaches zero (currently $3,000 per year maximum). While this is a simple example to illustrate the concept, in certain markets the potential exists for this strategy to help absorb much of the blow of taxes on the overall portfolio.

## Tax-Loss Harvesting Is Harder on Long-Term Assets

While tax-loss harvesting sounds like a useful strategy, there are some issues to consider. First, the longer you hold an asset the less chance there is that it will have an actual loss. Over long periods stocks, bonds, cash, and gold all tend to rise in value. Thus, apart from a *major* crash in an asset's value, it is unlikely that you would be able to harvest losses from an asset that you have held for many years. However, for assets that you have only owned for a short time, there are sometimes opportunities to take advantage of losses in one or more of your asset classes.

## Wash Sales

When reviewing opportunities to engage in tax loss harvesting, you must be aware of *wash sales*. The IRS defines a wash sale as selling an asset for a loss and then buying the *same asset* back again within 30 days. Losses generated by wash sales are not deductible. For example, assume that you own the Vanguard Total Stock Market index fund and sell it for a loss of $10,000 on the first of the month and then buy it back on the twenty-eighth. That would be a wash sale because you sold the asset and bought it back within 30 days. Under the wash sale rules, you would not be permitted to recognize the losses from this transaction on your taxes. However, if you had waited until the thirty-first day after the sale to buy back the asset, the tax loss would be perfectly valid.

Being forced to sit out of an asset class for 31 days does introduce the risk to your portfolio of missing out on market gains in that asset class.

However, using tax-loss harvesting in conjunction with a portfolio rebalancing can be a useful tool for minimizing the overall tax effects from rebalancing your portfolio. There are some strategies that recommend swapping similar (but not identical) funds in lieu of waiting the 31 days to keep from missing big moves in the market. However, it is least likely to cause problems if you simply wait 31 days before buying an asset back if you want to take advantage of the tax-loss harvesting rules.

**WASH SALES AND DIVIDEND REINVESTMENT**  Dividend reinvestment was discussed earlier as something you generally do *not* want in your portfolio. For a taxable investor seeking to take advantage of the tax-loss harvesting rules, dividend reinvestment can cause a specific problem if the reinvestment happens during the waiting period following a sale. Such a dividend reinvestment counts as a purchase and will trigger a wash sale! For example, assume that you sell your fund on the first of the month and plan to wait 31 days before repurchase. On the fifteenth of the month, a dividend is issued on your remaining shares in the fund and it is automatically used to buy shares of the same exact fund. That's a wash sale and the loss harvest cannot be used!

When determining the potential usefulness of tax-loss harvesting or any other tax-management strategy, it is recommended that you seek the advice of a qualified tax professional. Everyone's situation is different and these strategies may not be a good fit for every investor.

## Final Thoughts on Taxes

Although specific opportunities for tax savings vary by state and country, the general principles are going to be the same:

- Interest and dividend payments present constant tax challenges. Sheltering this income from taxation is a tremendous benefit.
- Capital gains are normally not taxed until a sale occurs, which allows you to control when you recognize a gain on an asset that has gone up in value.
- Tax-deferred accounts should be used for the least tax-efficient assets first. Assets should go into tax-sheltered accounts in the following order: bonds, cash, stocks, and gold.
- Keep some of your cash and gold outside of tax-deferred accounts for emergencies.
- Keeping some of your cash and gold inside tax-deferred accounts can allow you to rebalance the portfolio without triggering current taxation of overall portfolio gains.

Over the years tax laws will change and every investor's individual tax situation is unique. Please consult a qualified tax professional to determine the best way to apply the strategies outlined in this chapter to your portfolio.

## Recap

Taxes can absorb a significant portion of your annual investment returns without effective tax planning. Sensible use of tax-planning opportunities such as tax-deferred retirement accounts can protect your assets and allow them to grow more quickly over time.

Since bonds and cash are usually the least tax efficient Permanent Portfolio asset classes, you should try to put them into your tax-deferred accounts first. Next, you can place your stocks into your tax-deferred account if you still have room. However, a broadly based total stock market index fund is relatively tax-efficient when held in a taxable account if you don't have room for it in a tax-deferred account.

Gold is the most tax-efficient Permanent Portfolio asset since it does not pay interest or dividends. Also, you can delay the recognition of capital gains by not selling until rebalancing is needed. These two factors suggest that gold should go into your tax-deferred accounts last. Even then, putting all your gold into your tax-deferred accounts is not recommended in case you need to access it in an emergency. Also, keep some cash outside of tax-deferred accounts for emergencies as well. You may consider keeping at least a portion of each asset class in tax-deferred accounts to facilitate tax-free portfolio rebalancing.

Each individual's tax situation is different. Consult a qualified tax professional regarding your specific situation to identify all relevant tax planning opportunities.

CHAPTER 14

# Institutional Diversification

The Permanent Portfolio encourages investors to obtain maximum diversification in terms of economics and market environments (i.e., prosperity, recession, inflation, and deflation) and avoid risks where it doesn't add to the bottom line. These goals are achieved by splitting assets in the portfolio among the four asset classes in ways that will enable the growth *and* protection of your wealth.

Unfortunately, there are also risks to your wealth outside of what the markets are doing. These risks can show up in the form of institutional failures, manager incompetence and outright fraud to name just a few.

These risks fall outside of the typical metrics used by academics and many investment advisors to gauge a portfolio's diversification and performance. Yet, these risks can affect an investor's wealth just as seriously as more conventional risks, and sometimes more so. For instance, what's the point of trying to chase an extra 1 percent gain a year if a fund manager is taking risks behind the scenes that could cause a 50 percent loss if he makes a mistake? Or what about a problem at your brokerage that locks all customers out of their accounts for a period of time? Spreadsheets and financial models don't show these risks but it doesn't mean they can't show up at any moment.

This chapter describes ways of mitigating these extra-market risks through institutional diversification.

## What Is Institutional Diversification?

Institutional diversification simply means dividing your money among several funds, brokerages, banks, and other institutions to diversify against risks from the people and organizations holding and managing your assets.

This approach may seem overly cautious, but it is not. Financial history is filled with examples of strong banks going broke, fund companies mismanaging assets, and trustees proving untrustworthy. Diversification against these types of events just makes good sense.

## Why Institutional Diversification?

In the United States there are strict laws, regulations, and insurance in place to prevent the loss of assets by customers in the event of a bank, brokerage, or mutual fund company failure. These protections allow individual investors to have a degree of confidence that their assets will be protected in case the worst comes to pass.

Just because laws are in place, however, doesn't mean that your assets can't become entangled in a problem at an institution. In some cases, funds could be subject to limited access for an extended period of time while regulators and/or courts sort things out. In the worst cases, some kinds of failures can lead to either partial reimbursement or a total loss.

As much as the government may attempt to provide comprehensive protection against all calamities, no such system is ever truly airtight. Below is an overview of some of these threats.

## Exceeding Insurance Limits

One reason to have multiple brokerage accounts is to keep your account balances below the Securities Investor Protection Corporation (SIPC) limits, which are currently capped at $500,000 total (and $250,000 in cash). The SIPC is an insurance program similar to the FDIC in some respects, but it differs in important ways.

SIPC will protect assets in a brokerage account that are missing due to fraud or theft by the broker. It does not, however, protect you against investment losses due to normal market fluctuations or manager mistakes, nor does it protect certain types of assets such as commodity futures contracts. The SIPC website has more information on what protection it offers and how investors can be sure they are covered (www.sipc.org). Using different brokerages is one way to allow you to maintain full coverage when your accounts reach a certain threshold.

With the above said, many brokerages also carry insurance that covers other risks or adds to the existing SIPC limits. Spreading your money across two or more brokerages makes it more likely that you will remain below the limits of any other insurance coverage that may be provided by a financial institution. Since this varies by brokerage, it is a good idea to inquire about what insurance your particular provider has for customer assets.

## Manager Mistakes and Incompetence

As outlined in Chapters 6 through 9, a fund company can manage money in a completely legal manner, but still rack up large losses due to manager mistakes. For example, the cash chapter went over some money market funds that experienced tremendous losses during the 2008 market crash when managers took on too much risk. Stock and bond funds have had similar experiences when a manager made a risky bet that simply didn't turn out well.

The problem is that insurance coverage and government regulations will not protect you from these kinds of losses if they should happen. It is viewed simply as market risk and it is the investor's burden. This is true even if the fund managers are the ones responsible for risky behaviors that caused the problem. It may be that a fund company could compensate investors in the event of a very bad problem in one of their funds, but it is also true that they may not (and probably won't).

Although this risk is mitigated by using low-cost index funds and by following the advice outlined in this book, such risks have even shown up in very well regarded funds (Vanguard's Total Bond Market fund undershot their index in 2002 due to manager mistakes for instance). The simplest way to diversify against fund manager mistakes is to split your money among

different fund companies to protect yourself against problems that may occur in any one of them.

## Failure and Fraud

**MF GLOBAL** As discussed in Chapter 9 on Gold, in 2011 MF Global collapsed
almost overnight and defrauded investors by using their assets in ways not
authorized and clearly against the law. When MF Global's insolvency came
to light, customers found their assets frozen as multiple parties laid claim to
them (MF Global had apparently used customers' assets as collateral for their
own trades, among other activities). As of 2012, many of MF Global's
customers are still waiting for these matters to be resolved and they could
be waiting for years more. Many customers may only get back pennies on
the dollar if they get anything at all.

Figure 14.1 is a clipping from one of MF Global's marketing brochures
about customers' custody accounts. This brochure talked about the separation of customers' assets from those of the firm. This separation apparently
didn't prevent the accounts from being used inappropriately, however. *The
Street* reports:

> *MF Global is still missing an estimated $600 million more than a week
> after it filed for bankruptcy, and at least one high-profile accounting
> expert said Wednesday he is beginning to sense fraud may be the
> explanation.*
>
> *"My concern is that at the very end as things got very dire, as liquid-
> ity dried up, that you had some people in collusion go in and commit
> fraud here and I don't know that that did occur, but that's what it's*

**Stability**
Stability based on 225 years of experience.

**Separation**
Strict physical separation of client assets from
MF Global accounts.

**Protection**
FDIC insurance for all clients with assets
deposited into banks via MF Global.

SIPC insurance for all clients with securities
accounts.

**FIGURE 14.1  MF global marketing brochure about separation of customers' assets.**

*starting to smell like," Lynn Turner, former chief accountant at the Securities and Exchange Commission told* Bloomberg Television Wednesday . . .*

*. . . "It's amazing that we're sitting here today trying to find out today what happened with $600 million," Turner said. "It's like it just vanished into thin air and the fact that people today can't tell us where the $600 million went is not a good sign. The fact that they were held in custodial accounts that someone should have been on top of only further complicates the issue and makes it even more concerning."*[1]

**BEAR STEARNS AND LEHMAN BROTHERS**   During the credit crisis and market panic of 2008, there were some very notable failures among prominent financial institutions. Following the failure of Bear Stearns earlier in the year, the 160-year-old firm Lehman Brothers folded almost overnight as many bad investments seemed to turn sour all at once. Investors exposed to Bear Stearns and Lehman Brothers debt took tremendous losses, while customers with accounts at these institutions faced a variety of risks and sleepless nights as events unfolded.

## Identity Theft

Criminals have become incredibly sophisticated in their efforts to steal and access investment and/or bank accounts of individuals. There are a variety of ways this type of fraud can occur, from theft of account statements and other correspondence from the mail to sophisticated electronic theft of account information credentials. Sadly, identity theft often doesn't even happen with anonymous criminals but relatives, caregivers, and others with close intimate knowledge of the victim. Brokerages and banks normally carry insurance and have policies to deal with these events, but it could take some time to clear up such a mess if it should happen to you.

If you spread your money across more than one institution it reduces the likelihood that *all* of your assets would be affected by a single act of identity theft. Furthermore, if a portion of your assets were ever the subject of a criminal fraud, having access to assets at another institution could provide you with needed funds while you worked with law enforcement and the institution where the fraud occurred to resolve the matter.

---

[1] Dan Freed, "MF Global 'Starting to Smell Like' Fraud: Ex-SEC Accounting Chief," *The Street*, November 9, 2011, www.thestreet.com/story/11305806/1/mf-global-starting -to-smell-like-fraud-ex-sec-accounting-chief.html.

## Natural Disasters

Hurricanes, earthquakes, tsunamis, and other natural disasters are also a threat to financial institutions and the data centers where customer information is located. Most financial institutions have multiple backup "hot sites" to handle these and other emergencies. A hot site is a backup data center that is ready to come online at a moment's notice. The idea is that a company encountering a data breach or loss of data will be able to continue operations if the main data center should experience a problem.

The reality, though, is that account access can be affected in many different ways by a natural disaster. It's one thing to have a hot site backup data center. It's another thing when the *people* that handle the day-to-day operations of the company can't manage it any more due to their local situation. In other words, until a company is able to figure out a way to put in a backup CEO, board of directors, managers, and employees in hot-spare status the company will be subject to risks from natural disasters, no matter how much redundancy there is in the data systems.

## Terrorism

The perpetrators behind the September 11, 2001, terrorist attacks stated that the viciousness of the attack was designed to not only strike a symbolic blow, but also to disrupt the financial operations of Wall Street and impact the U.S. economy. Wall Street was, in fact, shut down for a week following the tragedy as the nation absorbed the scale of the destruction.

Events such as 9/11 can never be fully anticipated and protected against. Investors can, however, reduce the likelihood of losing all access to funds during an emergency by having accounts at more than one institution and preferably not all based in the same major financial center.

## Cyber Attack

Beyond the threat posed by terrorism to buildings and infrastructure, various online groups and governments have stated intentions to target stock exchanges electronically in cyber-warfare operations. In many cases, the damage that can be done through an electronic attack on a computer network can exceed the damage done by targeting a physical structure. For example, virtually all of Wall Street's records are in electronic form and a computer system attack could cause serious problems, including potentially large financial losses.

The financial networks of the world are interconnected in a relatively fragile way. A problem in the trading systems of one firm can cause a cascade effect in the world markets. In spring of 2010 the U.S. stock markets experienced a "Flash Crash" during which the Dow Jones stock index sunk by 1,000 points within five minutes before quickly recovering. During this time, automated trading systems piled on sell orders, making the problem escalate quickly before finally coming back under control (some investors who had set stop losses in their accounts took large losses as they were automatically traded out of positions that recovered almost immediately and other bad trades were later backed out and canceled).

The Flash Crash was reportedly caused by a combination of automated and high-frequency trading systems gone awry. However, if such an event can occur by *accident*, it could certainly occur again as a part of a *deliberate* attack.

By dividing your money among different institutions you have a better chance of accessing at least some of your funds if any of these events were to occur. Financial firms have a diverse set of systems, each of which are unique to the firm that created it. A wide-scale attack taking down all firms at once is not very likely, but taking down one firm, at least for a short period, is plausible.

Craig has a lot of real-world experience in computer security: "Early in my career I worked at a network security auditor. I was paid to break into computer networks and did work at financial firms, among others. While banks and financial institutions obviously have safeguards in place to prevent problems, it is always possible that a very knowledgeable outsider or (more likely) an insider could cause trouble.

"When you spread your money between at least two institutions it is unlikely that they are going to share the same infrastructure and each will have their own security policies, protections, and procedures. The diverse set of hardware, software, and internal controls between companies works in your favor against the likelihood of a single attack taking down multiple institutions at once. Do yourself a favor and spread your money outside of just one company to be safe."

## How to Divide Your Money

Institutional diversification is not difficult to accomplish and most investors are probably at least halfway there already. The most basic approach to institutional diversification is to simply have accounts with at least two brokerages or mutual fund companies and split your funds between them more or less evenly.

### Tax-Deferred Accounts

If you have an IRA or other tax-deferred account at one institution, you can open up an account at another company. Once you have opened up the new account you can simply transfer a portion of the account(s) to the new institution. Check with your broker for the forms and process to perform such a transfer. If done properly, such a transfer will not trigger any tax consequences.

## Taxable Accounts

If you have a taxable account you can transfer shares to another brokerage without incurring capital gains on assets that have appreciated in value since their purchase. Your brokerage will have the details on how to initiate a transfer of shares in this manner. The shares will simply be deposited at your new brokerage account and no taxes will be due because no sale has taken place. Contact your brokerage and ask them about transferring a portion of your shares to another brokerage and how to go about it. The process varies by company, but it is not a difficult thing to do.

## Fund Diversification

In addition to diversifying across institutions, it's a good idea to do it across fund providers as well as discussed in Chapter 10, Implementation. This type of diversification is achieved by not owning funds that are all provided by the same company. Split your money among different fund companies to be safe.

> Split your money among different fund companies to be safe.

For example, don't own just Vanguard funds when you can easily purchase shares of funds offered by Vanguard and another company like iShares. This approach is not to suggest that there is anything wrong with any particular fund provider (both Vanguard and iShares have good reputations), it's just a nod to financial history that unpredictable events can happen anytime and anywhere even to the best companies.

# Recap

The idea behind institutional diversification is to simply split your money among more than one bank, brokerage, or fund provider. This can protect against threats including fraud, incompetence, identity theft, natural disasters, cyber attack, terrorism, or other future unknown calamities.

While keeping all of your money at one bank or brokerage is often the simplest approach for many investors, financial history suggests that splitting it up among institutions is a good idea. When splitting your money, pick at least two brokerages you are comfortable with and use them to hold funds appropriate to the Permanent Portfolio. It is also a good idea to use funds from different companies to build your portfolio to diversify against manager risk in the funds.

If you have a tax-deferred account you can transfer part of your funds to a second provider with no tax consequences. Contact your provider for more information. Likewise, taxable funds can also be transferred to a second broker with no tax effects. The fund assets will simply be transferred into the new account. Contact your broker for the specific steps involved in this process.

# CHAPTER 15

# Geographic Diversification

An important element of the Permanent Portfolio strategy involves keeping some money outside of the country where you live. This chapter will go over the reasons why geographic diversification is a good idea and present some options to do it safely and conveniently in today's environment.

## Then and Now

When Harry Browne was writing, his advice for geographic diversification was to own gold coins in segregated storage in a Swiss bank. This advice was once relatively simple to implement and Swiss banks offered low minimums and were willing to accept customers with nothing more than a letter, deposit check, and basic information.

Sadly, the above situation no longer exists and a wider number of options and more creative strategies need to be considered, even if they do not perfectly fall in line with Browne's original recommendations. These new options each have pros and cons.

The topic of geographic diversification could be a book by itself, so all possibilities cannot be covered. However, we present several very viable options for the smallest up to the largest Permanent Portfolio amounts. It was important for the authors to present a wide number of easy and safe ways to achieve geographic diversification, even if it did not meet the ideal (which is no longer easily accomplished). Readers will need to decide which method achieves the right amount of geographic diversification to meet their individual needs.

## What Is Geographic Diversification?

Geographic diversification means simply holding some of your wealth outside of the country where you live. This type of diversification protects against the most extreme risks that an investor is likely to face. Such risks can appear in the form of anything—from major natural disasters that disrupt the financial markets regionally, to government actions aimed at confiscating property held within the nation's borders.

The purpose of geographic diversification is *not* hiding money from tax collectors, which is illegal. The purpose of having some of your wealth outside of the country where you live is to give you *options* to deal with certain extreme events if they should occur.

## What Assets Should Be Kept in a Foreign Account?

Physical gold is the best asset to keep in a foreign account for the following reasons:

- It is easily stored.
- It doesn't pay interest or dividends so there are fewer accounting issues.
- It rarely needs to be rebalanced.
- It is the most liquid asset in a true emergency.

Keeping other assets in a foreign account rarely offers any benefits. There are usually higher taxes, more accounting issues, and likely less liquidity in an emergency. Of the four Permanent Portfolio assets, gold simply works the best for geographic diversification.

## Why Geographic Diversification?

### Terrorism

As Chapter 14 on Institutional Diversification touched upon, by having some of your wealth in another country it is protected against terrorist incidents at home (especially if that incident is designed to impact the financial centers of your home country). In the United States, many large banks and brokerages are based in the New York City region, which has been targeted multiple times for terrorist attack. Other industrialized countries have similar concentrations of financial services firms in a handful of large cities. A major disaster in any of these locations is almost guaranteed to make accessing assets in an emergency difficult.

### Natural Disasters

Natural disasters that affect the financial centers of the United States could disrupt operations in many ways. Such threats were discussed in Chapter 14 as well. Having a portion of your wealth in a foreign location makes the likelihood very low of a natural disaster affecting all of your wealth at once.

## Government Confiscation

Governments have been known to react to emergencies by confiscating assets and/or implementing capital controls to prevent assets from leaving the country. It has even happened in the United States, with a sweeping gold confiscation in 1933 that was followed by controls on gold ownership that lasted until 1974. Other countries have implemented capital controls to prevent investors from removing assets from within a country's borders, nationalizing assets, and/or freezing bank accounts of all citizens.

**1933 U.S. GOLD SEIZURE** The clipping in Figure 15.1 is from the *New York Times* in 1933. It shows the Secretary of the Treasury offering a less-than-

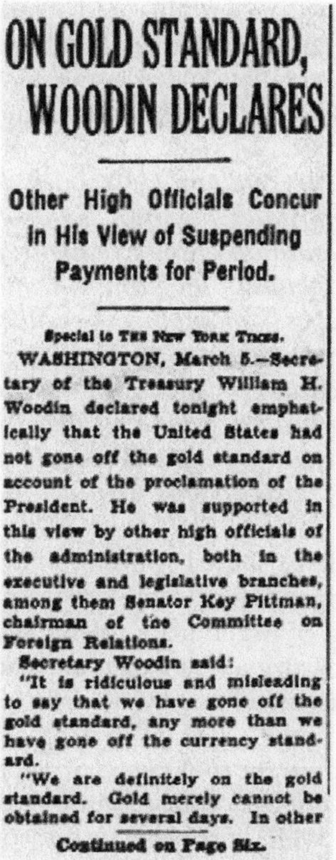

# ON GOLD STANDARD, WOODIN DECLARES

### Other High Officials Concur in His View of Suspending Payments for Period.

*Special to* THE NEW YORK TIMES.

WASHINGTON, March 5.—Secretary of the Treasury William H. Woodin declared tonight emphatically that the United States had not gone off the gold standard on account of the proclamation of the President. He was supported in this view by other high officials of the administration, both in the executive and legislative branches, among them Senator Key Pittman, chairman of the Committee on Foreign Relations.

Secretary Woodin said:

"It is ridiculous and misleading to say that we have gone off the gold standard, any more than we have gone off the currency standard.

"We are definitely on the gold standard. Gold merely cannot be obtained for several days. In other

Continued on Page Six.

**FIGURE 15.1** A clipping from the *New York Times* in March 1933 shows the Secretary of the Treasury misrepresenting Roosevelt's gold confiscation policy.

truthful (actually, he was flat-out lying) explanation of the illegal gold seizure order by Franklin D. Roosevelt in an effort to delay reactions by citizens. Roosevelt's gold seizure order prohibited conversion of paper notes into gold, as had been promised by the Treasury (which was effectively a U.S. government default). It also prohibited general storage of gold bullion by Americans.

> Although Secretary of the Treasury Woodin claimed that "Gold merely cannot be obtained for several days," the reality was that U.S. citizens wouldn't be able to obtain gold legally for the next 40 years (until 1974).

Although Secretary of the Treasury Woodin claimed that "Gold merely cannot be obtained for several days," the reality was that U.S. citizens wouldn't be able to obtain gold legally for the next 40 years (until 1974). The effect of this action was to end the gold standard for Americans, even though it did nothing to ease the effects of the Great Depression. All it did was usher in an era of price inflation that continues to this day. Here is what the *New York Times*, in March 1933, reported, as quoted from Figure 15.1:

> *Secretary of the Treasury William H. Woodin declared tonight emphatically that the United States had not gone off the gold standard on account of the proclamation of the President. He was supported in this view by other high officials of the administration, both in the executive and legislative branches. Among them Senator Key Pittman, chairman of the Committee on Foreign Relations. Secretary Woodin said: "It is ridiculous and misleading to say that we have gone off the gold standard, any more than we have gone off the currency standard. We are definitely on the gold standard.* **Gold merely cannot be obtained for several days.***" (Emphasis added)*

**ARGENTINA'S LITTLE CORRAL**   Other countries have more recently implemented capital controls right before confiscating citizens' assets. In 2001, for example, the government of Argentina implemented the *corralito* ("The Little Corral"). The *corralito* froze all bank accounts and devalued the peso by 66 percent. Citizens there saw almost two-thirds of their life savings vanish overnight.[1]

Some Argentinians thought they were protected by holding accounts inside the country that were denominated in U.S. dollar and euro assets instead of the peso. They were surprised to find out that part of the bank freeze was also a government decree that those accounts be converted to

---

[1] Argentina's 2001 *Corralito*, http://en.wikipedia.org/wiki/Corralito.

the peso before the devaluation, ensuring that *they* lost 66 percent of their life savings as well. Only citizens who had some assets outside the country had any protection against these policies.[2]

**IT'S FOR YOUR OWN GOOD** Argentina returned to this type of action in 2008, when it announced that private retirement funds within the country were to be seized by the government (for the protection of the citizens, of course). The *Wall Street Journal* reported:

> *Argentine President Cristina Kirchner announced this week that her government intends to nationalize the country's private pension system. If Congress approves this property grab, $30 billion in individually held retirement accounts—think 401(k)s—managed by private pension funds will become government property.*
>
> *That the state could seize retirement savings no doubt seems outrageous to Americans. But it is a predictable development in a country where government intervention in the financial system is the norm. With Washington now expanding its role as guarantor in American banking, that's something to think about.[3]*

Even if you believe that the current leaders in power are the best in the world and would never take such actions, how about the leaders five years from now? Or ten? The reality is that emergencies can happen in any country at any time and with little warning. Waiting to move property outside the gates when they are closing is simply not going to work. Assets need to be in a safe location *well before* trouble occurs.

## War and Civil Disorder

While we like to think that a war or major civil disorder will never happen within our own borders, history teaches that these events can break out anywhere, no matter how peaceful or prosperous a nation may be.

> Oddly, the idea of keeping all of your money inside your own country is more prevalent in the United States than in other parts of the world, probably because no major war or revolution has happened inside U.S. borders since the Civil War over 150 years ago.

---

[2] From personal discussions with Argentinians who experienced the 2001 incident.
[3] "Argentina's Property Grab," *Wall Street Journal* Opinion Page, October 23, 2008, http://online.wsj.com/article/SB122471757680560465.html.

Oddly, the idea of keeping all of your money inside your own country is more prevalent in the United States than in other parts of the world, probably because no major war has happened inside American borders since the Civil War more than 150 years ago. If, however, you were to ask people in Europe or Latin America about geographic diversification and political risk, you would hear stories of invasions, revolutions, and government confiscation of assets. These events might have occurred within their own lifetimes, or the lifetimes of a parent or grandparent. In fact, the idea of geographic diversification seems pretty wise to many with these life experiences.

An Amazon.com review of Harry Browne's last investing book, *Fail-Safe Investing,* relates "Steve's" experience:

> *I first read [Harry] Browne's advice a couple of decades ago when I was living overseas and had just had the fun of going through a coup against the government that involved three days of firefights between government troops and rebels inside the bank where every dime I owned was kept.*
>
> *Mr. Browne is right. Nobody knows what will happen next. If you have money you can't afford to lose, you have to be ready for anything, and Harry Browne gives you the tools to do so.*

One way to diversify against this type of risk is to hold assets outside of the country where you live. This approach serves as an ultimate safety net in case the political situation close to home becomes volatile and dangerous.

### You'll Sleep Better

It may sound strange, but with part of your money outside of the country where you live you'll sleep better. Events in the news will have less of an impact on you emotionally. You'll know that even if everything goes wrong where you live, you have a safety net in another part of the world for you and your family.

## Geographic Diversification and a Warning for U.S. Citizens

It is important to understand that geographic diversification is *not* a secret numbered Swiss bank account like you might see in an old James Bond movie. The reality is that foreign accounts are just a tool that can fill an investor's need for a certain type of diversification.

"It is unpatriotic to have foreign accounts!"

There are a variety of ways to get geographic diversification safely, cheaply, and legally. Unfortunately, some of the better ways of achieving such diversification are becoming harder and very expensive for ordinary Americans (especially in places like Switzerland). This is due to an ever-expanding reach of the U.S. government into the financial affairs of its citizens with many new laws and regulations affecting assets held in foreign accounts, and this trend has only accelerated over the past several years. These changes are making American citizens very unappealing as customers to overseas banks and much of the information written on this topic in prior years has become obsolete.

> The actions of the U.S. government in recent years can be interpreted in a number of ways. One interpretation is that a form of de facto capital controls are being put in place incrementally through red tape instead of overt legislation.

The actions of the U.S. government in recent years can be interpreted in a number of ways. One interpretation is that a form of de facto capital controls are being put in place incrementally through red tape instead of overt legislation. One day it may no longer be possible to find a foreign financial institution that is willing to do business with U.S. citizens, even if it is still *technically* legal to hold assets outside of U.S. borders.

Given how quickly the options have narrowed for U.S. citizens, consider these changes as evidence of the urgent need to open an account *now* and get some assets outside of the United States while it is still possible to do so. There is a better chance of maintaining an existing account than opening a new one in many cases. While not intended to be alarmist, the U.S. government has taken bold steps in recent years to limit individual citizens' freedom to move *their own money* outside U.S. borders. Regardless of the pretext offered for these restrictions, the lessons of history suggest that such measures should not be taken lightly.

## Even Politicians Do It

Recently, 2012 GOP presidential candidate Mitt Romney disclosed a fully legal and legitimate account at UBS Zürich worth $3 million that was shut down in 2010. You can be certain it wasn't holding Swiss chocolate and it wasn't likely holding only foreign currencies as reported in the *Boston Globe*:

> *In early 2010, as Romney advanced toward a second presidential campaign, [money manager R. Bradford] Malt decided to close the $3 million UBS account he set up in Switzerland seven years earlier, realizing it could become a political issue. In 2009, the U.S. government sued UBS to obtain the names of thousands of Americans who secretly held billions of dollars in Swiss accounts.*
>
> ***Malt said he opened the Swiss account not to hide assets, but to diversify Romney's investments into foreign currencies. If the value of the dollar declined, for example, a rise in the Swiss franc might offset it.*** *The account, Malt stressed, was listed on Romney's 2010 tax return and Romney paid taxes on the interest, just as he pays taxes on all the earnings from other foreign investments. (Emphasis added)*[4]

We are *not* critical of Mr. Romney's decision to have a foreign account. In fact, the authors *congratulate* Mr. Romney and his money managers for having the foresight to use geographic diversification in his portfolio.

---

[4] Todd Wallack, "Boston Lawyer Keeps Steady Hand on Romney's Holdings," *Boston Globe*, January 30, 2012, http://articles.boston.com/2012-01-30/business/30676371 _1_malt-romney-offshore-accounts.

We are *not* critical of Mr. Romney's decision to have a foreign account. In fact, the authors *congratulate* Mr. Romney and his money managers for having the foresight to use geographic diversification in his portfolio. It is, however, unfortunate that U.S. policy in recent years has made it so expensive (and often impossible) for ordinary Americans to do these things. As a further aside, it is *very unlikely* that Mr. Romney is the only prominent political leader who holds money outside of their own country.

## The Reality Risk Spectrum

Before going any further with the discussion, it's important to address a key concept we'll call the "Reality Risk Spectrum." The idea with the Reality Risk Spectrum is that it is never a good idea to take actions in an attempt to protect assets that actually *increases* the risk to those assets. In other words, don't go so overboard trying to secure your money that you run into trouble that never would have occurred if you had just kept things simple.

> Don't go to such extremes to protect against a relatively rare event like government property seizure that you allow yourself to be victimized by the *much more common* con artist or scam.

Don't go to such extremes to protect against a relatively rare event like government property seizure that you allow yourself to be victimized by the *much more common* con artist or scam. Figure 15.2 breaks down some of these realities. Keep things simple and don't outsmart yourself.

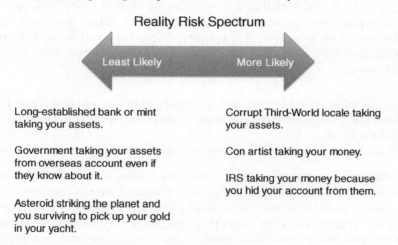

FIGURE 15.2  The Reality Risk Spectrum of account risks.

The main point of the observations above is this: keep overseas accounts as simple as possible and don't let fear of extreme events make you fall into the jaws of more common risks.

Here are some ground rules for storage of assets in foreign accounts:

1. Only deal with first-world countries with stable governments and legal systems that provide strong protections of private property.
2. Avoid dealing with institutions where accountability rules are opaque or unclear.
3. Try to do business in legal jurisdictions that support financial privacy.
4. *Always follow all legal disclosure requirements.*

Rule #1 is that you should only do business in first-world countries. There is no advantage to putting your money in third-world financial institutions, but plenty of risk that your money may never be returned to you. Any locale with lots of corruption, an unstable government, or history of not protecting private property rights should be avoided.

Rule #2 is that if you can't trace with certainty how an institution is regulated, insured, audited, and held accountable to its customers then you should avoid it. Any foreign jurisdiction you are considering should also have robust laws in place to deal with problems that financial institutions can encounter and provide methods of recovering assets if something goes wrong. The last thing you want is to put your money in some tiny, offshore haven only to find that if it goes missing you have no legal recourse (and the judge hearing your case is the uncle of the person who took it).

Rule #3 is the idea that a foreign locale should have bank privacy rules in place that prevent disclosure of account details without a valid order issued by a court in that country. These laws will prevent sharing information with those that are conducting fishing expeditions with no valid cause.

> In sum, stick to well-established institutions in places where it is safe to drink the water and you're less likely to encounter problems. Don't outsmart yourself.

Rule #4 is to follow all disclosure laws. Hiding assets can trigger stiff penalties, including the loss of the assets that are being hidden, and even the loss of your freedom. Just because a government knows you have an overseas account does not mean they can just go in and grab the money. Foreign jurisdictions have their own laws that cover these situations that you can leverage to protect yourself if needed.

In sum, stick to well-established institutions in places where it is safe to drink the water and you're less likely to encounter problems. *Don't outsmart yourself.*

## Types of Geographic Diversification

Below are the ways in which one may obtain geographic diversification of his gold holdings. These range from least protective up to the most protective.

**Least Protective**

- Gold ETF that holds gold overseas
- Closed end fund that holds gold outside the country
- Online gold storage services

**Medium Level of Protection**

- Gold certificates for an overseas institution or bank
- Unallocated account at an overseas institution or bank

**Most Protective**

- Allocated gold account at an overseas institution or bank
- Segregated gold account at an overseas institution or bank
- Safe deposit box at an overseas location

### Foreign Gold ETFs and Closed End Funds

These are financial products that in some cases store gold outside the country where you live. As discussed in Chapter 9, this could be physical gold with a closed-end fund like Central Gold Trust that stores assets in Canada, or perhaps an ETF like SGOL that stores its gold in Switzerland.

The plus with these funds is that you have some diversification against natural or manmade disasters in the United States. The minus is a government emergency could still force repatriation of funds against your wishes. Another minus, discussed in Chapter 9, is that an ETF or gold fund is held in a street name, not yours. Proving direct ownership to the ETF or fund, even if it offers physical gold redemption, is likely going to be difficult (especially in an emergency).

> Though gold funds offer convenience, they only offer minimal geographic diversification and won't be covered further in this chapter. For geographic diversification purposes, just remember that these funds are primarily for convenience, not safety.

A gold ETF or closed-end fund is useful for rebalancing your portfolio because it is so easily traded. It may make sense to keep a small portion of your gold allocation in a gold fund for this purpose and hold the rest using a more secure method. An example of such an approach would be to put 5 percent of your portfolio in a gold fund and put the remaining 20 percent in a foreign account. This approach would help prevent transactions on the overseas account, lower trading costs, and reduce bookkeeping matters.

Though gold funds offer convenience, they only offer minimal geographic diversification and won't be covered further in this chapter. For geographic diversification purposes, just remember that these funds are primarily for convenience, not safety.

## Online Gold Storage Services

In recent years some companies have started offering overseas gold storage services. These services allow investors to buy and sell gold online and have it stored in several locations around the world (New York, London, Zürich, etc.). These services have various terms and conditions aimed at assuring availability of the metal for delivery, but may harbor other risks.

## Unallocated Accounts

Institutions providing gold storage offer different types of accounts. One method is an unallocated account. The term "unallocated account" means the entity storing the gold is obligated to provide the gold on demand, but may not have it actually set aside for the depositors at all times. This approach weakens the overall security of the gold ownership because an investor doesn't actually own any specific gold; instead, he owns a claim to a portion of a gold pool held in a storage provider's vault or vaults.

## Allocated Account

A second type of gold storage is known as an "allocated account." This type of account involves the storage of physical gold in which the metal is specifically allocated to each customer in a single large pool. So if you buy 10 ounces of allocated gold the institution will add 10 ounces to the single large pool of gold they hold for everyone. When you want your gold, the institution simply removes 10 ounces from the pool to get you the funds.

Allocated accounts are appealing because they offer a high degree of safety and assurance that the asset will be there for each registered owner.

Since banks and other storage providers are only acting as a custodian (these are called "custody accounts"), the assets are not legally the property of the institution that holds them and can't be promised to creditors. Therefore, allocated gold account holders usually have more protection against the insolvency of the custodian.

## Segregated Storage Account

Segregated accounts take things one step up in safety. Instead of a large pool of gold where you can claim a certain amount of gold, the custodian will actually take out your purchased gold and set it aside for you specifically. Segregated storage accounts are the safest kind of gold storage and the best option for a Permanent Portfolio.

Segregated accounts are, however, more expensive than some other forms of gold ownership, since vault space is specifically set aside for these accounts and more handling is required. Also, many institutions no longer offer segregated gold storage as they did in the past and only offer allocated accounts now.

## Foreign Safe Deposit Box

Foreign safe deposit boxes can either be at a bank or private depository that specializes in providing this type of service. The plus with this type arrangement is that you will have direct control over the assets in your safe deposit box, since you will have to go there and put it in the safe deposit box yourself. This method also offers a private way to store a portion of your wealth that you know you won't need to touch for a long time.

The downside of this approach is that you will need to visit the actual foreign location to conduct your transactions, including buying and selling the asset if you need to rebalance your portfolio. Just like a bank safe deposit box in the United States, a foreign bank will not enter a safe deposit box without good reason (although there has been at least one case of a blanket safe deposit box opening and confiscation of assets in the U.K.).[5] Another minus of this approach is that you will need to carry insurance on the asset because safe deposit box providers normally do not insure the contents of deposit boxes. Finally, your relatives and heirs may not know about the safe deposit box and in the event of your incapacitation or death they may not be able to get to it (though some may consider this a plus!).

---

[5] "What Do You Keep in a Safety Deposit Box?," *BBC*, March 7, 2011, www.bbc.co.uk/news/uk-12248666.

## Overseas Gold Storage Options

### Online Gold Storage Services

As discussed above, there are services that specialize in storing gold for investors in various locations (London, New York, Switzerland, etc.). Examples of these services include:

Gold Money—www.goldmoney.com
Bullionvault—www.bullionvault.com

These companies offer an alternative for gold storage, but it's not clear whether they offer a more secure storage option than gold ETFs and closed-end funds.

Bullionvault does not provide a physical delivery option for the gold it holds. You can only sell the gold and withdraw deposited funds. As a result, there doesn't seem to be much benefit over owning an ETF that holds the gold for you in a location such as Switzerland.

Gold Money does provide the option of physical delivery of the gold it holds, but their corporate offices are located on the British channel island of Jersey, so legally it's not clear what recourse investors would have if there were to be some kind of problem with the company. For example, in the event of a legal dispute would you have to hire a Jersey islands attorney to sue Gold Money in a Jersey islands court? From a safety perspective, the Jersey islands don't offer anything especially compelling to a foreign depositor. Prior to 2009, for example, the Jersey islands didn't even offer depositor insurance and today its coverage levels are still quite low. As a custodian account perhaps it doesn't matter, but it might.

These services are not a top-list recommendation and better options exist if you are able to access them.

# New Zealand

New Zealand is a very stable country located in the south Pacific with a population of around 4 million. New Zealand features a British-based legal system and strong property rights. New Zealand also boasts a low crime rate, very low corruption, and one of the highest standards of living in the world. These are all favorable attributes of a country you are considering for a gold storage location.

### New Zealand Mint

The New Zealand Mint is actually a *private* bullion storage facility based in Auckland, New Zealand. It has no connection with the New Zealand government. The mint provides services to its customers including allocated storage or a private safe deposit box, a key to which is supplied to the customer.

*Website:* www.nzmint.com

*Account Types:* Allocated gold or safe deposit boxes.

*Account Minimums:* None. You can buy a single gold coin if you want and they'll store it.

*Account Costs:*

- 1 percent per year for allocated gold storage
- Minimum $30 charge per year
- $200 per year for small safe deposit box and $250 for large
- Discounts for very large quantity (over $500,000 USD) are available
- Their commissions on gold purchases are higher than industry norms

*Accepts U.S. Customers?* Yes

*Accepts Non-U.S. Customers?* Yes

*Requirements to open an account:*

- Two forms of ID (passport, etc.)
- Confirmation of address
- Agreement with New Zealand Mint's terms and conditions

*Reporting:*

- It is the customer's responsibility to disclose accounts and any tax liabilities he or she may have with the mint. The mint only responds to lawful requests from the New Zealand government to divulge customer information.

The New Zealand Mint is a private company and has no affiliation with the New Zealand government. It has been in business since 1967 and mints gold and silver currency for the south Pacific islands of Fiji, Cook, Niue, and Tuvalu. It also mints its own line of commemorative bullion coins such as the gold Kiwi. Additionally, it has its own *Star Wars* bullion coins (which are not recommended for Permanent Portfolio purposes due, in part, to the small market for Darth Vader and Luke Skywalker gold coins). They mint some coins in-house and respected mints such as PAMP Suisse or Sunshine Mint in Idaho USA do others so the quality is very high. New Zealand Mint also operates a private vault at their headquarters in Auckland.

The mint offers two services of interest: allocated gold storage and safe deposit boxes. The allocated gold storage service is available in person or over the phone when you place a bullion order. Once an account is opened you can purchase gold under the terms of the agreement and the mint will store it for you in their vault in your name and the gold is fully insured. The agreement is simple in terms of describing what assets the mint holds for you and the terms involved. The mint holds the bullion as a custody account and are not assets available to creditors if the mint were to have a problem financially.

If you prefer a safe deposit box the mint can also assist you with that service. You will, however, need to show up in person in Auckland to open it and place your gold in it (which you can buy right from their bullion desk). Further, as with most banks, safe deposit boxes at the mint are not insured because the mint has no way of knowing the contents. You will need your own insurance in that case.

Lloyd's of London insures allocated accounts for the full value of the gold. The insurance though won't cover things like terrorism and acts of war (which very few insurance policies cover anywhere). The gold held in your allocated account is accessible only by members of the New Zealand Mint staff for trading purposes on your behalf. The mint is insured against fraud and is audited by PricewaterhouseCoopers in compliance with New Zealand laws.

Customers can show up in Auckland to pick up their gold if they desire. More realistically, gold can be shipped to a customer's location if the customer pays for the transportation fees.

New Zealand's status as a small and remote island nation helps to insulate it from global issues. For one perspective on why the New Zealand Mint might be a good option for you, consider the following information from Mike O'Kane, head bullion trader for the New Zealand Mint:

> *The New Zealand government does not hold any gold reserves so there is little threat they'd confiscate it. We're also far away and surrounded by water. Nobody is going to come here and just walk away with the gold we store. The borders can be sealed off in an emergency. We're also largely an agricultural export economy. Since people need to eat, we're pretty well protected from global economic problems.*

One downside to the New Zealand Mint is that its commissions on gold purchases are high. They are around 9 percent or so (though these commissions may be negotiable depending on your purchase size).

One of the big positive points for this option is that the mint will handle even very small accounts for true allocated physical gold storage. Although not recommend, an investor could purchase a *single gold coin* and store it with the mint if he so desired. That option makes the New Zealnd Mint a viable choice even for the smallest investor who is looking for allocated gold storage overseas.

Overall, the New Zealand Mint's low minimums for allocated gold storage are very appealing for smaller accounts or those looking to diversify their holdings from other providers.

# Australia

Like New Zealand, Australia is a politically stable country with a British-based legal system and strong protection of property rights. Australia is also isolated geographically from most of the rest of the world. These are all good general attributes for a potential gold storage location.

## The Perth Mint

The Perth Mint is owned by the government of Western Australia and offers many gold-buying programs guaranteed by the government. The government of Western Australia is AAA rated by Standard & Poor's and the mint is conservatively managed with an emphasis on privacy and security. The mint has been in existence since 1899.

Western Australia has a very large mining industry and is a net exporter of natural resources to Australia and the world. The mint serves as a way to make the precious metals output from the mining industry available on international markets.

*Name:* Perth Mint

*Website:* www.perthmint.com.au

*Account Types:* Unallocated, allocated, and segregated held in either certificate or direct account form.

*Account Minimums:* $10,000USD minimum for the certificate program through authorized dealers (see website for current listing). Minimum $5,000USD for buys and sells. If you have over $50,000USD you can deal directly with the mint. Residents of Australia and New Zealand can contact the mint directly without going through a dealer for lower minimums.

*Account Costs:* There are costs associated with either the certificate program or if you deal directly with the depository.

*Certificate Program Costs:* Varies between approved dealers. Most approved dealers charge:

- 2 percent commission on Buy orders
- 1 percent commission on Sell orders

*Depository Program Account Costs:* For Australian/New Zealand clients with an account balance under $50,000AUD or international clients with an account balance under $250,000USD the mint will charge:

- 2 percent commission on Buy orders
- 1 percent commission on Sell orders

If the total value of your account balance (metal and cash included) is greater than the amounts mentioned above, no commission applies.

For both the Certificate and Depository Programs, an annual storage fee of 1 percent a year to hold allocated gold (lower costs for other account types) applies. For clients with significant assets, lower rates can be negotiated.

*Accepts U.S. Customers?* Yes
*Accepts Non-U.S. Customers?* Yes
*Requirements to open an account:*
- Notarized passport copy or other ID
- Confirmation of address
- Agreement with Perth Mint's terms and conditions

*Reporting:*
- It is the customer's responsibility to disclose information about accounts with the mint in compliance with applicable laws (which will vary based upon a customer's citizenship and residency). The mint will only respond to lawful requests from Australian courts to divulge customer information.

The Perth Mint deals with four main products of interest to a Permanent Portfolio investor:

- Gold Certificates
- Unallocated Gold Accounts
- Allocated (pooled) Gold Accounts (not currently available, but may be opened in the future)
- Segregated Gold Accounts

The Perth Mint Certificate Program (PMCP) is for account values less than $50,000USD. The certificates are sold through authorized dealers listed on the mint's website (there are several U.S. brokers and others around the world). The dealer handles the transaction for a fee that is usually 2 percent on buys and 1 percent on sells (which can be negotiated lower depending on the size of the transaction, but may be higher for smaller accounts).

The certificate and legal obligation the investor receives is not through the dealer, it is directly with the mint and is enforceable under Australian law. If the dealer goes bankrupt it does not affect the validity of the certificate. The investor can always deal directly with the mint as a certificate holder if there is a problem.

The certificates are for a specified amount of gold from the mint and are guaranteed by the government of Western Australia. An investor can get a certificate for unallocated, allocated, or segregated gold storage.

The biggest downside with the certificate is that the funds need to go through the dealer both on the buy and sell. This adds complexity to the transaction and potential exposure to problems with the dealer's dispersing of funds. However, if the dealer ever goes out of business an investor can simply deal directly with the mint and they will transfer funds back to the investor's account.

For accounts over $50,000USD it is recommend that investors skip the dealers and go straight to the mint. When this approach is used, an investor has the option to open an account directly and use the mint as the broker. This eliminates one more layer of paper in the transaction and provides access to the unallocated, allocated, or segregated account types as well.

The segregated account is recommended for the highest level of safety. When interviewed for this book, Bron Suchecki, the Analysis and Strategy Manager for Perth Mint, had the following to say about segregated, allocated, and unallocated storage options at the Perth Mint:

> *If you don't trust the counterparty [Perth Mint or otherwise] you shouldn't give anything to them. Allocated, unallocated or not.*

Mr. Suchecki's point is valid when you consider a gold storage service that would break its promise in one area would probably break promises in other areas as well. After all, what would stop them from going into the segregated storage vault and taking gold if they would break their other commitments?

Yet it's still more comforting to know that the gold for your Permanent Portfolio is already set aside under legal terms protecting the segregated holders in custody accounts and that is still the recommended approach. Again, it's just one less thing to worry about.

Why Perth Mint? Bron Suchecki explains it this way:

> *Australia has a British legal system. We're very stable politically with strong rule of law. We've never had a civil war and have high levels of social cohesion. Culturally we are laid back and don't worry and our roots as a British penal colony means we are naturally skeptical of government. All of the mint's metal is insured 100 percent and then we have the Government Guarantee on top of this, from an S&P AAA rated government.*
>
> *In terms of confiscation risks, Western Australia has a very Texas-like relationship with Australia's Federal Government. It is highly likely that West Australians would consider confiscation of gold as a seizure of "their" gold as it would have a big impact on our mining industry. We are a net exporter and it would hurt us economically*

*and thus could cause a huge blowback. The repeal of the Federal Resource Super Profit Tax in the face of a reported $22 million dollar ad campaign by mining interests is a possible template for the politics of gold confiscation in Australia, making it less than straightforward.*

In addition to the points touched on above, the Perth Mint is also prohibited by law from disclosing information about customer accounts. Only a valid court order issued by an Australian court can compel employees of the mint to discuss customer account details or disclose customer account information.

All Perth Mint accounts are guaranteed by the government of Western Australia and are insured by Lloyd's of London for the full value of their entire gold inventory, which provides one final level of strong protection for assets stored at the mint.

Overall, the Perth Mint is a very appealing option for safe and easy foreign gold storage.

# United States

Investors outside of the United States may actually want to work with a bank inside the United States for their geographic diversification needs. Additionally, some Permanent Portfolio investors may not feel comfortable working with a foreign gold storage provider and would prefer to keep their gold with a U.S.-based bank. It's just important to recognize that if gold were confiscated again storage vaults inside the United States would be the first to be seized. So for U.S.-based investors it's still recommended you use a foreign service for maximum diversification of this asset.

## Everbank

Banks in the United States generally do not offer gold metal accounts. Everbank, however, is an exception and offers some options in this area.

*Website:* www.everbank.com
*Account Types:* Unallocated and Allocated
*Account Minimums:* $5,000 to $7,500
*Account Costs:*
- 0.75 percent commission to buy or sell gold
- 1.5 percent per year for allocated gold storage
- No fee for unallocated storage

*Accepts U.S. Customers?* Yes.

*Accepts Non-U.S. Customers?* Varies. Call for details.

*Requirements to open an account:*
- Driver's license for U.S. residents
- Passport for non-U.S. customers
- Online account form completed

*Reporting:*
- Everbank is based in the United States and is subject to all reporting and disclosure requirements inside the United States.

Everbank has physical locations in the U.S. state of Florida and prominent Internet presence. The bank holds gold at six custodian vaults, domestically and globally. Because the assets belong to the bank's customers and the bank simply serves as custodian, the accounts are not FDIC insured. This is because the FDIC only insures *deposits* at the bank and the gold is not a bank deposit, but rather property of the customer that the bank is storing for a fee. The gold itself is insured at each custodian location and Everbank also carries insurance on the gold holdings. Everbank is regulated and audited at multiple levels, just like any other U.S.-based bank. All gold is stored as a custody account and it is neither part of the bank's balance sheet nor available to creditors in case of a bank failure.

Everbank offers its gold metal accounts in two versions. The first version is an unallocated gold account that has no fees, but the bank does store, ounce for ounce, all gold purchased by the customer, and this account can be converted to an allocated account with physical gold at any time. The second version is allocated storage where the customer can purchase actual coins or bars for the custody account that the banks will hold on the customer's behalf for an annual fee. The bank is also expected to begin offering segregated gold storage accounts in the near future. For the Permanent Portfolio, the allocated or segregated accounts are recommended for the highest level of safety.

Everbank does offer gold delivery for persons inside the United States. As of now, however, it does not offer gold delivery for international customers. However, in 2012 Everbank plans to start a new service tentatively called "designated storage." This feature will allow a customer to purchase gold and have it held at one of several globally distributed vaults. Once the account is set up, the gold will be held at the location selected by the customer in the bank's custody. With valid ID, a customer can pick up his gold at the designated location. This is an innovative new product to consider if you need to work with a U.S.-based bank.

When asked why someone should consider using Everbank, bank president Frank Trotter stated:

*We have the best value with low transaction fees and are a reputable institution. We also have offerings that allow you to diversify into global currency markets and domestic banking tools you'd find at any bank. We look at our offering as a "Toolkit for the Global Investor." In a lot of ways we've always believed in the Permanent Portfolio approach. We offer value, security and choice. Additionally, our employees understand the gold and currency markets and have expertise to back it up as they use these tools themselves. In 2012 we are going to be offering even more tools and services to investors. We are big advocates of diversification.*

Overall, this is an option for Permanent Portfolio investors that desire geographic diversification inside the United States (but again for U.S. persons a foreign location is preferred). The account opening process is simple with low minimums, which is an advantage as well. Plus, they offer more traditional banking services if you need them.

## Switzerland

As a location for foreign accounts, Switzerland has a certain mystique due to Hollywood movies and the fact that about 30 percent of all offshore wealth currently resides within its borders. Part of Switzerland's mystique is the result of the Swiss banking privacy laws that were created in 1934. These laws attached criminal penalties to disclosing customer account information. These laws were enacted, in part, to protect Jewish and other depositors against coercive measures that were being used to bring assets back into Nazi Germany. Unfortunately, these laws form a double-edged sword. The same laws that protect assets from confiscation efforts by rogue governments can also protect criminals who seek to conceal the proceeds of illegal activity.

Despite the Hollywood clichés about Swiss accounts, Swiss banks do have some special features, one of which it that a Swiss account places your money in a legal jurisdiction that has very specific and restrictive rules regarding who can access your account information and for what purpose.

> "Switzerland has never had a Bernie Madoff."—Otto Hueppi, Swiss American Advisors, AG

A second feature of Swiss banks is that oversight is very robust and Swiss banks do not have the history of corruption, failure, and fraud that has plagued other countries' banking systems (including the United States). As Swiss banker Otto Hueppi commented: "Switzerland has never had a Bernie Madoff."

In terms of absolute safety of bank accounts, Switzerland still represents a good choice if you can find a bank that will do business with you.

## Swiss Banking Realities for U.S. Citizens

Unfortunately, Swiss accounts are largely out of reach for most Americans today due to recent U.S. changes in account information disclosure requirements. There are some viable options that involve working through an intermediary (as discussed below). However, it is important to understand that Swiss banks today generally do not want to do business with American customers and even when a willing Swiss bank can be found, the account minimums have gotten much higher than in prior years, with current account minimums typically in the range of $250,000 and up. Even calling most Swiss banks from an American phone number will likely be enough for them to be unwilling to answer questions at all.

In recent years, one event in particular significantly changed the landscape for Americans wishing to open or maintain Swiss bank accounts. In 2008, a group of individuals at the multinational Swiss bank UBS deliberately aided a small number of Americans in criminal tax evasion schemes. When this tax evasion scheme came to light, UBS was pressured by the U.S. government to release the names of all of its U.S. clients (whether or not they had anything to do with the illegal tax evasion scheme). Facing the possibility of no longer being able to do business in the United States if it didn't cooperate, UBS turned over the names of its American holders of Swiss accounts, paid a large fine, and closed the Swiss accounts of its American customers. This incident made it clear that Swiss banking privacy today is no longer as robust as it once was.

Following the UBS incident, the U.S. government has continued to make demands of other Swiss banks to disclose customer account information. Faced with violating Swiss account privacy laws if such information was disclosed, and not wishing to close up their operations in the United States, most Swiss banks appear to have decided that American customers are simply not worth the trouble.

The Swiss view financial privacy as a basic civil right, and a set of banking practices have evolved over many generations that embrace this concept of privacy and security of customer accounts. The Swiss view the intrusion of government into the financial affairs of citizens in the same way that Americans view censorship of the press. The Swiss are not going to willingly comply with violations of banking privacy any more than an American newspaper would agree to censor stories to appease the Chinese government. This aspect of the Swiss banking culture is just something to remember when you read political spin about this topic in the newspaper framing the issue as a matter of going after tax evaders, drug dealers and terrorists.

The laws in Switzerland were *not* created to help tax evaders, drug dealers and terrorists. They were created to protect citizens against government abuses and illegal confiscation of private property. Nobody ever said freedom was without its problems, but it sure beats the alternative.

## Swiss Banking for Non-U.S. Citizens

If you are a non-U.S. citizen and reside outside of the United States, Swiss banks offer several secure ways of owning gold. The bad news is that many Swiss banks have raised the account minimums for non-Swiss citizens. Also, in some cases you may have to show up in person to open the account.

Ironically, even though Europeans are closest to Switzerland and most able to open a Swiss account, if you live in Europe it might make sense to think about storing your gold in a location outside of the European continent. This is just a nod to the history of Europe and the conflicts that have repeatedly erupted there.

Even with all of the limitations now in place when it comes to Swiss accounts, Swiss banks still have a lot of good attributes if you can work within the limitations and meet the high minimum account requirements. One bright spot for Swiss banking and U.S. citizens is that there are apparently discussions taking place between the U.S. and Swiss governments about entering into a tax treaty that might allow Swiss banks to resume doing business with Americans. For now, though, the situation is filled with uncertainty.

## Types of Swiss Banks

There are several varieties of Swiss banks:

1. **Multinationals**—These are the big banks like UBS and Credit Suisse. These banks have offices and operations all over the world.
2. **Private Banks**—The term "private bank" has a special meaning in Switzerland. Private banks mostly exist to serve high net worth individuals only. They mainly offer boutique services with high fees. They do business internationally, but many do not have branches outside of Switzerland.
3. **Cantonal Banks**—These are banks owned by the cantons in Switzerland (a Swiss canton is equivalent to a U.S. state). These banks have branches inside the canton and do not normally do business outside of Switzerland itself. They have reasonable fees and good service. However, most of them (but not all) will only do business with citizens living within the canton.

**CANTONAL BANKS—FOR NON-U.S. CITIZENS** Of the three types of Swiss banks, the cantonal banks are normally the best option for Permanent Portfolio investors for three primary reasons:

1. They are insured by the canton itself against failure.
2. They have limited operations outside the canton so it is harder for a foreign government to pressure them.
3. They have less financial exposure to external events because their business is concentrated in the canton.

The insurance that covers account holders at cantonal banks is provided by the canton itself. The depositor insurance provided by the Swiss version of the FDIC has much lower limits than provided in the United States, and thus the additional insurance coverage provided by the cantons is important to the overall safety of cantonal banks.

The second reason for the appeal of cantonal banks is what makes some of the other large Swiss banks, such as UBS or Credit Suisse, unappealing, and it involves the scope of their non-Swiss international operations. UBS's Achilles' heel in the recent IRS scandal (apart from its own employees acting foolishly) was the fact that it owned the U.S. broker Paine Webber and did a lot of business inside the United States. As a result of this arrangement, it was easy for the U.S. government to threaten to shut down UBS's U.S. operations if it did not comply with information requests from U.S. tax authorities.

Cantonal banks, however, do not do a lot of business outside of their local regions. These banks are chartered to primarily serve their canton residents. By not having assets exposed outside Switzerland, it is hard for foreign governments to apply pressure to disclose customer account information or otherwise interfere with their operations. They also are less exposed to risky foreign investments like U.S. and European mortgages that dogged UBS and Credit Suisse in recent years.

**RECOMMENDED CANTONAL BANKS** Some Swiss cantonal banks offer gold metal accounts only to *non-U.S. citizens who do not reside in the United States*. For an investor who falls into this category, this is often the best gold storage option available.

While there are many cantonal banks, most of them will not take foreign customers and exist to serve local account holders only. Calling them up and asking about opening an account as a foreigner is usually going to be met with a polite but terse "no thanks."

The banks listed next, however, will work with some foreign clients (though not Americans as of this writing in 2012).

**CANTONAL BANK OF ZÜRICH**  The Cantonal Bank of Zürich (ZKB—Zürcher Kantonalbank) is owned by the canton of Zürich in Switzerland. Zürich is the richest canton in Switzerland and ZKB has been in business for more than 140 years. The bank offers low-cost allocated gold storage accounts. It also offers safe deposit boxes if required.

> *Website:* www.zkb.ch
> *Account Types:* Allocated and safe deposit boxes
> *Account Minimums:* 250,000 to 500,000CHF
> *Account Costs:* Gold custody accounts are 0.5 to 1 percent per year depending on deposited funds. You can negotiate lower fees in some cases.
> *Accepts U.S. Citizens?:* No
> *Accepts Non-U.S. Citizens?:* Yes
> *Requirements to open an account:*
> - Passport
> - Proof of origination of funds
> - Bank account agreement
> - Must be physically present in Zürich at the bank
>
> *Reporting:*
> - Swiss bank privacy laws prohibit the bank from disclosing account details. Customers are responsible for all reporting and disclosure requirements applicable in their home countries.

ZKB is one of the strongest banks in Switzerland. It is run and insured by the Canton of Zürich and is a full service bank with branches throughout the region. It offers gold custody accounts for its customers in its vaults in Zürich for reasonable fees if you meet the minimums.

Unfortunately, the account minimums for non-Swiss account holders have become very high. Plus, the bank is not currently dealing with Americans. If, however, you can afford to use them, and meet their customer requirements, they are one of the best choices in the country for allocated gold storage accounts.

**BASLER KANTONALBANK**  Basler Kantonalbank is owned by the canton of Basel. They are another very old canton bank but, like ZKB, won't deal with Americans.

> *Website:* www.bkb.ch
> *Account Types:* Allocated and safe deposit boxes
> *Account Minimums:* Varies
> *Account Costs:* Gold Custody Accounts can be as low 0.30 percent per year but other fees may also apply

*Accepts U.S. Citizens?:* No

*Accepts Non-U.S. Citizens?:* Varies

*Requirements to open an account:*

- Passport
- Proof of origination of funds
- Bank account agreement

*Reporting:*

- Swiss bank privacy laws prohibit the bank from disclosing account details. Customers are responsible for all reporting and disclosure requirements in their home countries.

Basler Kantonalbank is not quite as highly regarded as ZKB, but it has a good reputation (certainly better than any major U.S. bank). However, the recent UBS scandal has brought it under scrutiny from the IRS and currently it absolutely will not deal with Americans. Non-U.S. citizens inquiring about accounts will need to discuss account minimums to determine whether an account at this bank is a realistic option.

# Intermediaries for U.S. Citizens

A niche industry has developed in which companies in Switzerland will work with local Swiss banks to open accounts for foreigners (even Americans in some cases). Fees and account minimums for this service vary.

Some intermediaries will simply open an account for you and from there the relationship is between you and the bank.

For Americans, however, using an intermediary is a bit more complicated. For American account holders, the intermediary will work as the agent in Switzerland, and the intermediary will open the account in the name of the American depositor. The bank account is held in the name of the American depositor, and is owned by the depositor. However, the reporting and disclosure matters are left to the intermediary so the bank is not in violation of Swiss law. An American account holder must sign an agreement stipulating that the intermediary is authorized to report activities to the IRS, fill out appropriate IRS paperwork for reporting, and maintain SEC compliance. The intermediary will charge an annual fee to perform this compliance work.

Adding an intermediary does add additional expense and complexity that did not exist before, though the overall fees are still within reason for an allocated gold storage account.

## Swiss American Advisors, AG (Sallfort Advisors)

Swiss American Advisors (formerly Sallfort Advisors, AG and renamed in 2012) is an SEC-registered agent in Zürich, Switzerland that opened in 2008.

Swiss American Advisors operates specifically to allow U.S. clients to have continued access to Swiss banking services with a fully SEC registered and IRS-compliant company. They are a full-service financial advisor and investment services firm and can access any SEC-registered investment product. They only work with American clients.

> *Website:* www.s-a-advisors.com
>
> *Account Types:* Allocated plus additional services
>
> *Account Minimums:* 250,000CHF is possible if the account will grow to 500,000CHF within the year
>
> *Account Costs:* Gold metal accounts have an annual fee of 0.73 percent
>
> *Accepts U.S. Citizens?* Yes. Only serves U.S. clients. SEC registered advisory firm
>
> *Accepts Non-U.S. Citizens?* No
>
> *Requirements to open an account:*
> - Notarized passport copy or other ID
> - Confirmation of address
> - Proof of origination of funds
> - Bank account agreement
> - Relevant IRS Tax forms, including Form W-9
> - Agreement with Sallfort Advisor's terms and conditions
>
> *Reporting:*
> - Swiss American Advisors requires filing of all required IRS forms, and they can assist with filing the annual foreign account disclosure form (FBAR) with the Treasury Department as well. Transactions are reported to the IRS for tax filing purposes.

Swiss American Advisors uses various banks to store customer gold. The accounts are in the customer's name and control. Swiss American Advisors handles paperwork regarding SEC and IRS compliance issues instead of the bank. Swiss American Advisors has authority only to trade inside the account at customer direction, and they have no access to the actual funds. They are a registered Swiss financial management firm and fully comply with Swiss Association of Asset Manager (SAAM) rules, which are typically stricter than SEC requirements. They are audited on a yearly basis by a Swiss firm. The Swiss bank that is custodian of all customer assets holds them in accordance with applicable Swiss law and account statements are provided by the bank.

Clients with gold accounts pay a reasonable 0.73 percent annual fee. This fee covers bank storage costs and overhead. By comparison, a gold ETF or closed-end fund can run in the 0.40 percent range. So for 0.33 percent more you can get true Swiss bank gold storage in an allocated account at a strong bank.

Why use Swiss American Advisors and hold gold in Switzerland? Managing Director Otto Hueppi explains it this way:

> *You get more security if you hold assets in Switzerland. For instance, brokers in the United States use a street name for your assets. In Switzerland they are held on your behalf with a street name but do not belong to the bank/broker. The assets are held in custody for you. They cannot be loaned out or used for other purposes. They are held for you on your behalf and this eliminates counterparty risk. No securities lending is allowed. This is why Swiss banks charge commissions and U.S. bankers don't. In the United States the cheap price you pay on gold and other assets is because the broker can use those assets for their own purposes to make money. In Switzerland gold is held in custody and is not usable by the bank or broker once purchased by the client.*
>
> *At Swiss American we have no direct access to assets. We can only buy and sell at the customer's direction. Withdrawals must come from the client only. Our auditing is yearly and must follow Swiss regulations SAAM [Swiss Association of Asset Managers] requirements, which are much stricter than the SEC. We are also audited on a yearly basis by a large Swiss auditing company. The Swiss bank ombudsman is available for any questions as an independent inspector as well. Finally, the bank is there and holds everything in custody and under Swiss laws. We don't own customers' accounts. It's all in their name at the bank.*

Although Otto Hueppi currently lives and works in Switzerland, he was born in the United States and lived there for a number of years. He has been working with Swiss banks for more than 28 years, 22 of which have been with private banking at places such as Zürcher Kantonalbank. Otto is familiar with the Permanent Portfolio strategy and the type of gold storage accounts that it requires.

## Swiss Gold Storage Services for U.S. and Non-U.S. Citizens

In recent years new services have emerged that work with large Swiss vault companies to buy and sell gold on behalf of customers and hold it in custody for them. They are not banks, but they are handling actual gold bullion and comply with Swiss laws requiring 100 percent coverage of the asset for all customer accounts that they oversee. These companies will normally deal with both U.S. and non-U.S. citizens.

## Global Gold, AG

Global Gold is a division of BFI Capital group, which opened in 1992. It is based in Switzerland. Global Gold began operation as a separate gold storage service in 2009. The people behind Global Gold wanted to deliver a service that would allow investors an easy and secure way to store gold in Switzerland without having to deal with banks that may not want their business.

> *Name:* Global Gold
> *Website:* www.globalgold.ch
> *Account Types:* Allocated
> *Account Minimums:* 50,000CHF for first purchase and 20,000CHF minimum for additional purchases
> *Account Costs:* 1.5 percent commission to sell and 3 percent to buy; rates go down depending on purchase amount
> *Annual storage fees are tiered as follows:*
> - More than 50,000CHF: 0.7 percent
> - More than 100,000CHF: 0.6 percent
> - More than 250,000CHF: 0.5 percent
> - More than 500,000CHF: 0.45 percent
> - More than 1,000,000CHF: 0.4 percent
> *Accepts U.S. Citizens?* Yes
> *Accepts Non-U.S. Citizens?* Yes
> *Requirements to open an account:*
> - Notarized passport copy or other ID
> - Confirmation of address
> - Proof of origination of funds
> - Agreement with Global Gold's terms and conditions
> *Reporting:*
> - Global Gold is not a financial institution. Customers are responsible for all reporting and disclosure requirements in their home countries.

Global Gold operates its service in cooperation with VIA MAT. VIA MAT is a large secure warehousing and vault service. The VIA MAT gold vault is located in the tax-free zone of Zürich's airport and gold transactions are not subject to Swiss taxes. Many other major gold ETFs and gold storage services use VIA MAT vaults in Zürich.

Global Gold acts as a broker for gold purchases, which means that when you wire money to Global Gold it will execute the buy order for physical gold for you. The gold is then stored at VIA MAT as part of Global Gold's holdings. Leftover funds from a trade are returned via wire to the originating account. *Global Gold is not a financial institution* and will not hold funds for you.

Assets held by Global Gold are audited by Ernst and Young and insured for the full amount by Lloyd's of London against common risks of loss. Global Gold is overseen by VQF, a Swiss financial services standards group, and complies with all applicable Swiss laws. Being based in Switzerland, Global Gold likely also offers some additional protection against foreign coercion or influence over their operations.

Global Gold does not offer segregated accounts until you reach the 5,000,000CHF mark. Assets are held in allocated Global Gold accounts and Global Gold manages the bookkeeping on the ownership of the metal for its customers. This is done because segregated storage at VIA MAT for each customer would be very expensive in terms of fees and bookkeeping. Global Gold does, however, maintain a 100 percent allocation to each customer.

Global Gold allows you to show up in person and take delivery of your metal directly if you so desire. You can also have it shipped to you, but you are responsible for all transportation fees associated with this service.

Claudio Grass, Managing Director at Global Gold, offers the following thoughts on Global Gold's services:

> *We are fans of Harry Browne. We created this service for institutional and private investors who are worried about keeping all their assets in the banking system. We are a 100 percent non-banking solution. Gold is bought 1:1 for each customer and physically allocated.*
>
> *Why Switzerland? We are the last island with direct democracy. We have a history of gold in the population here. We are the last place a government could pressure to take gold. The Swiss are not going to turn over our gold and gold was in our constitution up until 1998. Parents and grandparents still give gold to their children. Being a direct democracy, we can still say no to the Federal government. For the Swiss, we know that banking secrecy was created to protect people from government and we respect that tradition.*

The people behind Global Gold are familiar with the Permanent Portfolio strategy and the need for safe and secure foreign gold storage options. With many Swiss banks rejecting American clients, Global Gold offers a way to access the protection of gold storage in Switzerland without the hassle of dealing with a Swiss bank.

## Safe Deposit Boxes

For a higher level of privacy than allocated gold storage, a foreign safe deposit box is an option. The greatest problem with this approach is the requirement that you conduct all transactions in person. If, however, you are a frequent world traveler or have the means to travel to the site of your safe deposit box as needed, then this approach might be an option.

## Austria

If you want an anonymous safe deposit box, the services offered by Das Safe are highly regarded. Boxes start at 330 euros a year and go up depending on the size you require. Gold can be bought in Austrian banks over the counter for you to store in your safe deposit box. The website is www.dassafe.com.

## Switzerland

If you are non-U.S. citizen, a Swiss bank is an option for a safe deposit box. The cantonal banks listed in this chapter would be better candidates than the multi-national banks (although they do have safe deposit boxes as well). Swiss banks can supply gold bullion to deposit into your safe deposit box as well.

Most Swiss banks today will not take American clients for safe deposit box relationships.

## New Zealand

The New Zealand Mint offers safe deposit boxes at its vault in Auckland. Details are covered in the earlier section on the New Zealand Mint. The New Zealand Mint sells gold bullion over the counter that can be placed directly into your safe deposit box.

## Australia

Guardian Vaults in Melbourne, Australia offers not only safe deposit box services, but also gold bullion transactions. Gold can be held in allocated storage until you are able to transfer it to your private box. You can also use Guardian Vaults for insurance on the contents of the safe deposit box. The website is www.guardianvaults.com.au.

## Border Country

Finally, if you border a stable country and it is easy to access, you might consider opening a safe deposit box for gold storage. This option could provide some protection from events at home and may be easier to implement for your situation.

**TABLE 15.1** Geographic Diversification Matrix

| Storage Method | Allocated Storage | Convenience | Accepts U.S. Citizens | Cost | Account Min. |
|---|---|---|---|---|---|
| Gold ETF or Closed-End Fund | No | High | Yes | Low | Low |
| Gold Storage Service | Varies | High | Yes | Low | Low |
| New Zealand Mint | Yes | Mid | Yes | High[6] | Low |
| Perth Mint | Yes | Mid | Yes | Mid | Low–Mid |
| Global Gold | Yes | Mid | Yes | Mid | Mid–High |
| Swiss Intermediary | Yes | Mid | Yes | Mid–High | High |
| Swiss Bank | Yes | Low | No | Mid–High | High |
| Safe Deposit Box | Yes | Low | Varies | Low | Low |

## Geographic Diversification Matrix

Table 15.1 represents the range of options available for easy geographic diversification today. Based on this overview, consider the following guidelines when thinking about gold storage options:

**Gold ETFs and Closed-End Funds**—Not good for geographic diversification. You might, however, use them for a *portion* of your portfolio for rebalancing purposes so you don't have to rebalance your foreign account allocation as often.

**Gold Storage Services**—Similar to an ETF or closed-end fund in terms of safety. May have additional risks outside of an ETF or closed-end fund but likely not better protection.

**New Zealand Mint**—Good choice for smaller account holders who want simple and straightforward allocated gold storage. The purchasing commissions are a bit high, but for the convenience and geographic diversification it offers, it is a good option. It may also be a solid choice for larger account holders looking to diversify their gold holdings.

**Perth Mint**—A great option in terms of overall safety, cost, and geographic diversification. The dealer certificate program, however, is not as good as dealing with the mint if you meet the minimums. The government guarantee and longevity of the mint are appealing features as well.

---

[6] Commissions at the New Zealand Mint are higher than others. Otherwise, their costs are within reason for annual storage.

**Global Gold**—If you can meet the minimums and want your gold in Switzerland without dealing with a bank this is a good option.

**Swiss Intermediary**—If you are an American and want to have your gold stored in an actual Swiss bank this is a good option. If you can meet the minimums, the fees are reasonable and service is very professional.

**Swiss Bank**—If you are a non-American, dealing directly with a cantonal bank is a good option. It is, however, becoming very difficult logistically to work with them and account minimums are becoming out of reach for most investors.

**Safe Deposit Box**—Safe deposit boxes offer high levels of safety and privacy. However, the logistics of showing up in the actual country to manage the asset is not realistic for many investors. If you are able to travel to the safe deposit box location as needed, it may be an option to consider.

## Disclosing Accounts—U.S. Citizens

As a U.S. citizen it is illegal not to disclose foreign accounts. If you have an overseas financial account over a certain amount (currently $10,000 at any point in the year) you *must* disclose it annually to the IRS on the Form 1040, a new Form 8938 and to the Treasury Department using the Foreign Banks and Foreign Accounts (FBAR) form. Other countries may also have similar reporting requirements and you should check on applicable laws where you live to make sure you are in compliance.

*Don't use a foreign account to avoid taxes.* You may be caught eventually and at a minimum you are going to constantly worry about receiving an audit notice from the IRS (or worse). It's not worth it. Remember Rule #14 of the Golden Rules: Beware of tax-avoidance schemes. Comply with all laws and you can enjoy the benefits of a foreign account with no worries or regrets.

> As a U.S. citizen it is illegal not to disclose foreign accounts. If you have a foreign account over a certain amount you *must* disclose it annually to the IRS on the Form 1040, a new Form 8938 and Treasury Department using the Foreign Banks and Foreign Accounts (FBAR) form.

### How to Disclose

U.S. citizens must disclose financial interests in foreign accounts on the Form 1040, the new Form 8938, and the separate Treasury Department Foreign

Banks and Foreign Accounts form (FBAR—Treasury Form TD F 90-22.1).[7] The Form 1040 is submitted each year to the IRS as a taxpayer normally would with the appropriate box checked and disclosure of requested information. In 2012 a new form was added, Form 8938. This form has much more detailed disclosures than the Form 1040 alone. The form requirements are still being finalized as of this writing, but if you are utilizing foreign accounts for your Permanent Portfolio you should keep abreast of these filing requirements.

The FBAR form is submitted annually to the Treasury Department itself, and *not* with your Form 1040 that is submitted to the IRS. It is due by June 30th (as opposed to April 15th for the Form 1040). The 1040, 8938, and FBAR forms must be filed separately each year, and the FBAR filing address is different from the tax return filing address. You can download the FBAR form, fill in the requested information, and send it to the listed address via certified mail. Figure 15.3 shows the top of this form.

You can also file electronically by visiting the Treasury Financial Crimes Enforcement Network department website and registering for an ID here: http://bsaefiling.fincen.treas.gov/Enroll_Individual.html.

If you have any reservations about whether you are actually required to file these forms based on your own situation, just file the forms as if you were required to file them (subject, of course, to advice you receive from your attorney or accountant).

## Does Disclosure Jeopardize My Assets?

There is no use worrying about the ability of the U.S. government to get to your disclosed assets because not disclosing them is illegal and much more likely to cause you trouble than simply following the applicable disclosure

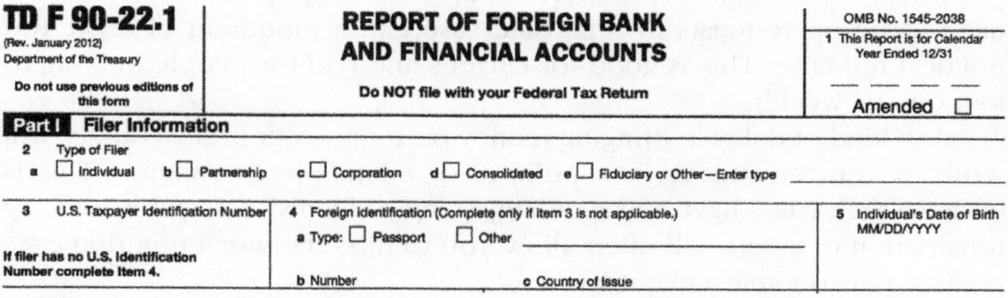

**TD F 90-22.1**
(Rev. January 2012)
Department of the Treasury

Do not use previous editions of this form

**REPORT OF FOREIGN BANK AND FINANCIAL ACCOUNTS**

Do NOT file with your Federal Tax Return

OMB No. 1545-2038

1 This Report is for Calendar Year Ended 12/31

Amended ☐

**Part I Filer Information**

2 Type of Filer
a ☐ Individual b ☐ Partnership c ☐ Corporation d ☐ Consolidated e ☐ Fiduciary or Other—Enter type

3 U.S. Taxpayer Identification Number
If filer has no U.S. Identification Number complete Item 4.

4 Foreign identification (Complete only if item 3 is not applicable.)
a Type: ☐ Passport ☐ Other
b Number c Country of Issue

5 Individual's Date of Birth MM/DD/YYYY

FIGURE 15.3 Treasury FBAR form. This form needs to be filed annually and is sent to a different address than your Form 1040.

---

[7] www.irs.gov/pub/irs-pdf/f90221.pdf.

requirements. But even if the government *does* know about your foreign account, it really doesn't matter that much for the following reasons:

1. You will have very few transactions in the gold allocation so taxes are not going to be significant. Also, gold doesn't generate any interest or dividends to pay taxes on either.
2. Just because the government knows about the account does not mean it can access it at will. There are foreign laws the U.S. authorities would have to contend with in addition to the applicable U.S. laws.

> Unless you are involved in drug dealing, terrorism, tax evasion, or other serious crimes, the U.S. government is not going to be worrying about you and your foreign account. Don't outsmart yourself.

Unless you are involved in drug dealing, terrorism, tax evasion or other serious crimes, the U.S. government is not going to be worrying about you and your foreign account. Don't outsmart yourself.

## Emergency Options

Any government that is keeping its citizens from moving money out of the country (or requesting that it all be brought *back*) is sending a signal that prudent investors should not take lightly. Don't be naive about these requests and fall for patriotic calls to do your duty and lose everything over events you weren't responsible for causing. History shows that decisions to control capital are frequently done to protect entrenched special interests and political leaders and *not* ordinary citizens.

Having money overseas means that the foreign jurisdictions can be used to tie up requests to repatriate assets in a mountain of legal and political red tape. This is good for citizens and bad for people looking to loot others' wealth.

Any kind of delay in bringing money back into your home country will work to your advantage in a political or economic emergency. This is because such crises have a way of happening suddenly. Being able to delay repatriation of assets will often allow you to miss the worst of a domestic political or economic emergency.

If you are faced with an emergency situation involving your assets, hire an attorney where you reside and in the country where your assets are stored. Use them to assist with either preventing the repatriation of your assets or at least delaying the repatriation for as long as possible. The longer you can delay bringing back assets, the better your chances you have of not losing everything. Part of having assets outside the country is to give you options to deal with these kinds of emergencies that people keeping all their assets inside the borders won't have. Take advantage of your options if they become necessary. Always remember that the time to make emergency plans is before the emergency arrives.

## Other Options

There are other options available for foreign gold storage. If it's not listed above it is probably because of one of the following:

1. The authors have no experience with it.
2. The authors have looked into it and think it is too complicated or risky to recommend to readers.

Just do your own due diligence, remember the advice given early on about the Reality Risk Spectrum, and you might also take another look at the Golden Rules of Financial Safety. Typically, going with a well-known, well-funded, and well-established provider in a first-world country is the safest and best option.

## Recap

Keeping some gold outside of the country where you live provides geographic diversification against natural or manmade disasters and other emergencies like government confiscation of private property. Geographic diversification can be obtained easily and safely by only considering foreign gold storage locations with stable governments and legal systems that provide strong protection of property rights.

For non-U.S. citizens, Swiss cantonal banks offer good gold storage options and reasonable fees, though in recent years they have increased their account minimums dramatically. There are also options inside the United States as well for allocated gold storage in a U.S.-based bank.

U.S. citizens can use a Swiss intermediary service if they can afford the high minimums. Otherwise, there are Swiss gold storage services that take lower minimums and avoid the hassles of Swiss banks. United States and European investors should also strongly consider alternative locations for foreign gold storage, such as Australia or New Zealand.

There are some online gold storage services, but it is unclear if they offer any significant advantage over a gold ETF or closed-end gold fund and may have some additional risks that are not currently well understood.

Despite what some may think, most governments around the world are probably not interested in your foreign accounts unless you are actively engaged in criminal activities. Keep your foreign gold allocation simple and in a safe location and it is much more likely to be there for you if you should ever need it in an emergency. Also, follow all applicable disclosure and reporting laws in your home country. The purpose of foreign gold storage is to make your investments safer, not riskier by having the authorities chasing after you.

Finally, don't outsmart yourself!

# CHAPTER 16

# The Variable Portfolio

The last piece of the Permanent Portfolio strategy is something called "the Variable Portfolio." As discussed, the Permanent Portfolio strategy has now provided four decades of stable returns with low volatility. It's boring, but profitable. In addition to this stable allocation, Harry Browne also realized that it's good to have an outlet for those times when you want to play the markets. What if you want the excitement of stock trading? Maybe you have a good hunch on the price of gold? Suppose you have some money and want to do some gambling? What to do? Simple: You want the Variable Portfolio.

*The Variable Portfolio is for speculation. Only money you can afford to lose should be allocated to it.*

Variable Portfolio money should be money that if you were to wake up tomorrow to find it gone it wouldn't affect your retirement, children's college savings, home down payment, and so on. It should be money that you're willing to put at risk of complete loss to satisfy a speculative itch.

The Variable Portfolio can hold any investment that you feel has merit. Speculative stocks, hot sector bets, artwork, and your cousin's startup company are all candidates. If you want to, use any market-timing scheme you think will work or maybe just follow the advice you see on TV or read in a magazine. If you're not a market timer but you really think stocks are a good deal, then buy some extra of a total stock market index fund. Or if you feel like doing nothing, then hold it all in cash until something catches your attention.

A word of warning though: All investors have different risk tolerances and unfortunately many investors don't find out what their risk tolerance actually is until after it has been exceeded by unforeseen losses. The Variable Portfolio should be approached with caution and an investor should make sure that the money he allocates to it is money that he *truly* can afford to lose if his speculative bets don't turn out as expected.

# Why a Variable Portfolio?

The Variable Portfolio can complement the Permanent Portfolio strategy for some. Many investors have a desire to try their luck at beating the market, and some are successful (though most are not). A Variable Portfolio allows you to wager money in a way that can't compromise your core savings if you turn out to be wrong, but will allow you to enjoy some gains if your speculative bets turn out well.

It's up to you whether to use a Variable Portfolio. The Permanent Portfolio works fine on its own, but some investors have an appetite for more risk, and for such investors a Variable Portfolio can complement the Permanent Portfolio. Just make sure that your Permanent Portfolio is fully insulated from any losses that may occur in your Variable Portfolio.

# Three Rules for the Variable Portfolio

The Variable Portfolio has three basic rules:

1. It must be money you can afford to lose.
2. You cannot replenish the Variable Portfolio with money from the Permanent Portfolio.
3. You can't make investments that expose you to greater losses than you have in your Variable Portfolio.

The Variable Portfolio can be any percent of your entire investment portfolio that you would be comfortable *losing*.

For example, you could divide your investments so that 10 percent was in the Variable Portfolio for money you could lose entirely and 90 percent in the Permanent Portfolio for money you can't risk at all. On the other hand, someone else might decide that the right percentages for him were 40 percent in the Variable Portfolio and 60 percent in the Permanent Portfolio.

Yet, many Permanent Portfolio investors may allocate 0 percent to a Variable Portfolio because they don't have any funds that they would feel comfortable losing. The Variable Portfolio is *optional*, not required. Just don't violate the above rules and you can do whatever you want.

## Rule #1—Money You Can Afford to Lose

If you can't afford to lose a penny of your investments then you should not allocate any money to a Variable Portfolio. Anyone in this situation should simply keep all of his money in the Permanent Portfolio and never look back.

If, however, you happen to have an area of expertise or knowledge that you think could translate into large investment returns then there is nothing wrong with putting some of your money behind an idea or theory that you believe has great potential. The key is to make sure you don't commit more than you would be comfortable losing if things don't turn out as planned.

When Harry Browne discussed Variable Portfolio strategies he often suggested that an investor should take as much risk as possible if he thinks that he has a really good investment idea. The idea is to make sure the payoff is there if you happen to hit the winning number. When you have identified money that you can *truly* afford to lose, it can be liberating to actually look for risks in the market that hold the potential for large gains if they turn out well.

## Rule #2—No Replenishing from Permanent Portfolio

As tempting as it may be to dip into your Permanent Portfolio to replenish your Variable Portfolio following a run of bad luck, *you must not do this*. If you take a loss in your Variable Portfolio you can't dip into your core assets of the Permanent Portfolio to re-build your wager pool.

> Don't compromise your savings from your salary to dig yourself out of a hole created in your Variable Portfolio.

Any money that goes into the Variable Portfolio should either be money you have made on Variable Portfolio investments or new money you are putting into your investment accounts from your earnings. In either case it must still be money that you can afford to lose. Don't compromise your savings from your salary to dig yourself out of a hole created in your Variable Portfolio.

The deposits into your Permanent Portfolio should be thought of as a one-way valve from the Variable Portfolio. It is acceptable to move Variable Portfolio funds into your Permanent Portfolio, but it is never acceptable to move funds from the Permanent Portfolio to the Variable Portfolio. This is probably the most important rule to remember when thinking about the Variable Portfolio.

## Rule #3—Can't Lose More than Initial Investment

There are different kinds of speculative investing and some of them are very dangerous because they can cause you to lose more money than you initially put in.

One example of a type of speculative investment that should be avoided in the Variable Portfolio is shorting stocks. Shorting stocks involves making a speculative bet that certain stocks are going to go down in value. Shorting a stock involves borrowing shares of the stock from the broker, selling it at the current price, and promising to return it at a future date in the hope that its price will be lower. If the price goes down you buy it back and return it to the broker and pocket the difference.

The problem is that if the stock goes *up* instead of down you are still responsible for paying it all back still. For example, if you are expecting a stock to drop by 50 percent but it instead goes up 200 percent, then your loss is going to be very large (far larger than your initial investment). You will need to buy the shares back at a much higher price in order to return them to the broker to cover your short sale. The losses can add up quickly because although a price can drop to zero (which is good if you are shorting the stock), the price can also continue going up indefinitely (very bad for a short sale). The potential for loss is therefore unlimited with shorting (in reality the broker will issue a margin call and clean out your account to cover the losses before that happens). Since shorting stocks can result in larger losses than the initial investment, this activity should be avoided in the Variable Portfolio.

Likewise, there are some private business investments that can leave you on the hook for more than you invested. In particular, avoid any investment that makes you a co-signer for debt that is larger than what you have put in. Also be careful of partnerships that can allow creditors to come after you directly if the business should fail. These kinds of risks can cause you to lose far more money than you have invested if things don't turn out as planned. These investments are not appropriate for the Variable Portfolio. Be sure your liability is limited only to what you have invested and no more.

> Finally, never under any circumstances borrow money to invest. This is not allowed even for Variable Portfolio investments.

Finally, never under any circumstances borrow money to invest. This is not allowed even for Variable Portfolio investments.

The examples above are merely illustrative of several kinds of speculations that can lead to larger losses than the initial investment. Unfortunately, there are many such ways of losing more than you initially invested.

The idea with the Permanent Portfolio is that you should be able to go to sleep at night knowing that your money is not at serious risk of loss. The idea with the Variable Portfolio, however, is that you should be able to go to sleep at night knowing that your money *is* at serious risk of loss, but *only* the amount of money that you have allocated to the Variable Portfolio and no more. Make sure not to get involved in any type of speculation that could expose you to greater losses than your initial investment.

> If you don't understand an investment, don't buy it.

When in doubt, go back and re-read the 16 Golden Rules at the beginning of this book. And definitely remember one of the most important rules: *If you don't understand an investment, don't buy it.*

## Modifying the Permanent Portfolio

A common theme in discussions about the Permanent Portfolio involves various ways of modifying the asset allocation from the 4 × 25 percent split to something else. Although these efforts at improving the Permanent Portfolio's performance are presumably undertaken with the best of intentions, the Permanent Portfolio should not be tweaked in the hope of getting better returns or more safety out of the portfolio. What seems to happen in virtually every case is that the tweak to the allocation that seemed like an obvious way of making the portfolio safer turns out instead to make it riskier. As much as possible, try to resist this temptation. If you add another asset to your Permanent Portfolio, or change the allocation percentages, you should treat the departure from the 4 × 25 percent Permanent Portfolio allocation as part of your Variable Portfolio.

For example, do you think that you should hold more than 25 percent of your investments in stocks? If the answer is "yes," then feel free to buy stocks in your Variable Portfolio, but leave your Permanent Portfolio percentages in place.

Similarly, if you decide that a Permanent Portfolio couldn't possibly be complete without an allocation to another asset like real estate investment trusts (REITs), then feel free to act on this belief by buying shares of a REIT index fund. Again, make sure that you do it within the confines of your Variable Portfolio.

## Can You Really Ever Beat the Market?

It is an unfortunate fact of life that most speculators eventually go broke, and many of them do it repeatedly. Statistically, you are probably not going to be able to beat the market consistently and reliably over the long term by speculating. This doesn't mean that you won't have some success from time to time, including hot streaks where everything seems to go right for you for a while. It is just important to understand the odds of the game you are playing are stacked against you, and if you play long enough you will probably lose.

The urge to speculate can be powerful, especially when some people seem to make it look easy. One of the reasons that everyone knows about certain high profile billionaire investors is because they are so rare. If everyone could pick stocks and pull in big market-beating gains then we'd all be billionaires. It's also important to remember that in the investment lottery, some people just flat-out get lucky. And yes, luck has a lot to do with stock speculation and beating the market.

When thinking about your prospects for long-term success as a speculator, don't think about the image of the smiling lottery winner as he receives his million-dollar check; rather, think about how hard it would have been to pick him out as the one who was going to win the lottery prior to the drawing. Successful speculation requires that a person be able to consistently pick winners before the drawing occurs, and this is extremely difficult to do.

A realistic approach to speculation can help prevent disappointment when the market refuses to cooperate with you. The Variable Portfolio provides you with a framework for speculating that can potentially lead to gains, but will in all cases prevent you from taking losses that you can't afford in your overall portfolio.

Just keep in mind that if you hit a particularly good streak of luck in your wagering, it does not mean you should increase your Variable Portfolio by taking money from your Permanent Portfolio. In fact, it probably means it would be a good idea to take some of the profits and put them back into the safety of the Permanent Portfolio. The markets have a way of taking gains away from speculators over the long term.

## Recap

The Variable Portfolio provides a framework for making speculative investments outside of the Permanent Portfolio and should only be used with money you can afford to lose.

If you can't afford to lose any money, or simply don't want to speculate, then all of your money should be kept exclusively in the Permanent Portfolio allocation.

If you do start a Variable Portfolio, follow these basic rules:

1. It must be with money you can afford to lose.
2. Losses in the Variable Portfolio cannot be replenished from funds in the Permanent Portfolio.

3. Never invest your Variable Portfolio in a way that could result in losses that are greater than the amount of the initial investment.

Beating the market is extremely difficult over the long term. If you have a run of good luck in your Variable Portfolio, you may want to consider putting a portion of your winnings into your Permanent Portfolio.

# CHAPTER 17

# Permanent Portfolio Funds

I f the idea of running your own Permanent Portfolio seems like too much trouble, there are currently two commercial funds that utilize variants of the strategy:

- The Permanent Portfolio Fund (Ticker: PRPFX)
- The Permanent ETF (Ticker: PERM)

While these products are convenient, they also have some drawbacks as well. We'll cover the performance, pros, and cons of using one of these funds so you can decide if they are the right kind of investment for you.[1]

## The Permanent Portfolio Fund

**Fund Name:** The Permanent Portfolio
**Fund Ticker:** PRPFX
**Fund Website:** www.permanentportfolio.com

In 1982 Terry Coxon and John Chandler (who were Harry Browne's newsletter editor and publisher, respectively) opened a fund that mimicked an early version of the Permanent Portfolio concept. Terry Coxon had co-written *Inflation Proofing Your Investments* with Harry Browne in 1981. This book was a significant departure from Harry Browne's thinking during the previous 10 years. Over this period Harry Browne had been a staunch hard-money advocate and had advised clients to purchase gold, silver, and Swiss francs to protect against the inflation that had afflicted the economy since the early 1970s.

---

[1] The authors have no financial interest in, and are not receiving any compensation from, either of the funds discussed here.

In the 1981 book, Harry Browne and Terry Coxon presented the idea that inflation would soon be coming under control and a more balanced portfolio might be needed going forward. They were right. By the time the book went to print the inflation that had plagued the United States for a decade was reaching its final stages and was poised for a steep decline (though no one knew that at the time). The disappearance of inflation would trigger large declines in the value of gold, silver, and Swiss francs. The new Permanent Portfolio allocations (there are minor variants described in the book), however, held assets that were able to profit from whatever this unknown future might bring.

The fund based on the early version of the Permanent Portfolio has held the following allocation since inception, with only minor modifications:

- 20 percent gold
- 5 percent silver
- 10 percent Swiss francs (held in the form of short-term Swiss government debt)
- 15 percent real estate and natural resource stocks
- 15 percent aggressive growth stocks
- 35 percent U.S. Treasury Bills and bonds

## Performance

Over the years the Permanent Portfolio fund has turned in reliable performance for a conservative fund of its type (though in recent years the fund's performance has been better than in its earlier years). Since its inception in 1982 the fund has performed as shown in Table 17.1 compared to the 4 × 25 percent Permanent Portfolio allocation presented in this book.

The fund has had very few down years, and in those years where it did post negative returns the losses were often mild in comparison to those seen by competing funds. In 2008, for example, the fund posted a loss of 8.36 percent when other conservative funds were posting losses of 20,

**TABLE 17.1  Permanent Portfolio Fund Versus 4 × 25 Percent Version Presented in This Book from 1982 to 2011**

| Fund Type | Annualized Returns | Real Returns |
|---|---|---|
| Permanent Portfolio Fund | 6.8% | 3.8% (est.)[2] |
| 4 × 25 percent Permanent Portfolio | 8.5% | 5.3% |

---

[2] Annualized inflation from 1982 to 2011 was 2.96 percent and is used to estimate this real return.

30 percent, or worse during the depths of the crisis. Over time, the real returns of the fund have been good—a nearly 4 percent average inflation-adjusted return over the life of the fund.

Compared to the Permanent Portfolio mutual fund, Harry Browne's 4 × 25 percent Permanent Portfolio allocation presented in this book (and based on Harry Browne's advice from 1987 forward) has provided higher historical returns, possibly as a result of holding more growth assets (stocks and bonds) versus those that just match inflation over time (cash and gold). This difference in returns is shown where the 4 × 25 percent fund had significantly higher returns over the same time period (and better real returns as well). Overall, however, the fund offers wide diversification in a single package. Compared to the myriad of other funds on the market, it is a good choice if the convenience of a single fund is important to you.

## Pros and Cons

All funds have their pros and cons. For convenience you usually give up something in return. Below is a short list of benefits and limitations of the Permanent Portfolio mutual fund.

**MANAGER RISK** In the case of the Permanent Portfolio fund you will give up autonomy over the asset classes it holds and you must rely on the manager to make prudent decisions with respect to the operation of the fund. So-called manager risk has been discussed in previous chapters, and it is a risk associated with *all* funds and is not unique to the Permanent Portfolio fund.

Manager risk is simply one of the inherent risks with any actively managed mutual fund. In contrast to the manager risk with this fund, if you use the do-it-yourself method of implementing your Permanent Portfolio described in this book, you can have more control over the assets and how they are owned.

**STOCK PICKING** The Permanent Portfolio fund uses active management for its stock allocation. As discussed earlier in this book, over time any actively managed stock portfolio will be expected to lag a broad-based stock market index that is not actively managed. Stock picking also increases trading costs internally and may result in higher turnover. The appeal of this fund should be in the wide diversification it holds in stocks, bonds, cash, and hard assets and not the manager's ability to pick winning stocks.

**TAX MANAGEMENT** The Permanent Portfolio fund is managed very well for taxes. The fund currently ranks #1 in Morningstar's ratings for 5, 10, and 15 years for after-tax returns and tax management in this category. This is a great result.

Even back to inception the fund has been managed to turn over as little in taxes to the government as possible. So in terms of holding a single fund in a taxable account, the Permanent Portfolio fund would be a great option if a fund's tax efficiency is an important consideration to you.

**EXPENSE RATIO**  The fund currently charges an expense ratio of 0.78 percent a year, which is below average, but not as cheap as index funds. In recent years the fund has seen a large inflow of new money, which has allowed the fund to continually bring the fees down and its efforts on this front are to be applauded. However, 0.78 percent a year in management fees is still significantly higher than a typical 4 × 25 percent Permanent Portfolio costs to operate. Therefore, the fund's management fees will affect overall returns, compared to a 4 × 25 percent allocation using low-cost ETFs and index funds. But again, part of what you are paying for is the convenience of an all-in-one fund and to some investors that is worth the small expense difference.

**EMPHASIS ON INFLATION ASSETS**  The Permanent Portfolio fund tends to overweight inflation-fighting assets like gold, silver, and Swiss francs (which together make up 35 percent of the fund's total allocation). This inflation tilt is going to affect performance during periods when inflation is not a problem. It also means in deflationary environments, such as 2008, the fund will tend to suffer compared to the 4 × 25 percent allocation because it doesn't hold a full 25 percent allocation to long-term U.S. Treasury bonds.

In terms of inflation assets, the gold allocation in the fund provides the same protection that is provided in the gold allocation in the 4 × 25 percent Permanent Portfolio. Gold has a clear monetary link and responds well to high inflation. The fund also holds silver, but silver is more of an industrial than monetary metal and may not respond as well as gold under all economic conditions, especially during periods of crisis.

The Swiss franc allocation in the fund no longer provides effective inflation protection. Although once tightly linked to gold, by the early 2000s the Swiss had severed this connection, and in 2011 the Swiss National Bank went so far as to threaten to peg the franc to the euro in order to, among other things, protect Swiss exports as discussed in Chapter 9 on gold.

The surprise 2011 Swiss National Bank announcement resulted in a dramatic decline in the value of the franc. The Swiss franc today is essentially another paper currency that is subject to central bank manipulation in the same way as any other currency. While the Swiss franc allocation was a good idea when the fund was started (the Swiss franc was a refuge from other currencies that were in the process of being devalued), the franc today does not serve the original purpose any longer.

The fund's overall emphasis on inflation protection means that it may lag the 4 × 25 percent Permanent Portfolio allocation if the dollar is strong and the economy is doing well. However, if you believe that inflation is going to be the primary economic and monetary problem going forward, this fund holds assets that should offer a good level of protection.

**CLOSING THOUGHTS** The Permanent Portfolio fund will not allow you to achieve geographic diversification because the gold is all held by the fund. Also, institutional diversification is limited because the same fund company holds all of your assets. If these considerations are important to you, then you'll have to skip the fund and do it yourself. Finally, this fund concentrates its assets in the United States so it is not appropriate for international investors unless a lot of exposure to the U.S. dollar and U.S. assets is desired.

The Permanent Portfolio fund has been around for 30 years and has followed the stated objective of stable growth in a portfolio. It also has managed to avoid any large losses as many other funds have had.

While the fund likely won't match the performance of the 4 × 25 percent allocation over time (especially during periods when stocks are performing well), it is a good choice for those who are looking for a safe and stable portfolio with little hassle. It also has a very long-established track record through good and bad markets. In an industry where funds come and go every few years, the Permanent Portfolio fund is likely to stick around.

## Global X Permanent ETF

**Fund Name:** Global X Funds Permanent ETF
**Fund Ticker:** PERM
**Fund Website:** www.globalxfunds.com/permanent

In February 2012 a new ETF became available with an allocation that is similar to the Permanent Portfolio's 4 × 25 percent split. This ETF is called the Permanent ETF, and is offered by Global X.

This ETF uses the following allocation to achieve 25 percent in stocks, bonds, cash and gold:

9 percent—U.S. large-cap stocks
3 percent—U.S. small-cap stocks
3 percent—International stocks
5 percent—U.S. real estate stocks
5 percent—U.S. and foreign natural resource stocks
25 percent—U.S. Treasury long-term bonds

25 percent—U.S. Treasury bills and notes
20 percent—Gold ETFs
5 percent—Silver ETFs

## Performance

This fund is so new that no long-term performance information exists. While it is expected that the fund will come close to the 4 × 25 percent allocation in terms of performance, there are many factors that could prevent this outcome depending on how the fund is operated. At this point, there is simply not enough data to know how it will perform.

## Pros and Cons

**MANAGER RISK**  Just as with any fund, the Global X Permanent fund has manager risk. The prospectus, however, narrowly limits what activities the managers can engage in. However, with 60 days' notice to shareholders the operation of the fund can be changed. Whatever constraints are placed on manager discretion, a bad manager decision can affect performance just as it can with any fund, so this is always a risk to take into consideration.

**FUND OF FUNDS**  The Global X fund is a so-called "fund of funds", which means that instead of holding actual gold and silver, it holds shares of gold and silver ETFs. Similarly, its stock holdings are in the form of shares of sector ETFs that correspond to the asset classes the fund targets in its stock holdings. In effect, the manager risk of the underlying funds owned by the ETF now comes through to the Global X ETF as well. A mistake in the gold ETF could impact shareholders in the Permanent ETF, for instance.

**STOCK PICKING**  The fund uses passive management for the stock allocation, so that is good news. In addition to matching the respective stock indices closely, it is also a low-cost approach. The fund does divide the stock allocation into smaller pieces to try to boost performance, however. While a single, broadly based index fund is probably a better choice for the stock allocation, the fund's approach to its stock allocation will probably work reasonably well, though investors will know more when the fund gets a few years of experience under its belt.

**TAX MANAGEMENT**  This fund is too new to have any information on taxes. One concern is that once a year the fund will automatically rebalance back to 25 percent each into the base stock, bonds, cash, and precious metals components. If this is not handled correctly, it could generate a lot of capital gains and dump the bill into taxable shareholders' laps.

Taxable investors should therefore be cautious about this fund until it has a few years of track record demonstrating how well it works from a tax efficiency perspective.

**EXPENSE RATIO** The fund has a very low 0.49 percent expense ratio. This includes the expenses of the underlying index funds it holds. Although this is a low fee, it is still not as low as an investor could do by using a do-it-yourself approach, as outlined in this book. However, for the convenience of a single fund it is a very reasonable cost.

**LONGEVITY RISK** Unfortunately, in the investment industry many funds have a relatively short life. Unlike the Permanent Portfolio Fund, which was started in 1982, the Global X Permanent ETF does not have a multi-decade history behind it or a large asset base. There is always the chance that in a few years the fund could close down if the operators do not think the fund is making enough money to keep it open. If this were to occur, investors would have their assets returned. For taxable investors this could also include a large tax bill if there are significant gains in the fund's underlying assets over that time.

**CLOSING THOUGHTS** Like other funds, the Permanent ETF will not allow you to achieve any kind of geographic or institutional diversification. Investors who want these features will need to look elsewhere. Also, as with the Permanent Portfolio fund discussed above, this ETF concentrates its assets in the United States so it is not appropriate for international investors unless there is a desire for a lot of exposure to U.S. assets and the U.S. dollar.

This ETF shows promise, but for tax management purposes (and until the fund has more of a track record) it's only recommended for investors who are able to hold it in a tax-deferred retirement account. This approach will provide protection in case the fund has large distributions due to poor tax management. This fund is something to keep on the radar, but it's not something we would feel comfortable putting more than a small amount of money in right now until it gets a few years of experience behind it.

# Recap

There are two commercially operated funds that use variants of the Permanent Portfolio strategy.

First, the Permanent Portfolio Fund has been around since 1982 and has a long track record of consistent performance. The Permanent Portfolio Fund tends to favor inflationary economic environments and may underperform during prosperous markets compared to the 4 × 25 percent split. This fund is well managed for taxable investors and could be a good all-in-one fund choice in a taxable portfolio.

Second, a new Permanent Portfolio ETF emerged in 2012 that more closely mirrors the 4 × 25 percent split presented in this book. However, this ETF is too new to make any determinations about long-term performance and tax efficiency. Investors should approach the ETF with caution and perhaps give it a few years to mature and see if it sticks around. Taxable investors should be especially cautious about the new ETF until the fund's tax efficiency can be determined.

Both of these funds concentrate assets in the U.S. markets and may not be appropriate for international investors unless they desire a lot of exposure to U.S. markets and the U.S. dollar. Also, neither of these funds allow for geographic or institutional diversification since a single fund company holds all of the assets. Both funds also all have higher fees and manager risk than a do-it-yourself approach, but if convenience is important to you, they are good options.

# CHAPTER 18

# Conclusion

T his book has covered everything we know about the Permanent Portfo-lio strategy. Yes, it's a lot of information. However, it was important to cover each topic thoroughly to make sure readers had all of the details and information needed to implement their own Permanent Portfolios. The in-vesting markets can be risky, but they don't need to be terrifying. The ability to grow and protect your savings means you can enjoy life and stop worry-ing about your nest egg.

The Permanent Portfolio is the best method we've come across to achieve stable inflation-adjusted returns across all market conditions. If you are one of those people who simply must engage in a little market specula-tion, there is also the option of setting up a Variable Portfolio to complement your Permanent Portfolio.

Investing should be a pleasurable process of steadily moving toward the achievement of your financial goals without major setbacks occurring on a regular basis. The Permanent Portfolio is one way to create this kind of ful-filling and productive investment experience.

We really appreciate you taking the time to read this book. We hope it was informative and useful to you. If the knowledge and suggestions shared in these pages helps you in your quest to grow and protect your hard-earned savings, we will have achieved our goal in writing it.

# Recommended Resources

## Books

In the realm of investing and economics there are a myriad of books available. Here are some recommended ones:

*Fail-Safe Investing*—Harry Browne's culmination of 40 years of investing, writing and consulting. *Fail-Safe Investing* is a quick read that presents the Permanent Portfolio as laid out in this book with less detail, but with the same message.

*Why the Best-Laid Investment Plans Usually Go Wrong*—Harry Browne was a passive-investing advocate for many years and this book is one of his best on the subject. A great book that breaks down the earlier formulation of the Permanent Portfolio and the assets it holds. Also contains a blistering critique of active-trading strategies, such as market timing and technical analysis. The book was written in 1987, which means some of the advice is dated in parts (index funds weren't widely available then and weren't in the recommendations, for instance) but still relevant in many aspects.

*Economics in One Lesson*—Henry Hazlitt's masterpiece explains economics easily and in lay terms. Written nearly 70 years ago, it is just as relevant today as it was back then. In fact, many of his insights into economic cause and effect are more prevalent than ever. The Permanent Portfolio has an economic foundation that aligns closely with Hazlitt's. The ideas presented in Hazlitt's book also allow you to avoid many economic fallacies.

Many of Harry Browne's books and writings are available in electronic form from Trends Action website: www.trendsaction.com. His books are also available in eBook format from Amazon.

## Podcasts

Harry Browne made a series of investing podcasts in 2004 to 2005 before his death in 2006. These podcasts cover the Permanent Portfolio strategy and other topics relating to free market economics. Because the Permanent Portfolio is a passive strategy, the podcasts are timeless in that they do not discuss current market conditions or trading ideas. The concepts presented in these podcasts are therefore very relevant today:

> Original Archive:
> www.harrybrowne.org/Archives/Archives-investment.htm
> Mirror Archive at Craig's blog:
> www.crawlingroad.com/blog/harry-browne-permanent-portfolio
> -archives

Craig occasionally releases podcasts as well that discuss the Permanent Portfolio strategy (The Crawling Road Podcast). It is also available at iTunes:

crawlingroad.com/blog/category/podcast/

# Websites

## Readers' Forum

An investment forum exists to discuss the Permanent Portfolio strategy. There is also an area to discuss speculative Variable Portfolio strategies. You can reach the forum here:

> www.gyrsoscopicinvesting.com/forum

## Author's Blog

Craig has been running the Crawling Road blog for years; it discusses the Permanent Portfolio and other random non-investing topics from time to time. Craig's blog provides updates about the portfolio, general comments, and annual performance reviews of the strategy:

> www.crawlingroad.com

## Brokerage Firms

There are many brokerages that can hold your Permanent Portfolio assets. The following companies, however, all have good reputations for service:

> www.vanguard.com
> www.fidelity.com

www.schwab.com
www.tdameritrade.com

## For the Gold Investor

If you intend to hold some physical gold bullion it may make sense to visit a local coin shop and see how their commissions compare to other dealers, but if this is not possible then ordering over the Internet is a viable option and these dealers have good reputations. Stick to modern production gold bullion coins with no collector value outside the gold content:

www.ajpm.com
www.amark.com
www.coloradogold.com
www.golddealer.com
www.kitco.com

If you are looking to buy gold from private sellers and not a reputable dealer it is be a good idea to test the coins. These two companies offer devices that can quickly validate common gold coins:

www.goldcoinbalance.com
www.fisch.co.za

Please see Chapter 15 on Geographic Diversification for more information regarding gold storage options. Also speak to a qualified tax professional to ensure you are disclosing your accounts as required by law.

Perth Mint Australia:
www.perthmint.com.au
New Zealand Mint:
www.nzmint.com
Global Gold Switzerland:
www.globalgold.ch
Swiss American Advisors (formerly Sallfort Advisors):
www.s-a-advisors.com
Zürcher Kantonalbank Switzerland (non-U.S. persons only):
www.zkb.ch
Basler Kantonalbank Switzerland (non-U.S. persons only):
www.bkb.ch
Everbank United States:
www.everbank.com

# About the Authors

**Craig Rowland** is a software entrepreneur with multiple successful start-ups and sold his previous company to Cisco Systems, Inc. in 2002. His company produced a real-time network attack response and analysis system. Craig began his career working for the Chief of Naval Operations, U.S. Pentagon. Eventually, he joined up with a group of individuals from the Air Force Information Warfare Squadron at WheelGroup Corporation which sold to Cisco Systems in 1998. At WheelGroup he was an early-stage employee hired to break into computer networks for a living and write network attack tools for their security auditing software. Later, Craig was an early-stage consultant to TippingPoint Technologies where he worked with the CTO on strategy and design on their next-generation security product. TippingPoint was sold in 2004 to 3Com Corporation. These companies all focused on computer and network security and he holds several patents in the field.

Currently, Craig works with start-ups where he helps turn ideas into new businesses. Craig's experience includes software development, project management, marketing, sales, venture capital fundraising, and executive management.

**J. M. Lawson** is an attorney in Dallas, Texas, and works on retirement plan design, administration and compliance issues. He also provides consulting around retirement plan investment selection, asset management, and related matters. His interest in the Permanent Portfolio grew out of a desire to find a safe and simple investment strategy that could help investors manage their retirement savings more effectively.

# Index

# Stay in touch!

Subscribe to our free Finance and Accounting eNewsletters at
**www.wiley.com/enewsletters**

Visit our blog: **www.capitalexchangeblog.com**

 **Follow us on Twitter**
@wiley_finance

 **"Like" us on Facebook**
www.facebook.com/wileyglobalfinance

 **Find us on LinkedIn**
Wiley Global Finance Group

**WILEY** Global Finance
WHERE DATA FINDS DIRECTION

Printed and bound by CPI Group (UK) Ltd, Croydon, CR0 4YY

16/04/2025

14658514-0004